For My very good friend
Wash Larsen with
Much appreciation for
that friendship over so
Many years

J B Beulah
May 18, 2017

HOUSE CALL

A Doctor's Time in Medicine and Government

J. ROY ROWLAND, M.D.
WITH SELBY McCASH

To my wife Luella, who is mainly responsible for any successes I've had, and my parents, who led me in the right direction from the beginning.
—J. ROY ROWLAND

To my partner Claire and daughter Moira, with love.
—SELBY McCASH

ACKNOWLEDGMENTS

We thank Sheryl Vogt and the staff at The Richard B. Russell Library for Political Research and Studies for their invaluable research assistance; Claire Cole Curcio, for her advice and countless hours of editing; Jim Comerford, Bill Stembridge, Kathy Hennemuth, Barbara Schlein, and Becki Brady, for sharing their memories; Johnny Isakson, Sanford Bishop, Saxby Chambliss, Jean Sumner, M.D., and Peter Buckley, M.D., for their encouragement and support; Luella Rowland, for her participation throughout the project; Jim Rowland, for his chauffeuring and support; Naren Aryal, Daniel Wheatley, and the creative team at Mascot Books.

J. Roy Rowland especially thanks Selby McCash for proposing this project and for his commitment in helping make it a reality.

www.mascotbooks.com

House Call: A Doctor's Time in Medicine and Government

Hospital vector graphic by Vecteezy! (www.vecteezy.com)

For more information, please contact:
Mascot Books
560 Herndon Parkway #120
Herndon, VA 20170
info@mascotbooks.com

Library of Congress Control Number: 2017900708

CPSIA Code: PBANG0417A
ISBN-13: 978-1-68401-191-9

Printed in the United States

CONTENTS

FOREWORD

by U.S. Rep. Sanford D. Bishop, Jr.

Debate is a natural consequence of a representative democracy. Gridlock is not. Sitting down with those across the aisle is not just an act of placing faith in political and ideological adversaries. It is an act of placing faith in our democratic system of government, a system founded on the art of creating consensus in order to move forward.

One of the country's great leaders, Martin Luther King, Jr., once said a genuine leader is not a searcher for consensus but a molder of consensus. Dr. J. Roy Rowland proved to be such a leader when I had the privilege of serving with him in the U.S. House of Representatives. He was ranking Democrat in the Georgia House delegation when I arrived as a rookie in 1993. I soon learned J. Roy and I shared the same vision about the meaning of leadership.

We served at a turning point in history, a time when extreme antagonism and partisanship was on the rise. We believed the country was taking a wrong turn when its leaders put partisan politics ahead of the values and interests of mainstream Americans. We were less swayed by the leadership of either party than by the needs and concerns of the people we represented and the country at-large. We believed our job was to fix, not just fight.

In *House Call*, J. Roy Rowland relates his struggles in medicine and politics during a lifetime now spanning nine decades. At the core of his story is a compelling plea for the country to return to the days when governmental leaders dutifully sought to resolve differences and avoid gridlock when addressing the country's vital economic and security needs. Although the health care reform plans he co-authored became a casualty of the growing partisan conflict, they still provide a model for Congress to follow in current efforts to create a sound health care system.

Many folks might suppose bipartisanship is dead. They cry out for a government driven by beliefs that transcend partisan politics. They desperately want the leaders they elect to be truthful, put the country first, govern for the future, be responsible, and work together. If Americans forcefully speak out as Dr. Rowland has done, the day will surely come when a patriotic spirit of bipartisanship is again alive and well.

FOREWORD

by Former U.S. Sen. Saxby Chambliss

When I first ran for Congress in 1992, I did not personally know the incumbent I wanted to unseat, U.S. Rep. J. Roy Rowland. What I did know was that the 1990 census put my home town of Moultrie into a new Republican-leaning congressional district. Although I wasn't successful in the primary race for the Republican nomination that year, I learned during my short campaign that Republicans and Democrats alike had nothing but positive things to say about Dr. Rowland. Even if I had won the nomination, I realized it would have been an uphill battle in the general election.

Fortunately for me, J. Roy retired from public life in 1994, opening the way for my election to Congress. We belonged to different parties. But, in many respects, our political careers were strikingly similar.

Although we held conservative views about government spending and regulation, we both worked with colleagues on the left and right to reach bipartisan solutions to the country's critical problems. I helped organize and lead the so-called Gang of Six in the Senate, a bipartisan group seeking agreement over a politically-thorny proposals to reduce the nation's out-of-control national debt. Rep. Rowland helped organize and lead the so-called Gang of Ten in the House, a bipartisan group seeking agreement over health care reform.

We both came under attack. We were criticized by people on both ends of the political spectrum. Leaders within our own parties even attacked us.

As our coalition pointed out, the only way for Congress to get a handle on the national debt is to make the hard votes on spending reduction, entitlement reform, and tax reform to stimulate revenue. But there were those on the left and right who refused to budge. As Rep. Rowland's coalition pointed out, the only way for Congress to succeed in extending health care access and coverage in an efficient, economically sound way is to resolve the conflict between those on the left advocating government control those on the right advocating free market principles. But he also encountered unyielding opposition.

Although we can point to a number of successful outcomes during our years in public life, the bipartisan efforts to reduce the debt and reform the health care system ended in gridlock. But I believe we fought the good fight. Working across the aisle is the way Congress is supposed to operate, and in doing so we affirmed our oath to defend the Constitution against all enemies, foreign and domestic, none of which are more threatening to our well-being than the failure to effectively address the national debt and the deep flaws in health care.

In *House Call*, J. Roy Rowland not only tells about his life in public service from his combat experiences as a teenage soldier to his return to medicine after his years as a lawmaker, but he continues the good fight by appealing for unity at a time of national turmoil.

CHAPTER ONE

As one of two medical doctors among the 535 members of Congress, I was about to help President Clinton transform the country's health care system from one of the industrialized world's most impaired systems to one worthy of a great nation. Or so I believed on the day Congress convened for the 1993-94 term.

From a historical viewpoint, the odds looked daunting. Presidents and members of Congress had repeatedly attempted and failed to establish a more secure and inclusive national health care system for nearly a century. None of them could resolve the fundamental disagreement over how much control should be apportioned to the government or the free market. But now the odds looked favorable. President Clinton had stirred up a nationwide groundswell for health care reform by making the issue a centerpiece of his presidential campaign, and his defeat of Republican President George H. W. Bush had confirmed how strongly that promise resonated with the American electorate.

Although America's patients receive the best care in the world, our health care system is beset with problems including the plight of millions of Americans lacking insurance coverage and adequate access to care; the insecurity of coverage troubling many; the counterproductive regulations hindering the care provided by medical professionals; and the extremely burdensome costs confronting government and many individuals and businesses. Just like today, most Americans urgently wanted the president and Congress to correct the system's deficiencies one way or another.

It wouldn't be easy. Although Democratic majorities controlled the House and Senate, I didn't think the president could solidify the diverse Democratic membership in Congress enough to pass a plan with Democratic votes alone. All Democratic members wanted to support some kind of plan, but they were divided. Some vowed only to support a plan based on strong government control while most would only support a plan based more on market forces. Aside from a faction planning to conspire against any health care reform, Republican members also wanted to support a plan. But they intended only to support a market-based plan while opposing anything they construed as socialized medicine.

From conversations I had with Democratic and Republican colleagues, I believed most members would support a fiscally-responsible, bureaucratically-restrained plan designed to make substantial improvements in a way that would be acceptable to most of their constituents. The messy details would have to be worked out. But I was convinced most members wouldn't want to oppose a cause as popular as health care reform and would join in supporting a substantial bipartisan agreement. *Washington Post* reporters David Broder and Haynes Johnson quoted Republican pollster and strategist Bill McInturff as privately saying the Democratic majority wouldn't be dumb enough to go home without reaching agreement over something, even if it wasn't exactly what the president wanted.

I was entering my sixth term as a member of the U.S. House of Representatives when the 1993-94 term began, a moderately-conservative Democrat representing a sprawling area of middle and South Georgia. I had practiced medicine as a family physician for 28 years, mostly in the mid-size city of Dublin, near Macon, before stunning the pundits in 1982 as a dark horse Democrat challenger who defeated a Democratic incumbent for the state's Eighth Congressional District seat. Mainly motivated by the sorry state of the health care system, I had turned to politics six years earlier in a successful race for a seat in the Georgia House.

Sixteen years later, I viewed the upcoming debate over health care system as the opportunity of a lifetime. Rep. Jim McDermott of Washington State and I were the only MD's serving in the House or the Senate, and I thought President Clinton and his health care reform team would welcome our input. If I could help the administration prepare and pass comprehensive health care reform, it would be the capstone of my political career.

Like me, President Clinton identified as a moderate. He served as a centrist governor and ran a centrist campaign for president. He had been a leader in the Democratic Leadership Council, the party's centrist wing. When the 1992 presidential campaign was getting underway, Georgia Gov. Zell Miller invited several members of Georgia's U.S. House delegation, including me, to a private meeting with the personable Democratic candidate at the Garden Room, a state hospitality and conference facility near the Georgia Capitol in Atlanta. I hadn't made up my mind about the presidential race. One option was to focus on my own race and not take a position in the presidential race.

I had become casually friendly with the elder President Bush through our mutual friendship with House Veterans' Affairs Committee Chairman Sonny Montgomery of Mississippi when Bush came to the House gym to play paddleball with Sonny during Bush's years as vice president. When president, he did me a favor by holding a White House signing ceremony for a minor bill I sponsored to establish "Infant Mortality Awareness Day." Although I didn't want to vocally oppose my party's presidential candidate by publicly supporting President Bush, I could have remained neutral. But when Bill Clinton confirmed his identity as a "New Democrat" favoring market-based solutions over big government, I pledged to support him.

As it turned out, I didn't have a clue about what lay ahead. No one did. Beginning in an outburst of lofty, optimistic rhetoric, the health care reform debate devolved into an intensely-rancorous political and ideological conflict before fizzling out without the full House or Senate ever voting on any health care reform. Squandering one opportunity after another, a few leaders on the left and right paralyzed the process rather than consider worthwhile bipartisan compromise plans that potentially could have passed. Oddly, these bitterly-antagonistic rivals unwittingly collaborated to produce the dispiriting result, gridlock.

The end came late in the 1993-94 term. When Congress returned to work on September 19, 1994, following a long Labor Day recess, I learned Democratic House Majority Leader Dick Gephardt of Missouri had decided to shut down the debate in the House. It was apparent neither the government-driven Clinton plan nor any of its variations could pass and he wasn't willing to give a bipartisan compromise a chance. Democratic Senate Majority Leader George Mitchell of Maine wanted to bring a bipartisan compromise to the floor. But he was pressured into terminating the debate in the Senate on September 26 when confronted by a late-developing Republican filibuster threat.

It might well have been a different ending if either body had voted on a bipartisan compromise immediately following the recess. Even if most Americans had become thoroughly disillusioned by the debate at this point, I think most members of Congress would have voted for a politically-acceptable compromise if the Democratic House majority leader hadn't first pulled the plug in the House and a Republican faction hadn't compelled the Democratic Senate majority leader to pull the plug in the Senate.

The debate began to go wrong the moment President and Hillary Clinton abandoned a bipartisan centrist approach, insisting on everything on their health care reform wish list and resisting any realistic compromise. All of their goals were important. But the specific means for achieving everything at once proved to be highly controversial as policy, and absolutely toxic politically. Most Americans and most members of Congress in both parties opposed a plan proposing to control costs with a massive new government bureaucracy and to fund its new and expanded benefits with deficit spending and a mandate requiring businesses to provide and help pay for employee health care coverage.

As the Clinton plan foundered, I emerged as a leading House Democrat in efforts to enact a bipartisan alternative based on managed competition principles. The two bipartisan plans I cosponsored would have moved the country closer toward universal care and addressed a number of the system's distressing problems. The national limelight briefly focused on me as a principal author of a plan recognized by many in Congress and the media as the only one attracting enough support to pass if Democratic House leaders would let it out of committee. They didn't. My earlier attempts to help the president and first lady develop a plan offering managed competition solutions had been politely rebuffed. Although I opposed the Clinton plan for its unfunded costs and excessive bureaucracy, I was told at one point the president would grant me any political favor if I would vote to bring the Clinton plan out of the committee where it had bogged down. I turned down the offer.

A challenge I had welcomed turned into an ugly intra-party confrontation. Dick Gephardt and House Energy and Commerce Committee Chairman John Dingell of Michigan, key backers of the Clinton plan, dismissed every bipartisan proposal introduced in the House during the two-year debate, including those I cosponsored, calling them worse-than-nothing distractions to divert support from "real" reform. This was a time when the congressional environment was becoming more rigidly and angrily polarized. With many Republicans attacking the Clinton plan as socialized medicine, I felt Gephardt and Dingell viewed Democrats taking a lead in bipartisan efforts as party heretics.

After maintaining friendly relations with members across the ideological spectrum for years, I began to feel a chill when in the company of some of my Democratic colleagues on the left. Although the Democratic Party umbrella had traditionally covered a range of liberals and conservatives, anyone straying from the Democratic congressional leadership line too often now risked becoming a party outcast. At one point several Democratic House members wanted the Democratic House Caucus to punish me for alleged party disloyalty by stripping me of the subcommittee chairmanship I held on the Veterans' Affairs Committee. Fortunately, the respect and friendship I shared with both liberal and conservative Democrats prevented the ill-conceived attack from gaining traction.

Although I had done the best I could to maintain a constructive working relationship with my party's leadership, I was an independent lawmaker who was sometimes criticized by those on the left as too conservative and by those on the right as too liberal. More often than not I positioned myself somewhere in the middle, seeking compromises to achieve positive results for all sides.

A spirit of collegiality existed when I entered politics that enabled lawmakers to resolve differences on vitally important issues. The congressional environment changed dramatically during the 1980s and 1990s, a period when the two parties became more ideologically uniform and sharply divided. Led by my brilliant fellow Georgian, Newt Gingrich, this was a time when many Republicans embraced a more confrontational style of governance and Democratic leaders reacted by becoming more confrontational themselves. These were years when tension between the two parties and members on the left and right within the same party stretched tighter and tighter, finally reaching a breaking point in the 1993-94 debate over health care reform.

Has extreme partisanship led to dangerous dysfunction at the federal level? Like most Americans, I think so. Most Americans say we need to stand up for our beliefs. I agree with them. I also agree with those who say we need to work together when the chips are down. I particularly agree with those who understand strongly-held beliefs and the art of compromise aren't incompatible.

Resolving deep differences isn't easy. But history proves it can be done. What happened in the 1993-94 health care reform debate was a tragedy for millions of people without coverage or adequate access to health care; a deflating experience for Americans whose faith in their government was undermined more than ever; a major step toward a new era of extreme political polarization; and a political disaster for the Democratic party which lost control of both houses of Congress in the next election.

Without question, it was one of the great debacles in the history of our governmental process. And the political reverberations are still being felt. If Congress had passed a substantial bipartisan alternative to the Clinton plan, it would have preempted the need for President Obama's Affordable Care Act (ACA) as we know it. If there had been no Affordable Care Act, it would have eliminated an issue that cost Hillary Clinton a significant portion of the vote in the 2016 presidential race. Some have surmised public concern over the ACA was one of the principal factors that cost her the election.

If the failure to enact health care reform was my most disappointing experience in public life, our effort to reach a bipartisan compromise was the proudest. As chairman of a bipartisan coalition, I helped produce a politically-viable plan that could have led to cost-effective universal access to care. The whole story of how our efforts to bring all sides together went astray in the 1993-94 health care reform debate has never been told from my perspective in the center. I'll relate that story in detail later. By reflecting on the partisan pitfalls of the past, I'm hopeful it will help those in power overcome them as they try to correct the deficiencies in the health care system in the future.

The outcome also contributed to my decision to retire from public life. Moderately conservative Democrats like me were becoming marginalized. It was time to hang it up.

Unlike lawmakers with a theatrical flair, I was a low-key politician who depended on hard work, perseverance, and a positive relationship with colleagues. My brief period of fame was an exception. Although I expressed strong views on many issues and was involved in highly controversial issues from the beginning, I didn't attract a lot of media attention.

The media tended to focus on politicians who were verbally confrontational and took positions at either end of the political spectrum. Nevertheless, the record shows I had more legislative wins than losses. I may have been an obscure political figure to most people outside my district, but behind the scenes I helped make a historic difference as a link between the left and the right.

I was among the white Southerners in Congress who voted for the Dr. Martin Luther King, Jr. holiday bill, helping break through a wall of opposition that had prevented passage of the measure, a major step toward racial reconciliation. I coalesced with other fiscal conservatives to trim deficit spending, often clashing with leaders of both parties. After long supporting President Reagan's policy of supplying weapons to the Contra guerrillas in their revolution against the Marxist-influenced Sandinista regime in Nicaragua, I cast a decisive swing vote to stop the flow of U.S. military aid to a foreign insurgency in order to preserve an election leading to the peaceful ouster of the Sandinistas. I brokered compromises between environmentalists and the business community on landmark clean air and water bills, making passage of the measures possible. I teamed with other farm-area members in a united effort to sustain family farming.

Among the bills I authored or co-authored that became law, all with bipartisan support, were those creating a national AIDS commission, intensifying the fight against the disease; banning Quaaludes, a dangerous drug costing thousands of lives; helping save endangered rural hospitals by equalizing the federal reimbursement rate; establishing programs to lower the country's shameful infant mortality rate; providing benefits denied to veterans suffering from diseases attributable to exposure to nuclear radiation while serving in the military; and eliminating unnecessary and burdensome federal health care regulations.

As a Georgia legislator I was able to tighten the limit on state borrowing and sponsored the legislation imposing the country's first ban on Quaaludes.

Looking back, whatever I accomplished wouldn't have been possible if I hadn't earned the trust and friendship of others; respected other points of view and remained open to reasonable compromises; and pursued goals tenaciously.

My mother described my younger brother Joe and me as "true-blooded Rowlands." This was her way of saying we could be astonishingly stubborn. People describe me as good-natured, courteous, and soft-spoken. But if I'm as mild-mannered as they say, it conceals something inside that drives me to succeed. Years ago I participated in a charity pool tournament at my hometown Elks Club and defeated everyone until reaching the finals. When I lost the final match, I bought a pool table and practiced for a year. After winning the following year, I donated the pool table to our church. This might seem a little compulsive, but I've always challenged myself, sometimes even in small ways. On rare occasions I've changed course when a goal appeared to be unreachable. I withdrew from the governor's race in 1982 and ran for Congress instead. But with few exceptions I've always pursued improbable goals regardless of the odds.

I've never forgotten a slogan posted on my high school hallway bulletin board that read, "Do right because it is right and not because you are afraid to do wrong." We were reared to be truthful, work hard, respect and help others, and never get too big for our britches. The idea of common sense and common decency somehow stuck. If I ever deliberately lied, it would wear on my conscience. If I did something I felt was wrong, it bothered me until I tried to make it right.

In spite of my in-born persistence, I've listened to others and sometimes changed my mind. After entering politics, and listening to the needs of individuals and the country at-large, my view regarding the boundaries of government responsibility shifted more to the middle. When I thought government had a responsibility to act, I found a willingness to balance conflicting interests to be essential in getting things done.

My life couldn't have been as fulfilling if it hadn't been for my wife of more than 70 years, the former Luella Price, my partner in everything I've done; my loving children and grandchildren who have enriched our lives;

my parents, extended family, and mentors who shared their knowledge and implanted their values in me; and many people whose friendship and support made so many things possible.

Everyone's life is an adventure. As I grow older, I realize how adventurous mine has been—and continues to be.

CHAPTER TWO

With the help of a great uncle, Dr. Earl Brinson, Mama delivered her first-born son on February 3, 1926, in the back bedroom of our home in Wrightsville, a town of about 1,700, founded in 1858 as the governmental seat and trading hub for newly-created Johnson County in the midst of a cotton-growing and turpentine-producing area of east middle Georgia.

My parents—James Roy Rowland and the former Jerradine Marilyn Brinson—christened me James Roy, Jr., calling me "J. Roy" to distinguish me from my father who went by his middle name. As a skinny high school football player, my teammates would nickname me "Slim." Some members of Congress would refer to me as "Doc" when I served in the U.S. House. Political opponents would call me all kinds of names. But mostly I've always been called "J. Roy," with the "J" and the "Roy" pronounced as one word. The family expanded to four when my brother Joe Wesley Rowland arrived on Christmas day almost three years later. The family numbered five when joined by Rex, a dog of uncertain lineage, and later Bucky, a white English setter.

Joe and I were lively youngsters who stretched the rules from time to time, earning an occasional spanking when we were kids and stern talks when we were older. But we were mostly mindful of our elders and our upbringing couldn't have been happier. Mama and Daddy were the most loving and nurturing parents imaginable. They were also among the area's most gifted and prominent citizens.

Our mother, called Jerradine, the daughter of a pharmacist, was a musician who long served as pianist, organist, and choir director for the Wrightsville Methodist Church. She once played professionally as the background pianist in the days when Wrightsville's movie theater featured silent movies before the coming of talkies. After graduating from high school in 1919, Mama earned a degree in music and voice in 1923 from a Methodist institution, LaGrange College in west Georgia. She taught school as a music teacher for two years in the south Georgia town of Douglas where her sister and her sister's husband lived, Ida and Emmitt Roberts.

After carrying on a long-distance courtship by mail and telephone, she returned home to marry my father. They had known each other growing up, attending the same schools and church in Wrightsville. She later became Johnson County's welfare director, serving in that capacity from the 1930s until her retirement in 1971, handling all of the cases in a chronically poor area with the help of one secretary. She served as church music director until the age of eighty-five when her health began to fail. She entered an assisted care facility two years later where she passed away.

Our father, the son of a farmer, businessman, and longtime state legislator, was an attorney who gained widespread recognition as defense counsel in several sensational civil and criminal trials. After graduating from high school, he served in the Army for about a year before his discharge at the end of World War I. Entering Mercer University Law School in Macon, he received his law degree in 1923, opened a law practice in Wrightsville, married my mother, and went on to serve as city attorney and solicitor of the City Court in Wrightsville, solicitor general of the multi-county Dublin Judicial District, and as an elected superior court judge. When defeated by an opponent from a larger community after serving on the bench for four years, he resumed his Wrightsville-based law practice.

Two of his high-profile trials involved a wild West-style gunfight on the streets of Wrightsville. While delivering newspapers early on a weekday morning, I heard sharp bangs as I was riding on Elm Street and pulled to a stop at the town's main intersection of Elm and Marcus streets. I realized the bangs were gun shots. A couple of them ricocheted off a building. Although the streets seemed empty at first, I noticed a well-known local citizen walking up the Johnson County Courthouse stairway across the street. Holding his stomach, he was apparently looking for help. A moment later a second well-known citizen appeared right in front of me as he crossed the street toward Brantley's Drug Store where Dr. J.G. Brantley maintained a medical practice. Holding a bleeding arm, he looked straight at me and exclaimed, "I got the SOB."

Reportedly feuding over a property transaction, their encounter had fatal consequences. The victim who suffered the stomach wound died later that day. The incident was widely publicized and the ensuing trial packed the courtroom. With my father defending him, the assailant was acquitted on a plea of self-defense. Later, my father's client was shot as he left a Wrightsville barber shot, allegedly by a son of the deceased in retaliation for his father's death. Although this time the shooting wasn't fatal, the son was charged with assault. My father was again retained as defense counsel.

This was just after World War II when the undeclared Japanese attack on Pearl Harbor was still fresh in everyone's memory. In his summation, Daddy told the jury the defendant feared an attack by the man who had fatally shot his father and took preemptive action for self-protection—pointing out this was something the U.S. might have done to prevent the bombing of our Naval base in Hawaii. The argument struck a receptive chord with the jury. Daddy again won an acquittal. His Pearl Harbor defense was talked about for a long time, especially among Georgia attorneys.

My father received statewide and even national attention as the attorney for a future governor and U.S. senator, Herman Talmadge, in Georgia's infamous three governors' controversy. This was a time when Talmadge's legendary father, Gene Talmadge, dominated Georgia politics. The state was bitterly divided between rural voters who supported Gene Talmadge as the champion of dirt farmers and small towns and urban voters who opposed Gene Talmadge as the enemy of "progress" and big cities, particularly Atlanta. After his election to a fourth term as governor, Gene Talmadge died from cancer before being sworn into office. Although the state constitution designated the lieutenant governor as the successor if the governor's office was prematurely vacated, pro-Talmadge legislators claimed the General Assembly had the authority to name the next governor since Gene Talmadge hadn't yet taken the oath of office.

The legislature named his son Herman as governor, bypassing Lt. Gov. Melvin Thompson who wasn't in the Talmadge camp. Herman Talmadge seized control of the governor's office with the help of the State Patrol. Thompson occupied the lieutenant governor's office, insisting he was the rightful governor. The incumbent governor, Ellis Arnall, said he would remain the state's chief executive until the dispute was settled, moving into another capitol office. Georgia had three gubernatorial claimants, a political soap opera that made news throughout the country.

Thompson sued and Talmadge asked Daddy to represent him. My father was a natural choice. He was a noted trial attorney and his father, my grandfather Papa Rowland, had helped engineer the legislative decision in favor of Talmadge as a member of the General Assembly. In a ruling handed down in March 1947, the Georgia Supreme Court held that Thompson would serve two years of the four-year term and the voters would chose the governor in the next general election. In a letter dated April 8, 1947, Talmadge told my father "I have read your brief very carefully and I think it is the best one I have ever read. The people with whom I have talked believe we got a political and not a legal decision."

A few years later my father was appointed legal advisor to a colorful governor, Marvin Griffin of Bainbridge. But Daddy resigned a year later. The Griffin administration was caught up in allegations of misusing state funds. Integrity meant everything to my father. He wouldn't have been comfortable in an environment where wrongdoing was evident.

One day in March 1956, the car Daddy was driving to Macon on legal business skidded off the road and overturned. Suffering extensive injuries, he was brought to a hospital in Dublin where I practiced medicine. Needless to say, this was a terrible shock and heartbreaking time. We brought in a capable surgeon but we were unable to save him. If some of the procedures we recognize now were known back then, he might have pulled through. He died on March 15 at the age of fifty-six. The law library at the Johnson County courthouse is dedicated to my father.

Joe and I were mostly buffered from the poverty and inequality experienced by many people around us. Like any family we went through periods of stress. But what I mostly remember is the fun we had together. Daddy often led us on summer Sunday outings to picnic and swim following church. We regularly gathered around Mama at the piano, singing popular songs at the top of our lungs if not always on key. Although I played the accordion from my teenage until my early married years, my mother's musical talent unfortunately eluded me. Our parents certainly looked after us. Mama once ran onto a football field in full view of the spectators to make sure I was okay when I was lying on the turf with a minor injury. That's how concerned she was about our well-being. When Daddy thought I had been treated unfairly in my military recruitment, he pursued the issue all the way to Congress.

Church was a big part of our lives. Unless seriously ill, our well-groomed attendance at both Sunday school and church services at the Wrightsville Methodist Church was as certain as the sunrise. We were Methodists on both sides of the family for as far back as anyone could remember, a tradition Luella and I have continued.

On typical evenings the whole family, including Rex or Bucky after Rex's sad demise, settled in my parents' back bedroom of our two-bedroom, one-bath frame home to listen to programs like Jack Benny, Fred Allen, Fibber Magee and Mollie, Lum and Abner, Amos and Andy, and the Hit Parade on our table model Philco radio. Joe and I stretched out on the floor playing games like Fiddle Stix and Monopoly while we listened.

On cold winter evenings, we kept a coal fire going in the bedroom fireplace, the only source for warmth. Our home was heated by coal-burning fireplaces in most rooms and by a wood-burning stove in the kitchen and cooled in hot weather by a black rotating fan. One of my regular chores was hauling coal and firewood inside from the backyard stockpiles. Our hot water supply came from the kitchen stove which heated a water tank connected by pipes to the sinks and the bathtub. Although a GE electric heater was placed in the bathroom, this helped only if we were directly in front of it. Joe and I took our required evening baths just before bedtime with amazing speed, getting the scrubbing done before the steaming water cooled down too much, and rushing to our unheated front bedroom to bury ourselves under heaping mounds of quilts and blankets. On cold mornings, Daddy always arose first to light the kitchen stove, returning to bed until the kitchen warmed up enough for everyone to eat breakfast and start preparing for the day in relative comfort.

I was born during a period of economic well-being. But the Great Depression descended on Wrightsville and the world when I was three and persisted throughout my youth. Although professionally successful, our parents struggled financially at times as did many families even more affluent than ours. This was a time when my mother earned a depression-era salary and many of my father's clients found it difficult to pay their legal fees. We always lived comfortably. But sometimes we went without material things. I remember how disappointed I felt when I asked for my first bicycle one Christmas at the age of about nine and didn't receive it because my parents couldn't afford it at the time.

Fortunately, our Christmases and other holidays were so full of excitement I didn't stay downcast too long, and I was thrilled when I received a second-hand bike the following year.

In later years I learned The Bank of Wrightsville once threatened to foreclose on our home. The bank had purchased the mortgage and demanded payment of the loan right away. W. Herschel Lovett, a leading businessman who served in the Georgia Senate for many years, my mother's uncle and my great-uncle, headed the bank. If this seems like an especially hardnosed business decision, I suppose banks were going through hard times just like many families. The crisis was averted when Mama's father, the grandfather I knew as PaPa, paid the loan in full, apparently from savings.

Serving mullet for supper was one way Mama economized. Salt water mullet was trucked to Wrightsville from the Georgia coast and retailed in Wrightsville for five cents a pound. Although preserved on ice during its long ride and stay in the market, the mullet wasn't exactly fresh by the time it reached a consumer's plate. One evening I refused to touch the mullet when Mama served the odorous fish with grits.

"Some little boy in China would like this," Daddy sharply said. I'll never forget how angry my normally calm and thoughtful father became when I retorted, "I wish some little boy in China had mine." Uncharacteristically, he swatted me hard with his hand and I recoiled and went sprawling on the floor. My parents helped me up, saying reassuring things. I've always believed the incident reflected the severe pressure Daddy was sometimes under. He was also probably thinking less about the children in China than those nearby who didn't have enough to eat.

In our youthful world, rebelliousness was an unknown concept. Joe was an outstanding football player and valedictorian of his class. I was involved with sports and other activities and made decent grades. But we sometimes tested our parents' patience. They certainly didn't always appreciate my fondness for practical jokes. I remember the time I secretly acquired a realistic-looking fake dog dropping and placed the offensive item on a living room chair just before company walked through the door. What an uproar it caused when Mama spotted it. At first she blamed poor Bucky, but I confessed. Although I escaped with a rebuke on this occasion, sometimes our unruly behavior resulted in a more serious response.

Few parents believed in sparing the rod in our day. But spankings weren't administered very often in our household. When they were, they were usually more symbolic than painful. As Mama tried to slap me with a belt on the backside, I squirmed and dodged and her glancing blows would hardly be felt. We generally ended up laughing and in good humor. I only recall once behaving badly enough for my mother to call on my father to deal with the problem. When he returned home from work, he ordered me into the bathroom, locked the door, and applied several whacks with a belt that weren't hard enough to do any physical harm but definitely hurt. This wasn't quite what Mama expected. She pounded on the door, calling on Daddy to stop, which he did when he thought the lesson had been adequately learned. I don't remember the nature of the offense. But I'm sure it was never repeated.

Mama and Daddy gave us much more freedom than most youngsters have today. From an early age I roamed the countryside with friends on our bicycles; swam, fished, and camped out; built and flew impressively large model planes; shot marbles for keeps as kids and pool for pocket change as teenagers; played pick-up sports for hours on end; published a community newspaper; and found many creative and competitive ways to occupy our free time. We worked at youthful jobs, took part in Boy Scouts, and participated in school activities. The opportunities for fun and adventure in our small town seemed endless.

Our grandparents made some of these opportunities possible. In fact, one grandfather, PaPa Brinson, planted the seed for my career in medicine, and our other grandfather, Papa Rowland, for my life in politics.

Joe and I addressed our paternal grandfather, Joe H. Rowland, not just as Papa but as Papa Rowland. Papa Rowland owned a large farm a couple of miles from town run by an overseer. But he and Mama Rowland lived across the street. They kept chickens in a fenced-in area behind their house and cows for milking in a barn. Next door was a hog lot. Papa Rowland slaughtered three or four hogs every fall when the weather turned cold. Although a minimally painful process for the hogs, dispatching, cleaning, and butchering the animals produced a monumentally-awful odor. The perennial hog butchering produced a much-appreciated bounty for the family including hams, shoulders, and other cuts that were cured in a smokehouse; homemade sausage; and lard Mama Rowland used in cooking made by boiling the skin in a pot.

My father mixed hog brains with scrambled eggs. Although a breakfast delicacy for many in his generation, this was never to my taste. On occasion Mama Rowland produced a memorable dessert by creating cottage cheese from sour milk, squeezing the moisture out when it turned to clabber, and topping it with sweet cream, sugar, and nutmeg. I frequently crossed the road to fetch a quart of milk, half a pound of butter, and as many eggs as needed.

Born in 1869 on a farm near Wrightsville, Papa Rowland was a farmer, teacher, businessman, and a longtime member of the General Assembly who allied himself with the leading voice for Georgia's farmers, Gene Talmadge. He didn't drink, smoke, or play cards. If strictly pious in his personal habits, he was also famously generous. As owner of a farm supply business, he extended credit to struggling farmers, black and white, even when it put his own financial standing at risk. Black residents of the Buckeye community in Laurens County supported me when I ran for the legislature in 1976 because they hadn't forgotten my grandfather helped keep their families going during the depression.

He left the farm on which he was raised at 21 to teach school in Johnson County and was soon appointed school superintendent, a job that took him around the county in a horse and buggy to fix problems at schools for both races. His peak pay as an educator was $325 a year. To augment his income, he rented land to farm, eventually owning more than 2,500 acres. He later turned to business, founding and operating a saw mill, cotton gin, cotton warehouse, Wrightsville's second service station, and Wrightsville's first feed and seed store. He not only sold supplies to farmers, he gave them valuable advice. One year he urged cotton farmers to plant alternative crops when he foresaw a glut in the cotton market, which would drive cotton prices down. He made a big difference in the lives of many farmers who followed his advice.

Papa Rowland entered politics in 1904, serving two terms as the elected clerk of the Johnson County Superior Court, stepping down in 1908 to concentrate on farming and business. He returned to politics in 1937, serving three terms in the Georgia House and two terms in the Georgia Senate.

Between the ages of ten and twelve, I accompanied Papa Rowland on trips to Atlanta to serve as a legislative page. Joe also served as a page under our grandfather's sponsorship as soon as he was old enough. I rode in my grandfather's Studebaker to Georgia's capital city; stayed at the downtown Henry Grady Hotel, then one of Atlanta's finest, and participated in the hustle and bustle of the legislative sessions at the state Capitol for several days. Although we usually drove from the hotel to the Capitol, I was awestruck when we sometimes walked through the busy Atlanta streets. As an adult, I always thought I would like to be involved in politics, an idea rooted in those legislative experiences with Papa Rowland.

Our maternal grandfather, Jeremiah Wesley Brinson, Jr., was born in 1879. We called him PaPa, always spelling it with two capital P's. PaPa's father, a physician who earned his medical degree at a medical college then located in Savannah, had settled in the up-and-coming town of Wrightsville, then a stopping point for several railroads carrying farm commodities to larger markets. He had four brothers altogether—an attorney, a business man, and two brothers who worked in health care. One was a doctor, my great Uncle Earl who brought me into the world. PaPa and his other brother were pharmacists. Their father purchased the centrally-located two-story building where the drug store run by the brothers was established. The pharmacy's original name, Brinson and Sons, was changed to Brinson Drug Store when PaPa became the sole proprietor after the deaths of his father and brother.

Standing five feet, six inches tall, PaPa was a giant of a person. Examples of his generosity are too numerous to recall. He bailed out my parents, gave my bride and me our first car, and filled our unfurnished apartment full of furniture when I was a pre-med student. One of his customers, a

Wrightsville woman, regularly took advantage of his good nature. She would order a glass of Coca-Cola, which the soda jerk made by pumping syrup into a glass with shaved ice and filling it up with carbonated water. She would drink part of the coke and complain it didn't have enough carbonated water. When her glass was refilled, she would drink some more and complain it didn't have enough syrup. This would continue until she drank several glasses for the price of one, a nickel. PaPa would grumble and threaten to cut her off, but never did. He couldn't hurt anyone's feelings.

Beginning at the age of nine or ten, I spent much of my free time at Brinson Drug Store. Walking on my own, I regularly went there after school and during vacation. PaPa welcomed me and so did Mama Brinson, who helped PaPa run the drug store, recruiting me up as a soda jerk at the pharmacy's busy soda counter and compensating me with ice cream and sodas. I reached the handles to pump the syrup for soft drinks by stacking two empty Coca-Cola crates to use as a platform. The drug store provided curb service. When autos and pickup trucks parked along the curb in front and honked, I was often the designated car hop who went outside to take the orders and retrieve the trays attached to the vehicle windows when customers honked again. Another assignment was bringing PaPa a half dozen fried oysters, a "half fry," from Mallett's Meat Market every Saturday evening when the drug store was especially busy.

I became PaPa's pharmaceutical assistant. While standing by his side, he taught me to mix compounds from the separate liquids and powders that came in bulk. Some products simply required repackaging. Epsom salt, for example, arrived in wooden barrels and was retailed in nickel and dime bags. Under my grandfather's close supervision, I learned how to mix the compounds and fill the bags in precise amounts.

At the age of twelve, I decided to be a medical doctor when I grew up. If it hadn't been for the many hours I helped PaPa prepare medications, who knows whether medicine would have been the path I would have taken. Except for a brief period of uncertainty following World War II, I never wavered from this childhood dream.

In the early 1960s, while practicing medicine in Dublin, I purchased Brinson Drug Store. PaPa had passed away and I wanted the drug store that had meant so much to me to continue serving the community. I kept the store going for a couple of years, but it was difficult to keep qualified management and compete with the big chains. After nearly seventy years, my grandfather's drug store finally closed. But the old building still stands. The pharmacy's name, "Brinson Drug Store," painted on the side long ago, has now faded. But the words can still be plainly seen, stirring up memories whenever I'm visiting the town where I grew up.

CHAPTER THREE

Although barely a speck on the map, Wrightsville was a lively place to come of age during the years between the two world wars, especially on Saturdays when people who lived within the municipal limits and on the farms and settlements scattered throughout Johnson County and several surrounding counties gravitated to the center of town.

They came to shop; see a movie; eat out; play pool at the family-friendly pool room; have a treat at the drug store soda fountains; prepare for church by getting their hair cut or styled; and just to be a part of the spirited scene. Some stores remained open from early morning well into the evening. Although the blue laws required businesses to close by midnight, the barber shops always stayed open late into the evening to accommodate merchants who capped off the long work day by getting a twenty-five cent haircut and possibly a straight-razor shave, a shoe shine, and even a shower. Many homes lacked plumbing and two of the town's barber shops provided public bathing facilities.

Weather permitting, people swarmed along the sidewalks. Many of the men sat shoulder-to-shoulder on the curbs, conversing about crop prices, weather, politics, hunting and fishing, and the latest gossip. While parents shopped, teenage girls strolled outside in pairs or small groups, some wearing dresses made from chicken feed sacks designed with floral patterns. The homespun clothing was not only inexpensive, it was pretty and fashionable for the time. As a teenager, I regularly joined the dozen or so boys who hung out in front of the theater and next-door pool hall and sometimes whistled as the girls passed by. The girls didn't seem to mind and the adults paid no attention.

During football season, endless touch games took place on the lawn of the Johnson County Courthouse, a stately 1895 structure now listed as a national historic site. The Dixie Theater presented Saturday double-features for youngsters earlier in the day, followed by grown-up movies, and concluded with late-night horror films that drew a demographically-mixed audience. Joe and I were regulars in the pickup football games and at the Saturday movies.

The community's business, governmental, and entertainment epicenter was located at the intersection of East and West Elm Street and North and South Marcus Street, a site marked by the installation of Wrightsville's first circa-1930 traffic light. The intersection today looks much like it did back then with the courthouse standing on the northeast corner; the 1890s-era building that housed PaPa's pharmacy and Daddy's upstairs' law office on the northwest corner; the building where a cousin, Ethel Layton, ran the City Café on the southwest corner; and the Exchange Bank that rescued Papa Rowland from a financial crisis on the southeast corner.

While this intersection remains Wrightsville's downtown focal point where businesses and offices are still clustered, the variety of enterprises flourishing in the area when I was growing up was truly extraordinary. Among them were six grocery stores; four service stations; three drug stores; three dry goods stores; three barber shops and at least as many beauty salons; two cafes; two hardware stores; two banks; three automobile dealerships: Ford, Chevrolet, and Pontiac; a feed and seed store; the movie theater; the pool room; a fish market; a meat market with a take-out counter offering hamburgers, sandwiches and world class fried oysters;

and the Frost House, a boarding house on South Marcus Street for traveling salesmen and one or two fulltime lodgers, a place where our family went to eat family-style lunches and suppers for twenty-five cents a plate.

Our home was located on a residential stretch of South Marcus Street three and a half blocks away from the Elm Street intersection. We lived on a dirt road until I was about three when Marcus Street was paved, becoming one of the few surfaced roads in town other than Elm Street, Wrightsville's main highway. Although born in another nearby home, I was an infant when we moved to our South Marcus Street address. During my early years, our surroundings served as a playground. My friends and I perilously climbed the gnarled pecan trees in our backyard and played pretend games in the ditch running in front of our house.

We often played at the Wrightsville and Tennille Railroad crossing a block and a half south of our house. Adults called it the "Wiggle and Twist" railroad because of the meandering tracks. Kids called it the "Worry and Trouble" railroad. I'm not sure why. If our parents worried about us playing there they could have put it off bounds. But they never did. A wooden water tank stood near the crossing and the steam engines sounded like monsters huffing and puffing when they stopped for refills. We laid pennies on the tracks, ran and hid, and collected the flattened coins after trains passed over them.

The proximity of our home to the center of town made it possible for me to walk on my own to and from PaPa's pharmacy and the Dixie Theater, another place where I gained work experience. We were well-acquainted with the theater's management and no one objected when I volunteered to serve popcorn, drinks, and candy. Sometimes I took up tickets, a responsibility my friends envied.

Along with just about every youngster in town, Joe and I ritually attended the Saturday double features which included a western, a cliff-hanging serial, and an Our Gang comedy or a cartoon. When the Dixie Theater extended its Saturday hours in the mid-1930s from 10 p.m. to 11:30 p.m. to present horror films like *Frankenstein, Dracula, Wolfman,*

The Mummy, and The Invisible Man, Joe and I begged to go. I was about nine or ten years old and Joe was about six or seven. Our parents, apparently not too concerned about how the scary movies would affect our young psyches, gave in to our pleading and let us go on our own to most if not all of them. A ticket cost a modest ten cents.

There were no street lights on South Marcus. We walked to the theater and back in darkness. On our return home, I invariably tried to frighten Joe. We were already scared out of our wits by the horror movie and efforts to scare Joe only succeeded in frightening both of us even more. We always stayed in the middle of the road where it seemed safer and broke into a run as we approached the house.

In the summertime, we fished and went swimming almost every day, traveling on our bikes. The main swimming venue in Wrightsville and Johnson County was known as The Creek, a place Daddy called the best natural swimming pool on earth. The Creek was a spot in the Ohoopee River on the outskirts of Wrightsville where a natural spring fed into the river, creating a pool of bone-chilling water about thirty yards long and almost as wide that tapered to a depth of about ten to twelve feet. On one side was a sandy beach and on the other side an embankment. Youngsters swung off the embankment on a rope tied to a tree limb and plunged into the cold water with arms flailing.

On summer Sundays following church, The Creek was always crowded if it wasn't raining. Whole families, including ours, came with baskets loaded with picnic lunches. Occasionally, a local evangelical church conducted a baptism at the site, something everyone watched with appreciative interest.

As soon as I owned a bicycle, my boyhood chums and I traveled to The Creek on most summer days, sometimes remaining most of the day. We rode our bikes along the old Dublin Road, a dirt road running parallel to the nearby paved new Dublin Road. When we arrived at Mason's Bridge, an aging wooden structure crossing the river, we parked off the road and hiked on a well-worn trail along the river's edge to reach the swimming area. We behaved like youngsters have always behaved, engaging in noisy, high-energy rowdiness. But no one was ever seriously injured and I don't remember any serious conflicts. It was always fun for everyone.

Today the world's greatest natural swimming pool is overgrown and mostly forgotten, sadly missed by a dwindling few.

Another regular bike destination was Papa Rowland's farm located two miles outside of town. Farmed by tenants and managed by an overseer, the spread was known as a twenty-five horse farm because it took twenty-five horses or mules to farm it. The farm's forty-five acre pond was an excellent fishing site. My pal Arnold Hicks and I, sometimes joined by other friends, made many trips to the farm to fish, swim, and sometimes camp out. Mr. Jim Luck, the rural mail carrier and the only known owner of a motor boat in Johnson County, gave rides to Arnold and me and other friends when we happened to be there at the same time, a big thrill for us. Although we didn't know it at the time, the pond was found to be inhabited by cotton mouth moccasins when drained many years later. Fortunately, the snakes never bothered the humans intruding on their habitat.

Papa Rowland owned a country store located on the Kite Road, a pecan tree-lined road passing through his farm. I was among a covey of high school boys and girls who crammed into cars and headed for the store every once in a while to dance to the music of the store's juke box. It was a friendly place thanks to the manager, Leo Stewart, son of the overseer of Papa Rowland's farm.

Along with four or five pals, I took up building and flying gas-fueled model planes. Powered flight, still in its early years, held a strong allure for us. Our leader was Carroll Blankenship, a Tom Swift-like character who was keenly interested in short-wave radios and other science-related gadgets and machines, earning a small income by repairing radios and electrical appliances. Under his oversight, we built the models with balsam wood, tissue paper, and a small aluminum motor, some with four-foot wing spans. Traveling by bike, we carried the models outside of town where we could fly them in open fields, spending much of our time fixing them after crash landings.

In 1940, four friends and I entered the newspaper business. The partners were Carroll, seventeen; Alex Daley, sixteen; and Arnold Hicks, Rollie Smith, and me, all about fourteen. In later years we couldn't remember who originated the idea. But we enthusiastically agreed we should publish a weekly newspaper to compete with the town's professional weekly, *The Wrightsville Headlight*. When Joe, eleven, tried to join us, we shooed him away. He was younger and therefore deemed a nuisance. But he refused to be shooed and he became our typesetter or "printer's devil," performing the tedious task of setting type one letter, number, space, and punctuation mark at a time.

My parents allowed us to use our detached garage in back of the house as a base of our enterprise. The garage included a walled-off ten by twenty foot area used for storage. We cleared out the bric-a-brac and converted the space into a make-shift office. We scrounged up several rickety chairs, a couple of small tables, and an old cast iron coal and wood-burning stove to keep us warm while working in the winter, venting it through a broken window pane.

Pooling our limited resources, we purchased a hand-operated printing press used for light printing in homes or small businesses from the Johnson Smith catalogue. We stocked up on reams of inexpensive legal-size yellow paper and tubes of printer's ink. When the *Headlight* replaced its old hand-set press with a modern linotype machine, a *Headlight* employee, aware of what we were up to, surreptitiously let us have a collection of lead type that was supposed to be thrown away. He placed the wooden boxes containing the surplus type in back of the newspaper where we would find them. The *Star Flash News*, as we named the paper, was born.

We knocked on many doors to sell subscriptions and ads, accumulating more than one hundred subscribers for five cents a month and a number of regular advertisers for ten cents a column inch. We eventually earned enough income to open a bank account like any business. Later, Wardlaw Starling, a weekly newspaper publisher in Nashville, Georgia, who was married to my father's sister, Nancy, gave us a surplus professional hand-set printing press, enabling us to diversify our operation by providing businesses with stationary letterheads, invoices, and other material. After buying many cases of soft drinks, we qualified for wholesale prices, augmenting our newspaper and printing income by selling soft drinks to the many young people who crowded in and around our garage office after school and during the summer, mostly the twelve-ounce bottles of Pop Cola, RC Cola and Nehi orange and grape sodas.

By the end of 1942, after producing the *Star Flash News* for nearly two years, our zeal for the venture waned as we became more involved in other activities. The two oldest partners, Carroll Blankenship and Alex Daley, were called into the Army. Arnold, Rollie, and I were busy with Boy Scouts, jobs, and school sports.

One copy of the *Star Flash News* survives. The January 1, 1941, edition included stories about a car accident, a warehouse fire, wedding announcements, bowl game predictions, a brawl at a New Year's eve party among "fortune tellers" living outside Wrightsville that had to be stopped by police, and a "skyrocket" that slammed into an outhouse belonging to Mr. Charlie Roundtree, editor of the *Headlight*, while someone was shooting fireworks on Christmas eve. Fortunately the mishap didn't cause a fire and the structure was left intact. A story headlined "No News" made the following request: "We, the editors of this paper wish that people would give us news. We cannot print news when we do not have it. You do not need to bring it to us. When you see us on the streets just give it to us. We will appreciate it very much."

Many people gave us news, encouragement, and financial support. I still appreciate it.

Alex Daley not only helped produce a newspaper, he delivered one as well, *The Atlanta Journal*. I substituted for him on occasion and he recommended me for the route when he left for Army duty. Delivering newspapers isn't an easy job. I was up well before dawn every morning and rode on my bike to the Dixie Theater. The newspapers were brought to Wrightsville along with tins of new movies by a Benton Brothers Rapid

Film Express truck and left in a tied bundle in front of the theater. Carrying a heavy load of newspapers in a bag strapped over my shoulder, I delivered them throughout much of town in all kinds of weather.

The roads could be slippery and difficult to negotiate on rainy days. If it was pouring, Mama drove me in the car. But this was rare. It took an hour and a half to two hours to deliver the newspapers to an average of 140 subscribers. I paid fifteen cents and received twenty-five cents for each subscriber, giving me an average income of $14 a week. Collecting the subscription fee was often a challenge. Some subscribers always paid on time and some rarely did. It could be more difficult to collect from the wealthier citizens than from those of more modest means. I learned patience and polite persistence usually produced positive results.

I always had quite a few papers left over. Striking a deal with the grocery stores and the fish market, I sold the surplus papers for a penny a pound for wrapping fish. If I dreaded eating the mullet, at least I profited by selling the newspaper it came wrapped in. On Sundays, the employee in charge of the shoe shine stand at Moseley's Barber Shop, who had the owner's permission to open on Sunday morning to provide shines for church-bound passersby, keeping all the income for himself, agreed to sell the extra Sunday papers for me. This was a good arrangement for both of us. The newspapers helped attract shoe shine customers.

After completing the route, I returned home, cleaned up and ate breakfast, and, on school days, rode my bike to classes which began at 8:30 a.m. Joe eventually inherited the newspaper delivery job when I finished high school. Until then, I retained the route even when I started attending Boy Scout camp in the summers, recruiting friends to fill in for me.

My Boy Scout years began when I was twelve. At the time, Wrightsville didn't have a Boy Scout troop and I'm not sure how scouting came to my attention. The year was 1938, several decades after the Boy Scouts of America was established. When I heard or read about it, the idea of exploring the outdoors, earning merit badges, and wearing the uniform as part of a kindred group of youngsters captured my imagination. The closest Boy Scout troop was located sixteen miles away in Dublin. My parents drove me to the weekly meetings for about a year, and it must have been a relief to them when a Wrightsville troop was started.

Cliff Moye, the city postal carrier, was Wrightsville's founding scoutmaster. We called him by his first name. He was more like a friend than an adult supervisor. Cliff was dedicated to scouting and years later he became the country's longest continuous scoutmaster.

To become official, a prospective troop had to secure a charter from the Boy Scouts of America. A charter is granted by the national headquarters only if the applying troop is sufficiently well-organized and prepared to comply with the Boy Scout rules and standards. With the Wrightsville Lions Club serving as the troop's founding sponsor, we were confident we would meet the national qualifications. After the application was mailed, we waited. And waited. As the review process dragged on, our confidence wavered.

One day while playing touch football with a group of friends and fellow Boy Scouts on the lawn of the Wrightsville Methodist Church, I saw Cliff walking in our direction, waving an envelope. "I've got it. I've got the charter," he yelled. We ran and huddled around him, excited by the official-looking document in his hands. It was a memorable moment.

During my last three summers as a high school student, I attended Camp Ben Hawkins, the Boy Scout camp located near the town of Byron not far from Macon. This is where I earned most of the merit badges I needed to become an Eagle Scout, Wrightsville's first. Some of the merit badges required considerable study and effort, like the one for bird study. In my third and final season at Camp Ben Hawkins I was placed in charge of the kitchen, making me a part of the camp staff. Once a week I was entrusted to drive the camp's Chevy pickup truck to Macon to pick up supplies. I was also earning the Red Cross swimming instructor's rating and was offered the position of waterfront director for the following summer of 1943, the most coveted staff position. Although I strongly wanted to accept, the war would pull me in another direction.

I was a senior in high school when I succeeded my second cousin, Ervin Brinson, as chief projectionist at the Dixie Theater. I subbed for Ervin when he had to miss work, learning how to run the projector, change reels, splice film, and keep the movies running smoothly. When he was called into the Army, I was named fulltime projectionist, a prestigious position for a young person in Wrightsville. The job paid $12.50 a week. When added to my newspaper delivery income, I made about $26.50 a week, big money for a teenager in those days. This was a time of intense patriotism and I used some of my savings to purchase War Bonds which significantly helped finance World War II.

Although a dependable projectionist most of the time, I was distracted when my girlfriend, Luella Price, came to see a movie. The projectionist needed to be in the booth to change reels and fix the film if it broke. But there were periods when there was nothing to do but watch a film I had seen many times. When I spotted Luella entering the theater, the temptation to join her was too strong to resist. During idle interludes, I slipped out of the projection booth overlooking the balcony and scampered down a couple of flights of stairs to sit with her for as long as possible. While AWOL, I recruited a black youth a couple of years younger than me named Kyzer, who was normally in charge of maintenance, to keep watch in the booth. On a couple of occasions, Kyzer, who had worked hard at his own job, nodded off and the reel ran out. When the screen went blank, the audience invariably reacted with a clamor of whistles and catcalls. I rushed back to the booth to get the movie going again, wondering whether I would be fired.

Many years later I came to Wrightsville as a member of Congress to participate in a fourth of July celebration. As I was circulating among the crowd along the parade route, a tall black man approached and said, "Congressman, do you remember me?" It was Kyzer. We hugged like brothers.

My high school years were wonderful years. We liked our teachers and coaches who did their best to prepare us for the future. I was a founding staff member of the school newspaper, *The Taillight*. Although I didn't play much, I enjoyed being a part of the basketball team.

To this day, playing on the Wrightsville High School Tigers football team is one of my most unforgettable experiences. We played twenty games during my two seasons, winning seventeen, tying one, and losing two. We should have won the tied game and possibly one of the two games we lost. In a game against Swainsboro, one of our players, Henry Mallette, incurred three consecutive fifteen-yard penalties for personal fouls. Although Henry was an excellent player who helped us win many games, the penalties might have made a difference in a game we lost by two points, 9 to 7. In the tied game against Wrens, I intercepted a pass and was headed for the winning touchdown when Hoyt Martin, our quarterback who was much faster, hollered for a lateral as he ran beside me. When I tossed the ball, it resulted in a fumble recovered by Wrens. We were just whipped in our loss to Jesup, a team featuring an unstoppable halfback named John Donaldson who went on to star at the University of Georgia.

No post-season championships were played in high school football at that time. But with only two losses in two seasons, we established ourselves as one of the top high school teams in Georgia in our class. The whole community followed our games. At school, the players were treated like heroes. At the pre-game rallies in the school auditorium, we stood together in a place of honor while the cheerleaders and student body whooped it up on our behalf. Although I wasn't one of the team's stars, this was a big deal for a teenager.

I decided to try out for football in the fall of 1941, my junior year. Friends were playing and I wanted to join them. At 125 pounds, I wasn't much of a prospect. Coach Ed Schwabe assigned me to two positions, a linebacker on defense and center on offense behind our starter, Curtis Daniels. When Curtis broke his hand in our first game, and was unable to hike the ball in practice the following week, I became the starting center. In those days, before the introduction of the T-formation, it was the center's responsibility to snap the ball accurately and with some velocity to the quarterback standing a few yards behind the line. A center's hiking could make the difference between winning and losing. Many years later Hoyt Martin told me I never mishandled a snap. Although I was knocked around much of the time, I suppose my dependability as a hiker and my willingness to block and tackle as hard as I could enabled me to hold onto my starting positions.

While delivering newspapers early the next morning after my first game, I saw the coach standing on his front porch, waiting for me. He was one of my subscribers. As I handed him his newspaper, he greeted me by saying, "You played a good game last night." I've never forgotten that instant. His comment not only boosted my self-esteem, it deepened an innate conviction that if I fought tenaciously enough, good things could happen.

As a member of those Wrightsville High teams, my work ethic and determination were hardly anything special. We were a team of hard-working and focused players who had truly bonded as friends and teammates. We were fortunate to have a coach like Coach Schwabe who encouraged a close-knit environment. A number of opposing teams were bigger and better than we were. But none played harder or smarter or with more unity.

I was also a junior when I noticed Luella. After the ninth grade, students from the New Home community were bused to Wrightsville High, a distance of about ten miles, for their final two years of high school, which then consisted of only eleven grades. Luella was raised near New Home, one of seven siblings in a farming family that operated a country store and a cotton gin. After she transferred from the New Home school and made the girls' basketball team at Wrightsville High, I noticed her in games and around school. Although I wanted to get to know her, I was too shy to introduce myself.

Circumstances finally brought us together when we were seniors. It was a football friendship that facilitated those circumstances.

A teammate, Earl Ivey, knew I wanted to meet Luella. Earl's girlfriend was a New Home neighbor of Luella's, Bronnie Price, no relation. Earl had an idea. He suggested I join Bronnie and him on a Sunday ride in his pickup truck. We would show up unannounced at Luella's house and invite her to go with us as if it were a spur-of-the-moment occurrence. This sounded like a good plan to me. Earl, who lived on the Adrian road about six miles out in the country, picked me up in his pickup the next Sunday and we drove to New Home to meet up with Bronnie and hopefully Luella. When Luella agreed to join us, it was the first of many Sunday afternoon rides. Before long, Luella and I were a steady couple.

The military draft lay ahead. We were at war, a time when rationing and austerity were imposed on everyone. Yet the uncertain future didn't deter us from enjoying our final year in high school, a year highlighted by our graduation ceremony and our junior-senior prom. For many years afterward, everyone who was at the prom remembered an incident in which I intervened in an apparent fight. As it turned out, however, it wasn't a real fight at all.

The incident involved two of my friends from the football team, Henry Mallett and James Capshaw. Just about everyone in school knew they had bitterly argued over something and were threatening to do bodily harm to one another. But unknown to their friends, the two had reconciled through the mediation of our school superintendent, Mr. J.C. Oliff. When the prom was underway in the school gym, Mr. Oliff called Henry and James onto the stage and asked them to shake hands. Privately, Mr. Orliff had arranged a mock confrontation as a joke. Instead of shaking hands, Henry raised his arm to give James a pretend slap. The script called for Henry and James to then shake hands and have a good laugh.

Before that could happen, however, I bolted out of my seat and rushed onto the stage to stop Henry from hitting James. I remember Mrs. Oliff, the superintendent's wife, who was standing on stage with her husband, shouting "stop him, stop him," as I charged toward the startled group. Mr. and Mrs. Oliff intercepted me and explained the "fight" was all in fun. Naturally I became the butt of a lot of kidding. Although I was embarrassed, the incident somehow emphasized how much we had been through together and how close we were.

One day early in December 1941, Arnold, Rollie, and I were leaving the school building after working on the school newspaper. As we stepped outside, we saw Mrs. Oliff running toward the school from her home across the street where she and Mr. Oliff lived. "The Japanese have bombed Pearl Harbor," she called out. I knew Hawaii was a U.S. territory. But I didn't realize how that day was going to change our lives.

CHAPTER FOUR

With casualties mounting after two years of war on two fronts, Uncle Sam wanted fighting troops badly enough to sign me up for a college-based military educational program at the age of seventeen and send me into combat instead. My bait-and-switch Army recruitment is an amusing memory now. I'm glad I served on the frontlines in the Allied crusade against Nazism. But it wasn't funny then.

On the day I graduated from high school, my eighteenth birthday was seven and a half months away. The 1940 Selective Training and Service Act required males between the ages of eighteen and sixty-five to register for the draft, and those between the ages of eighteen and forty-five could be called to active duty unless granted an exemption or deferment. More than sixteen million Americans would serve in the armed services during World War II with exemptions granted to the disabled and individuals doing essential civilian work, and deferments to college students as long as they maintained passing grades.

I had planned to spend the summer of 1943 as waterfront director at Camp Ben Hawkins and start college in the fall while I would still have a few more months before becoming draft eligible. But my parents thought

I should enter college and qualify for a deferment without delay. Although disappointed, I followed their sensible advice and enrolled for the summer quarter at Emory at Oxford, a two-year division of Emory University, a private liberal arts institution founded by Methodists. The Oxford campus, located thirty-eight miles east of the university's main campus near Atlanta, had a much smaller enrollment than big universities and its student body lived in campus dorms, a good fit for a teenager from a small town.

Emory at Oxford was academically demanding. Although I completed the summer and fall quarters without flunking any subjects, I needed to take two remedial courses. I would potentially be at risk for the draft if I didn't improve my grades. By the end of 1943, I not only felt jittery about my academic standing, I didn't want to be a shirker.

Many friends were entering the Army or Navy. Arnold Hicks and Rollie Smith had joined the Navy at seventeen, the only age young people could voluntarily join a military service. After turning eighteen, they had to leave their fate to the draft, and most draftees were assigned to the branch with the greatest need, the Army. Arnold and Rollie had opted for a relatively comfortable ship over a cold, muddy foxhole while they had a choice. I wondered if I should do the same.

Although my mother wasn't too happy when I told my parents what I was considering, my father gave it some thought and agreed joining the Navy would be a prudent step. With parental acquiescence and assistance, we learned two military educational programs had been established as part of the war effort. In both programs, enlistees were placed on college campuses for extended academic training before they were deployed as regular soldiers and sailors. The Navy had created the V-12 program the previous July to train commissioned officers and the Army had launched the Army Specialized Training Program (ASTP) not long after the attack on Pearl Harbor to train enlistees in critically-needed fields such as medicine, engineering, and foreign languages.

I was shocked when the Navy wouldn't take me. I was color blind. Until then, color blindness had never been a problem. But it was a condition that ruled me out for enlistment in the Navy. The Army, on the other hand, wasn't as picky.

The Army recruiters I met were friendly and encouraging, assuring me I could join the Army ASTP Reserve right away, transfer to the regular Army at eighteen, and serve my military obligation on a college campus for a year and a half before being deployed for regular duty. I would wear a uniform and be under the same discipline as any soldier but would be stationed at one of the some 200 colleges participating in the program. Hopefully I would be assigned to the University of Georgia in Athens near home.

On January 5, 1944, my parents drove me to Atlanta where I was sworn in by a female major at a rather austere Army recruitment center in a downtown office building. I was advised to go home and await orders. The owner of a feed and seed store in Wrightsville, Duren Williams, who would give Luella and me a $500 television set after the war and tell us to pay whenever we could, kindly gave me a job to occupy my time during the interim. In March, my orders came by mail to report to Fort McPherson in Atlanta on April 14. As far as I knew, everything was proceeding according to plan.

This time I traveled alone by Greyhound bus, joining a swarm of incoming recruits. Although I didn't meet any other ASTP candidates, I figured we would be given our individual assignments after we were processed into the Army and I would soon contentedly be on my way to college. We were given physical exams, issued uniforms, drilled in formations, and attended orientation classes. After three days, we were bused to a train station in downtown Atlanta late one afternoon and loaded onto a jam-packed troop train.

We had no idea where we were going. We traveled all night, fitfully trying to sleep in the crowded coaches. After wearily reaching our destination the next day, we were transported to a military installation and assembled in formation. Facing us was a sergeant standing on a small platform who spoke to us through a megaphone.

"I want all of you to know you are in an IRTC (Infantry Replacement Training Center)," he informed us. The place, we learned, was Camp

Blanding near the town of Starke in central Florida. "You are to receive infantry basic training for the next seventeen weeks to replace those casualties that are occurring in Europe and the Pacific," he said.

Whoa, I thought. *This ain't what I signed up for.*

As soon as I had a chance, I called home to let my parents know where I was and what had happened. If we had known I could be summarily reassigned to combat training, I could have remained at Emory at Oxford and buckled down in an effort to retain my deferment. If I was going into combat if I volunteered for military service, the risk of flunking out and getting drafted wouldn't have been an issue. By signing me up for the ASTP, recruiters made sure I was immediately available for regular Army duty.

We now know the Army was planning to terminate the ASTP at the time I joined in order to use the soldiers enrolled in the program as casualty replacement troops. But no one mentioned any uncertainty about the program's future when I joined. Was the Army resorting to subterfuge? That's the way it appeared. But the Army was doing whatever was necessary to provide the troops needed to win the war as quickly as possible. Also reassigned to infantry combat duty following the D Day landing were soldiers serving in desk jobs, those stationed in the U.S. as a strategic reserve, and even aviation cadets.

My father contacted one of the most powerful political figures in the country, U.S. Rep. Carl Vinson of nearby Milledgeville, then chairman of the House Naval Affairs Committee. While making it clear he wasn't seeking preferential treatment, Daddy wanted to know if I had been treated legally and fairly and, if a mistake had been made, could it be corrected? My father was a personal friend as well as a supporter of Rep. Vinson. I'm sure Rep. Vinson would have asked the War Department for an explanation on behalf of any constituent and I know he did his best to get answers for my father and the Rowland family. But there was nothing Rep. Vinson could do.

He advised my father the ASTP would soon be shut down. Whether or not I had been misled, my assignment to infantry basic training was irreversible. From the ASTP's inception until its termination, approximately 150,000 soldiers participated. Many had already finished the 18 months of study and had been redeployed in the line of duty. But many were in the midst of studies when they were pulled off campuses and sent overseas to fight the war. I don't know how many other young people were recruited for the program and reassigned without setting foot in a classroom. But there was at least one—me!

Infantry basic training didn't leave me much time to worry about how I had been treated. We were up and on the go before the crack of dawn and went to bed exhausted. We marched day and night, sometimes through swampy terrain, carrying backpacks weighing up to forty pounds. We spent hours practicing at the firing ranges and learning how to clean and disassemble and reassemble our rifles and other weapons. We shined shoes and polished brass. We did countless pushups and other calisthenics. Within the allotted four months, they converted relatively soft young civilians into well-conditioned soldiers.

From Camp Blanding, we traveled by train to Camp Bowie near Brownwood, TX, where we joined the 13th Armored Division, known as the "Black Cats," a division preparing to join the fighting in France following D Day. Trained as a rifleman and machine gunner, I was placed in Company A.

While at Brownwood, a town bustling with soldiers, I searched several jewelry stores to find an engagement ring for Luella. I found one I thought she would like for $100, a huge expenditure in those days, and sent it to her by mail. This took every penny I had. Not having enough money left to buy a candy bar or go to a movie made me feel rather helpless and lonelier than ever. But buying the ring was a step toward what I yearned to do—return home, marry Luella, and get on with my medical education. It didn't look like that would happen anytime soon.

It wasn't long before the 13th Armored Division was on its way to Camp Kilmer in New Brunswick, NJ, the country's largest military processing center where many thousands of troops were dispatched for over-seas duty. I was getting used to long-distance train rides. New Jersey was a frigid place in December and I remember how cold my feet felt while standing on the frozen ground during morning formations. The base provided a variety of recreational facilities for troops awaiting departure including a movie theater and an auditorium where many celebrities per-formed. But the only experience I really enjoyed during my brief stay at Camp Kilmer was visiting New York City, a twenty-two mile train ride.

When told I would have a couple of days of leave, I called Luella and asked her to meet me in Manhattan. She was living in Greensboro, N.C., with her sister, Alma Gailey, where she was employed by a chemical company. Alma arranged for a friend to travel with Luella as a chaper-one. Neither Luella nor I had ever been to New York City. A buddy from New York suggested we meet at the New York Public Library on Fifth Avenue. Manhattan can be a bewildering place for any visitor, especially a small town teenager. When I walked out of the train station and into a scene of soaring buildings, loud horn-honking traffic, and crowds of people everywhere, I was apprehensive about finding Luella.

After arriving at the library and starting up the long stairway, I spot-ted Luella and her travelling companion standing near the entrance, an indescribably happy moment.

We wandered around the city, gawked at the buildings, admired the store-front Christmas decorations, and ate at a couple of restaurants. We found affordable rooms at the Summit Hotel near Rockefeller Center and did some sightseeing the next day. But I had to return to camp. Although just wishful thinking, I had hoped the Army would give me additional leave. I convinced Luella and our chaperone to remain in New York, which they did for two more nights. But I wasn't allowed to leave Camp Kilmer, the place where I first spent a Christmas away from home and family.

My next visit to New York City came a few weeks later. In mid-Jan-uary 1945, countless thousands of troops, including those of us in the 13th Armored Division, filed onto transport ships in New York's harbor for a voyage to France. As I stood at the ship railing and watched the Statue of Liberty fade from sight, I had an empty feeling in the pit of my stomach. Would I ever see home again? Although the troops didn't talk much about the danger ahead, I couldn't help thinking some of us wouldn't return alive.

My ship, the *USS General W.M. Black*, was part of a huge convoy of transport and escort ships, an awesome sight. The *USS General Black* was a Liberty Ship, one of about 2,700 ships rapidly built at a number of U.S. shipyards during World War II to carry troops and supplies to Europe and the Pacific. Some could carry as many as a couple of thousand troops and, believe me, they weren't designed for a pleasure cruise.

Soldiers were packed below deck. The eight bunks in each column were stacked so closely on top of one another it was difficult to turn over. It was a stifling place to try to sleep. The sea was rough at times and many of the troops, including me, suffered from sea sickness. I was miserably nauseated for much of the trip and ate very little. I was also a little nervous when we had U-boat warnings and were instructed not to bang against the hull. Although I didn't hear the noise, depth charges were dropped on at least one occasion when a German submarine was thought to be stalking us.

After nearly two weeks at sea, the convoy finally anchored at the port of LaHavre, France. I was over my sea sickness and feeling better. Although it took two days to unload all of the soldiers, I was fortunately among the first wave to disembark on January 28. None of us wanted to stay aboard those ships any longer than necessary.

What we saw when we landed was sobering. Little was left of the old port city except twisted metal and piles of rubble. One of the worst snow storms in years had hit the area and much of the debris was covered in a deep white blanket with drifts reaching six feet or more. It was painfully cold. Even wearing layers of heavy Army winter clothing, I couldn't believe how cold it was. Although I had experienced cold days in middle Georgia, and I had just been through a cold spell at Camp Kilmer, nothing had prepared me for the bitterly freezing weather we would endure during the next month or so.

My company and other units of the 13th Armored Division were loaded into cattle trucks and half-tracks and driven forty miles through snow and sleet into the interior of Normandy. An Allied staging area had been established between Dieppe and Rouen. This is where we stayed for six weeks to prepare for the missions ahead. Equipped with sleeping bags, we settled into tents, the backs of trucks, and some in houses and buildings.

Several of us found a barn to stay in. We built a small fire to get a little warmer. As a Boy Scout, I was confident we could build and maintain a camp fire without endangering the barn. But the structure had a thatched roof and the farmer disagreed about the safety. He emerged from his farm house with a bucket of water and doused the fire while scolding us in French. We argued in English but he wasn't interested in negotiating. Nor did he invite us inside. With a few more sharp words we didn't understand, he returned to his warm house while we climbed into our sleeping bags and made the best of it. This wasn't the welcome we expected. I remember thinking, *We're saving you from the Germans and you treat us like this!*

Not all of the French locals were unfriendly to the Americans. Some provided eggs, chickens, wine, and other products for small amounts of currency. But based on my contacts with the French people, I discovered some didn't particularly appreciate the Allied liberation in spite of years of brutal Nazi occupation. I suppose many people in France just wished all of the interlopers would go away so they could return to the life they had known before the war.

During the weeks we spent in the Dieppe-to-Rouen area, we unpacked weapons and equipment, checked vehicles for maintenance problems, and took care of the many details necessary to get the division ready. This is where I spent my nineteenth birthday. No one served me cake and ice cream.

CHAPTER FIVE

When we arrived at LaHavre, the Allied forces had stopped the Germans at the Battle of the Bulge a few weeks before and had begun the final Allied offensive across France and into Germany. I participated in the final three months of the eleven-month campaign from the D Day landings in Normandy on June 6, 1944 to the German surrender at a school house in Reims on May 7, 1945. I was one of more than five million Allied soldiers who took part in this superbly-managed military operation by the most mobile and powerful armed force the world had ever known.

They moved us by divisions, ninety-one of them, each approximately 11,000 strong. An average of twelve soldiers belonged to my immediate military family, the squad. Elements of the 13th Armored Division first experienced combat as they approached the German border two months after landing, firing at the enemy from the French side of the border. My squad came under fire after entering Germany, encountering pockets of resistance until nearly the end of the war a month later. Several of my squad members were among the 766,000 Allied soldiers wounded during the fighting in France and Germany and one was among the 200,000 Allied soldiers who paid the ultimate price.

Although the Black Cats were temporarily stationed in a fixed place a couple of times, mostly we kept moving, often traveling day and night.

In combat situations, I was a rifleman when walking and a machine gunner when riding in a half-track. When traveling in the half-track, I was appointed assistant driver, a responsibility placing me in the "jump seat" next to the driver. By riding closer to the engine, I was somewhat warmer than fellow squad members in back. Whenever we stopped, I climbed out with a grease gun and lubricated the bogie wheels, the wheels the track runs on. While traveling at night in a long line of military vehicles, we turned our headlights off in order not to attract enemy fire. The vehicles had a pinpoint light in back for other vehicles to follow. It was my job to keep an eye on the tiny light and help the driver stay on the road and not collide with the vehicle in front.

We suffered from exposure to cold and rainy weather. We experienced severe sleep deprivation, struggling to stay awake even while navigating in the half track, sometimes nodding off even when standing up. We coped with hours of boredom when not on the move and endured intense fear when under fire. We more or less got used to C-rations and K-rations, our main diet.

Moments of relaxation came when we drank strong black coffee warmed by the half-track exhaust and took breaks for cigarettes. Several cigarette brands were in plentiful supply. Maybe the many times I heard announcer Don Wilson recite the slogan, "Be Happy, Go Lucky," while listening to the Jack Benny Show in my parents' bedroom influenced my decision to take up smoking Lucky Strikes. Daddy sent me a "foxhole lighter" that lit a wick with no flame, a prize possession.

Although we occasionally had to stop to let supply trucks catch up with us, the Army did an amazing job of supplying food, ammunition, and other essentials to the vast forces almost constantly on the go. This included delivering the mail, which arrived in batches. If I didn't receive a letter from Luella, I wondered whether she still loved me. But sooner or later I always received a batch of her letters when the mail caught up with us. Mama forwarded my Eagle Scout award and it arrived in one of the mail deliveries. Because of the war, a Boy Scout Court of Honor hadn't been held to formally present the Eagle Scout award. This was a source of interest to other squad members who warmly congratulated me.

After our extended stay at the initial staging area, we were ordered in mid-March to move out. We drove for several hundred miles before bivouacking on the border of France and Germany in the vicinity of the French town of Avricourt where the 13th Armored Division headquarters was established. On the evening of March 19 and morning of March 20 our division's artillery opened fire on the Germans in support of the Seventh Army's attack on Saarbrucken, Germany, the first combat experience for the Black Cats. A few days later my company crossed the German border near Zweibrucken where we were temporarily assigned to police an occupied area. I remember waking up on Easter morning, April 1, 1945, in a foxhole dug on a hillside and looking out over the picturesque countryside. Although still chilly, spring was on the way. Although we didn't know it, this was the calm before the storm. We were about to experience the heat of battle for much of the remainder of the month.

On April 5, I climbed into our half-track to join the line of military traffic leaving the occupied area, heading for Germany's largest river, the Rhine. Although we expected to join Gen. George Patton's Third Army for its drive into German from the south, our division was temporarily diverted to the XVIII Corps to participate in one of the war's decisive campaigns, the encirclement and capture of the Ruhr pocket, the richest of all German industrial areas. This was Germany's last great arsenal. More than 430,000 Germans were defending the Ruhr region. When the region was surrounded and fell, hundreds of thousands of German soldiers were taken prisoner.

The Black Cats drove north along the Rhine until reaching Cologne, the point where we were to join the attack to close the circle. We encountered light-to-moderate German resistance at roadblocks, while crossing rivers and streams, and as we entered and passed through cities and towns, many of them in ruins. When we crossed an intact bridge over the Sieg River and entered the city of Siegburg, we heard heavy enemy artillery and mortar fire. The explosions weren't close enough to stop us and we continued until we reached the rubble of a blown-up overpass, blocking our advance. When Army engineers cleared a path through a railroad yard to bypass the debris-blocked road, we followed a circuitous route northeast of Siegburg and eventually connected with Germany's super-highway, the Autobahn.

We came under intermittent fire as we sped along the Autobahn. Several soldiers in my company, Company A, were wounded. When we stopped at a destroyed bridge over the Agger River, German artillery fire exploded in our vicinity and we fired back at the fields and buildings on the other side of the river with artillery, tank, and mortar fire, hitting a warehouse where ammunition was evidently stored, setting off intermittent explosions. The enemy guns were silenced and the Germans apparently pulled back, enabling our engineers to construct a temporary bridge. At another place where the enemy took a stand, we engaged in an intense thirty-minute exchange of fire, with artillery bursts and tracer flashes filling the sky in both directions. Again, the Germans abandoned their positions and retreated.

Over a period of about a week, we crossed four rivers, the Sieg, Agger, Duhun, and Wupper. At the Wupper River, we lost the 13th Armored Division's commander, Gen. John B. Wogan, who was wounded by German sniper fire while observing a bridging operation. He was replaced by Gen. John Millikin, whom I would later meet at a medal ceremony just after the Germans surrendered.

Somewhere along the way, a 240 mm mortar shell exploded in the street of one of the many German towns we passed through exactly where our squad had temporarily stopped. I was standing not too far from the explosion. When the thick dust and smoke cleared a little, I saw our squad leader, Staff Sgt. Leaton, sitting in the middle of the street, bleeding profusely and calling for help. He suffered a serious head wound and was replaced by Buck Sgt. Thompson. Two other squad members, George Dunseath, a friend, and Clinton George, suffered leg wounds from the shrapnel. Another squad member from Quebec I only knew as "Frenchy" was killed. The incident delayed us, but not for long.

Before we engaged in more fighting, the German defense collapsed and the battle for the Ruhr pocket ended in mid-April. The Black Cats were ordered to head south, cross the Danube River, and continue to the Austrian border, joining Gen. Patton's Third Army for its drive to make contact with the Russian armies entering Germany from the east. After traveling several hundred miles, we crossed the Danube where a sign placed by Army engineers said, "Just another damn river." The "Blue Danube" was a green, muddy color, and was far from beautiful to us. Although we heard German artillery fire in the area, engineers had bridged the Danube and we crossed without incident on April 27.

Overrunning several undefended roadblocks, we approached another large river, the Isar, a day later. The Germans were dug in on the other side. As we advanced, our officers learned a railroad bridge across the Isar had been destroyed but a highway bridge was still intact. But as our leading units reached the river on the afternoon of April 29, the highway bridge was blown up in their faces. The only way to reach the other side was to paddle across in open assault boats through enemy fire.

The 13th Armored Division stopped on the west side of the river with its forces spread out from Worth to Plattling. My squad and the rest of Company A were ordered to cross the Isar River at Landau, a city we couldn't see beyond the trees above the embankment on the other side. The river, about fifty yards wide at this point, swirled and raced at an alarming pace as a result of spring rain and the thawing of the nearby ice-capped Alps. With information coming from aerial sightings, we knew German forces were heavily entrenched on the other side and any crossing would be met with rifle, machine gun, and mortar fire.

During the pre-dawn hours of April 30, our artillery laid down a continuous barrage to clear away the concentration of German defenders. Hoping the enemy firepower was reduced enough to enable most if not all of our assault boats to cross safely and establish a foothold on the other side, we got the go-ahead for the advance to start at 4:05 a.m.

All of us in Company A had dismounted from our vehicles and were assembled by platoons in pitch-black darkness about one hundred yards from the river. It was so dark I couldn't see my hands in front of my face, although I could make out the silhouettes of the heads of some of the guys around me. Instructed not to make a sound, we stood in silence, listening to our artillery shells whistling as they passed overhead and landed in enemy territory.

There were three platoons in the company. The First and Second Platoons were chosen to lead the assault. My platoon, the Third, would go last. As the first two platoons moved to the river's edge, those of us left behind heard rifle and machine gun fire and explosions that sounded like mortar fire. We could tell it was German fire by the sound of the machine guns. The German machine guns had a more rapid pattern than ours—a bbbbbb sound compared to our b-b-b-b-b-b.

Soldiers in the First and Second Platoons were headed directly into that fire, I thought. I nervously waited. Soon it would be the Third Platoon's turn to cross the swiftly-moving river with the enemy shooting at us.

After quite a while, I overheard Company A's commander, Capt. Dickson, tell someone on his radio phone he wasn't sending any men across the river. Thank God, I thought. I later learned a number of our assault boats had been launched and about forty soldiers made it across in spite of the heavy German small arms fire. Some of the soldiers who reached the other side were wounded and all of them were trapped. The embankment on the German side was fairly steep and covered with growth. As long as our soldiers hugged the embankment, they were protected. Although a few German defenders tried to crawl close enough to toss grenades or shoot rifles down at the Americans clinging to the embankment, intense fire from our side kept them back.

By 8:30 a.m., Company A was under orders to do whatever was

possible to evacuate the trapped soldiers. Most of them scrambled along the embankment and took cover in the debris of the blown-out highway bridge. There was a fifteen-foot gap in the bridge. Anyone who tried to swim across would have likely drowned in the current. While they were relatively safe on the embankment or behind the debris, they would have also become open targets in the water. The first rescue plan was to toss a rope from our side of the river to the soldiers concealed amidst the rubble of the bridge in order to secure a lifeline over the gap. A soldier who crawled out on what was left of the bridge on our side in an effort to throw the rope was shot and killed. But a second soldier made a successful toss and the lifeline was secured.

With our guns blazing to prevent the Germans from getting a bead on the "aerialists," most of the trapped soldiers made it back one at a time, hand over hand, above the roiling river. But a couple of wounded GI's remained on the enemy side in extreme danger and someone had to go after them.

The Third Platoon had moved close to the river. Several small boulders were scattered not far from the edge and members of our squad, including me, had taken cover behind them. At the moment, the Germans had stopped shooting. Sgt. Thompson, our squad leader following the wounding of Sgt. Leaton, walked up to us from behind and asked for volunteers to retrieve the wounded. I don't recall agreeing to go. But I got up and joined two others who volunteered. We hurried to an assault boat tethered on the bank, climbed in, and pushed off.

The Germans opened fire as soon as we started across the river. Their bullets sounded like whips cracking above and around us. Fortunately the covering fire from our side prevented the German gunners from zeroing in accurately enough to hit their target. Although terrified, we focused on fighting the current. The assault boats were powered with paddles, and, trust me, we paddled as hard as we could. The boats that made it across earlier were carrying more soldiers and had more paddle-power. In spite of our furious effort, the current swept us fifty yards or so downstream, making the trip all the more frightening.

When we landed, we made our way along the embankment in crouched positions until we reached the spot where we expected to find our wounded. The heavy overgrowth made it a difficult walk. When we reached an assault boat pulled up on the bank, we saw a tech sergeant lying inside, someone I knew from up-state New York whose name I can't recall. He had suffered a severe neck wound. We cautiously crawled up the embankment and peered around for other casualties in the immediate area, but saw no one.

We didn't hear any firing as we paddled back. The German defenders who fired at us when we were headed in their direction must have pulled out. The medics took charge when we landed on our side. Although later told we rescued two soldiers, I only remember one. If there were two with us on the return trip, I'll blame my faulty memory on the hectic situation. But I know all of the trapped troops, including the wounded, made it back.

After returning to my squad, we prepared to travel. I don't remember anyone even mentioning our crossing under fire until a few days later when told I had been recommended for the Bronze Star, which surprised me. As I later read in the "Special Order" accompanying the medal, it was given for "heroic achievement in connection with military operations against the enemy on 30 April 1945…. Private First Class Rowland, rifleman, volunteered to cross the Isar River into enemy territory to remove wounded men trapped there. With others, he crossed the river in an assault boat under heavy enemy small arms' fire, and helped locate two severely wounded soldiers. These casualties were immediately evacuated for medical treatment. The courage and initiative of Private First Class Rowland resulted in the saving of two lives and the ultimate destruction of enemy emplacements that had impeded the Division's advance."

I appreciated the recognition for doing a difficult and dangerous job. But everyone who served in battle zones during the war risked his or her life. Those who suffered lasting wounds and who died in the war are heroes.

While we were stalled at the Landau crossing point, Army engineers installed a pontoon bridge at Plattling. This was where our company finally crossed the Isar River. On May 1, at 11 a.m., after assembling on the other side, we moved southward toward our destination of Marktl, a village on the Inn River near the Austrian border. Some advance units of the 13th Armored Division overcame lightly armed roadblocks between the Isar and Inn rivers and a few soldiers were wounded. The war wasn't quite over. But my squad and company traveled to Marktl without getting fired upon.

The Wehrmacht and SS troops were in a state of collapse. Many thousands were surrendering to the invading Allied forces, many no doubt wanting to avoid capture by the Soviets. We stopped in towns between the Isar River and Marktl, sometimes going door to door to root out concealed enemy soldiers. One of the German soldiers coming out of hiding with arms in the air told us, "Hitler kaput." Hitler had committed suicide, and the news had evidently reached the German troops. In one town, a German officer emerged from a building and approached me waving a white handkerchief. He was carrying a holstered pistol. Speaking good English, he handed me the pistol, said he was glad the war was over, and returned to the building where he would soon be rounded up. I still have the pistol, a weapon made in Yugoslavia.

As we entered one of the towns in southern Germany, I don't recall its name, we encountered scores of liberated inmates of a Nazi slave labor camp. The guards had fled. The survivors came running and stumbling down the main street and surrounded us. Their condition was horrific. If I wasn't fully aware of what the war was all about before then, this experience made it absolutely clear we were fighting pure evil. To this day, I feel angry and sad when I think about what I saw that day.

I was standing in the machine gun turret of our half-track when one of the liberated inmates came to the side of the vehicle. He had tears in his eyes and he reached up for my hand. I leaned over and took his hand in mine. He nodded without saying a word, apparently quietly telling me, "Thank you."

Historians say the Nazis established approximately 15,000 slave labor camps in Germany. The camp we overran may have been one of the sub-camps scattered around Bavaria connected to the notorious Dachau concentration camp. Some of the freed inmates were from Poland. The Nazis brought citizens capable of doing hard physical work from the countries they invaded to work in the labor camps, especially those from the Jewish population.

Along with the rest of Company A, I bivouacked in a field at Marktl. For a few days we were uncertain whether we would be ordered to cross the Inn River and continue mopping-up operations. All of us were thinking, *Am I going to be the last one killed in this war?* We learned on May 7 the Germans had formally surrendered. The surrender became official the following day, May 8, which was celebrated in the U.S. and much of the world as VE Day. We later learned joyful celebrations broke out in the U.S. and allied countries. But there was only a sense of relief among those of us camped in in that field outside the small German village.

We didn't know where we would be headed next. The U.S. would maintain a major military presence in war-torn Europe for a long time to come. But we already knew the 13th Armored Division would be re-deployed in the Pacific as part of an invading force to storm the shores of the Japan. While this wasn't official, it was a persistent rumor.

For the moment, at least, we could enjoy ourselves. Leaving our tents and sleeping bags, we were comfortably billeted in houses and buildings in and around Marktl. German military horses grazed nearby and some of us had great fun riding them through the countryside. We visited a number of sites including Branau, Hitler's birthplace; the old Austrian city of Salzburg; and The Eagle's Nest, Hitler's mountain re-treat. Now that we were no longer at war, the mountainous scenery was awe-inspiring.

Although it was May and spring flowers were beginning to bloom, at one point it snowed. I considered this quite odd. It surely wouldn't happen in Georgia where I desperately wanted to be.

Early in June, after serving as an occupational force for a few weeks, we rode in railroad box cars to Camp Atlanta near Reims where the surrender document was signed, passing through Munich where Hitler got his political start, a city now left in near-total destruction. Camp Atlanta was one of the staging areas named for U.S. cities or for cigarette brands established by the Army to send arriving troops into battle and then were used after the surrender as staging areas for troops returning to the states. Although we were allowed to keep Nazi souvenirs, one of my barrack mates quickly got rid of some jewelry he said he had found in one of the destroyed cities. We were warned soldiers caught with personal property that didn't belong to them would be court marshaled. None of us wanted our departure for home delayed for any reason.

The return voyage was about as uncomfortable as the one coming over. But knowing I would soon be reunited with Luella and my family and friends made it much more tolerable. We arrived in Hampton Roads, VA, and were transported to nearby Camp Patrick Henry. Although still at war with Japan, the country was celebrating the victory in Europe. Everywhere we went we were treated like heroes. Life was good again, although we expected it to be a temporary respite. At Camp Patrick Henry, I was given a thirty-day furlough. After that, my orders called for me to report to Camp Cook, CA, the staging area for sending troops to the Pacific. As far as anyone in the 13th Armored Division knew, the furlough could be the last time we would see friends and loved ones. I intended to make the most of it by getting married.

I caught a bus to Dublin, arriving after midnight. From the bus terminal, I called my parents in Wrightsville. They left for the sixteen mile drive to Dublin to pick me up. Instead of waiting, I took a taxi which had come to the terminal for the late bus arrival. About half-way to Wrightsville I spotted a car coming our way. It was my parents. Both vehicles stopped and I quickly paid the taxi driver and jumped out. We celebrated my homecoming at the side of the road in the middle of the night with everyone excitedly hugging and chattering.

Luella and I were married at the Wrightsville Methodist Church on August 3. Borrowing my parents' car, we drove to Jacksonville, Florida, for our honeymoon. Not having booked a place to stay in advance, we found a rental cottage on the beach. At first the lady who owned the beach house wasn't sure about us. But we convinced her we were newlyweds who would be trustworthy tenants. It was a perfect place. Maybe the fact that I would likely return to harm's way in a few weeks made us enjoy every moment all the more.

I've read a lot about the dropping of the atomic bomb on Hiroshima and Nagasaki, including a number of critical articles. It was awful for so many people to be killed and horribly maimed by the blast and by the long term effects of radiation exposure. But there's a good chance I wouldn't have survived the war if it hadn't been for those bombs. Many thousands of American and Japanese soldiers would have been killed in an invasion of Japan. Many civilians would also have lost their lives. We believed President Truman made the only decision he could have made. Soon after the bombs were dropped on August 6 and August 9, the war in the Pacific ended.

Military personnel were discharged when they accumulated enough points for duration of service, service overseas, combat service, exemplary service, medals for bravery, and other criteria. I was still well short of the threshold.

While stationed at Camp Cook, I was given a couple of furloughs with sufficient time to make the grueling train trip from California to Georgia, and back, which took several days each way. The trains lacked air conditioning and it was a grimy, extremely tiring trip. Sleeping in the coach seats night after night was exhausting. Sponging off in the train lavatory was the only way to get a little cleaner. In spite of the discomfort, I made two trips home.

Neither my family nor I could understand why I had to stay on the west coast. But the Army made it clear I would remain in California for the foreseeable future. I suppose the Army felt it made an exception for one soldier other requests for reassignment would have to be approved. Again my father contacted Rep. Vinson. This time the congressman's intervention on my behalf worked. The fact that I had been misled in my recruitment probably influenced the congressman. He was also told I was a newly-wed and he knew keeping me separated by thousands of miles from my wife and family wasn't serving any military need. Soon after Rep. Vinson was contacted, I was transferred to Fort McPherson in Atlanta and assigned to the Military Police Detachment.

They needed a typist at my Atlanta posting and I could type. This led to my promotion to sergeant, giving me additional points. After serving three months as a clerk-typist, I was eligible for discharge and I declined an offer to reenlist with the possibility of going to Officer Candidate School. I just wanted out after two years and two weeks of active military duty from my induction on April 14, 1944, until my official discharge on May 1, 1946.

CHAPTER SIX

Like many returning veterans, I faced an uncertain future. I couldn't have been happier when I learned Luella was expecting or prouder when our daughter, Lou, soon joined us. But, as parents, we had to face reality.

Although I still dreamed of becoming a medical doctor, we knew six years of pre-med and medical studies would require substantial out-of-pocket expenses for a young family of three and we would have to live close to the financial edge even with parental help and educational assistance under the GI bill. Moreover, we weren't sure I could immediately gain admission to a college at a time when veterans were surging onto suddenly-overcrowded campuses. Admission was especially problematic at the University of Georgia, my first choice for pre-med studies, a campus bursting with incoming veterans.

We moved in with my folks and I joined the "52-20 Club," a federal program paying jobless veterans $20 a week for up to fifty-two weeks. My "52-20" eligibility ended when I took a temporary job as Wrightsville's city mail carrier as a substitute for my former scoutmaster, Cliff Moye, who had undergone an operation and needed time off to recuperate. I learned a permanent position as a Johnson County rural mail carrier was expected to open up and it would probably be mine if I wanted it. I was seriously tempted. It would have provided job security, health care coverage, and a respectable income.

After making it through the war safely, I had a close call not long after returning home. My high school football buddy, Henry Mallette, had taken up flying as a senior in high school and joined the Civil Air Patrol. Henry served in the Army Air Corps during the war. I had visited him when I was stationed at Camp Bowie and he was training as an aviation cadet in San Antonio. Now back in Wrightsville, Henry regularly flew a nearly-new Piper Cub he rented from the owner of the air field in nearby Dublin, Bud Barron. Henry offered to give me flying lessons. My mail delivery duties left me plenty of free time and I jumped at the chance.

Henry was a good pilot. He also took chances. Attempting a perilous aerial maneuver during one of our lessons, we crash landed in a field in Wrightsville. The aircraft was significantly damaged. We suffered minor injuries and had to receive emergency treatment from a Wrightsville doctor. We were lucky. The consequences could have been much more serious. My father took it very seriously. In a man-to-man conversation, he told me I was a father with responsibilities and I would have to make up my own mind whether I should keep flying. But if I did, I wouldn't be welcome to stay under his roof. This ended my flying aspirations. I wish Henry had quit flying as well. Some years later, in his forties, he was killed while performing a flying stunt in an air show he had started.

My career as a postman ended when a cousin, J.W. Brinson, who was home for a visit, suggested I apply to the junior college he was attending in Douglas, South Georgia College. Douglas was the city where my mother taught school before marrying my father. As a youngster, I spent part of my summer vacations with Uncle Emmitt and Aunt Ida Roberts. I had enjoyed those visits in spite of suffering from hay fever from the tobacco dust that pervaded the town during tobacco season. By mid-1946, I had been accepted and Luella, Lou, and I were on our way to South Georgia College.

Under the GI bill signed into law by President Franklin D. Roosevelt three years before, veterans could receive assistance for tuition, books, and a small monthly allowance for four years of college. More than two million World War II veterans would attend college with the bill's help. When I enrolled, nearly half of the males attending college were veterans. Luella would remain a fulltime mother and supportive wife and I would remain a fulltime student for four of the six years it would take to earn my MD. Although my parents would help with living expenses for all six years, Luella would take a job, Lou would be placed in day care, and I would find ways to augment our income when the GI benefits ran out.

Would I have become a medical doctor without government help? Maybe. But it's more likely the dream I had held since my days helping PaPa at the drug store would have gone unfulfilled.

We temporarily moved into a South Georgia College dormitory on the campus a couple of miles outside of town. But we soon located an affordable furnished room for rent at a home within the town limits. In addition to kitchen privileges, we lived in one room. I studied on a card table. For relaxation, we often walked the half mile to the center of town, pushing Lou in a wicker stroller. I bought a girl's bike for $10 and pedaled to classes on a sandy unpaved road.

My chemistry teacher, Mr. Barnett, particularly tried to assist veterans. With his mentoring, I acquired a solid foundation in chemistry, a particularly important subject for an aspiring medical doctor. While I had studied fairly diligently at Emory at Oxford, I really bore down at South Georgia College and was rewarded with excellent grades. The two quarters I spent in Douglas gave me a basic grounding that prepared me for the increasingly difficult academic challenges ahead.

I applied for admission to the University of Georgia and was accepted, transferring to the Athens campus in the fall of 1946. The university provided us an unfurnished apartment on the first floor of a two-story wooden structure that once served as an Army barrack, one of a row of surplus barracks obtained by the university to house veterans with families. PaPa gave us furniture stored behind his home that belonged to his mother, my great-grandmother, and we borrowed Papa Rowland's truck to haul the furniture to Athens. The converted barracks were heated with kerosene. With fuel in short supply following the war, my parents saved us from running out several times by bringing us some from Wrightsville.

Our apartment was located on "Ag Hill" on the southern side of the large campus. Although I could occasionally catch a ride from a neighboring student, most of the time I walked to classes on the main north campus, a hike of about two miles each way, an even longer distance than my walks to classes at South Georgia College. I was rushed by SAE fraternity, the fraternity my father belonged to and my brother would later join. But I was too busy for fraternity life. Aside from rare breaks like the Saturday afternoon football games at nearby Sanford Stadium, I continued to study almost every minute I was awake and continued to do well academically.

The Medical College of Georgia in Augusta paid particular attention to grades in organic chemistry in selecting new students. I earned A's in both of my organic chemistry classes. Nevertheless, we weren't certain I would make the cut when I sought admission to medical school. The University of Georgia gave students IQ and aptitude tests. While my scores potentially qualified me for admission to medical school, I was told they were marginal and, if accepted, I might struggle academically. This made me even more determined to qualify.

Luella and I regularly socialized with the couple living above us, James "Spot" Hunt and his wife Avis. We had a lot in common. Spot was also a pre-med student and he and Avis also had one child. Spot and I applied to the Medical College of Georgia at the same time. While waiting for an answer toward the end of the school year, I frequently checked the mail at the post office on Lumpkin Street about a mile from where we resided. When the envelope bearing the medical college logo arrived, my heart pounded as I tore it open. It's a big understatement to say I was happy and relieved at my acceptance. I ran to our apartment as fast as I could to tell Luella.

Spot hadn't heard from the medical college. This seemed ominous. Since I had received an acceptance letter and he hadn't, he wondered whether he had been rejected. It was a tremendous relief for the Hunts when a letter of approval arrived the next day. Since we wanted our friends to join us in Augusta, this was good news for us as well.

Moving back to Wrightsville for the summer, we boarded part of the time with Luella's parents and part of the time with mine and drove to Augusta several times in a borrowed car to look for a place to live. It wasn't easy to find something suitable within our modest price range. We couldn't afford a car and I needed to reside within walking distance of the college. If we had taken the first thing we found that we could afford, my start in medical school might well have been much more difficult. But we were fortunate. Thanks to Luella's brother, Travis L. Price, Jr., who lived in Augusta, we had a place to temporarily stay while we searched for an apartment that was right for us.

As the opening of fall quarter neared, we located an affordable apartment on 15th Street about a mile from school. This was a lucky break for several reasons. Bill Martin, a senior at the medical college, and his wife Beth, who worked in the school's bacteriology department, were next door neighbors. Bill helped guide me through the first year. He owned a car and I often hitched a ride to class with him. Our friendship with the Martins also paid off two years later when my GI aid ran out and Luella needed a job. She replaced Beth in the bacteriology department with Beth's recommendation. The apartment was located directly across the street from the Theta Kappa Psi fraternity house, another lucky happenstance. Every medical student joined one of the four fraternities then connected to the medical college. Fraternity affiliation not only provided a social outlet, members helped each other scholastically. I joined Theta Kappa Psi.

Once we moved in, and I registered for classes, the difficult work began. My previous college studies didn't compare with the academic intensity of medical college. When not in class, I constantly stayed busy studying or doing clinical work. Flunking out became a real worry at times.

We were also never free from financial pressure, nearly running out of money at the end of every month. Anxiety and physical and mental exhaustion were the norm. If not as sleep-deprived as I had been as a combat soldier, fatigue was a routine part of my existence as a medical student.

If medical school sounds like an ordeal, it often was. But, in fact, these were probably the most enjoyable four continuous years of my life.

Meeting the academic challenge was the most gratifying thing I had ever done. But there was more to the medical school experience than personal accomplishment. Bonding with a community of bright and dedicated young people who shared a common purpose made it such an unforgettable time. Several of us in the freshman class once discussed what our place in the college's history would be and decided our class would probably be rated as the all-time best. Perhaps we were cocky. But it reflected our youthful exuberance and passion for medicine. We believed we were preparing not only for our own future, but to help usher in a brilliant new era in health care.

We would have scoffed if compared to Dr. Kildare, the fictional young doctor who confronted and overcame wrongdoing in books, films, radio, and a TV series. We knew these melodramatic stories weren't real life. But maybe all of us privately identified with the heroic idealism of Dr. Kildare. In retrospect, embracing a sense of dedication to the advancement of medicine and the care of patients was as important as the studies.

Our first year was devoted to basic sciences including histology, osteology, and physiology. We studied gross anatomy half a day, every day, for the first two quarters. To learn about the human anatomy, we worked with cadavers preserved in tanks of formaldehyde, with four students assigned to each cadaver. Every freshman smelled like formaldehyde. You couldn't scrub enough to wash the odor away. When freshmen went to a party or restaurant or any place where people gathered, everyone avoided them. I'm not exaggerating. But I didn't mind at all. It was part of our identity.

At the end of the school year, the first-year class traditionally threw a party called the "Freshman Brawl." Just as the name suggests, we really let our hair down. It was, after all, a major milestone in our lives. For the first time I consumed enough alcohol to really feel the affect.

Beginning my sophomore year, I felt I had arrived. I was now a veteran who welcomed and helped the newcomers. But this was my toughest year academically. I particularly struggled with physiology, a stumbling block for many students. We also studied bacteriology, parasitology, pathology biochemistry, pharmacology, physical diagnosis, and an introduction to clinical medicine. Bearing down harder than ever, I managed to do well in all my subjects in spite of moments of real uncertainty.

In the final quarter, I was awarded my white coat along with my stethoscope, percussion hammer, otoscope, ophthalmoscope, and blood pressure cuff. I also saw my first patient. The poor fellow had been seen many times by other medical students. His chart must have weighed five pounds.

When Luella took a job at the bacteriology department, she worked with our close friends Rhee Rabb and Mary Waters, wives of fellow medical students Roy Rabb and Raymond Waters. We were a virtual family. I worked in the summer between my sophomore and junior years cleaning newly-built brick homes with muriatic acid, which, believe me, is rough on the hands. I joined ROTC in my junior and senior years, receiving a small amount of additional pay for the college-connected military training. In my senior year, I also earned extra money working as a University Hospital extern.

My feeling of accomplishment and confidence as a budding physician was dramatically elevated as a junior. We studied medicine, surgery, endocrinology, OB/GYN, psychiatry, anesthesiology, urology, and orthopedics. This was also the beginning of my clinical years, a time when I began regularly seeing patients in the clinics and at the hospital.

About this time PaPa bought a new Buick and gave us his old car, a 1941 Plymouth sedan with running boards, the final model before the production of civilian vehicles was suspended during World War II. It was a dependable car requiring few repairs. With this new mobility, we were able to rent a small house located a little farther away from the college on Cumming Road for my final two years in medical college. The previous occupants, Don Dearing, his wife Marian, and their three children, had moved into a new house next door. Rather than sell, Don rented his vacated house to us.

Don was a motorcycle buff who owned two British-made BSA motorcycles. He invited me to join him on motorcycle jaunts around the immediate countryside. Although a neophyte, I improved. Don thought I was advanced enough to join him as a participant in a cross-country motorcycle race in Columbia, S.C. This sounded like great fun to me. Luella didn't think as highly of the idea, however. I was a few months away from graduation and, if injured and laid up, I might not have finished my classes and qualified for my long-sought medical degree. She was right, of course. Racing a motorcycle wasn't sensible. When my father heard about my plan to race, he called and said I would have to choose between continued financial help from home or racing.

I wisely didn't race and my motorcycle days were over. My father's blunt counseling might have saved me from serious injury or worse once again.

As a senior, I was given more responsibility. I now assisted in the operating room. This included delivering babies in the "Stork Club," a basement suite of the Newton Building where seniors like me attended to pregnant women who were charity patients, with help from an OB/GYN resident if needed. Various departments within the college offered externships for experience and income. I was given an externship assisting residents and attending physicians in surgery during the day and as an emergency room doctor at University Hospital at night. Because of a shortage of real interns, the responsibility I was given in the ER was comparable to a year of internship.

We learned late in the school year no final exams would be given. We would be graded by observations of the faculty. This was fine with me. I had finished near the top of my class, one of four seniors selected for the honor medical society, Alpha Omega Alpha, the medical school equivalent of Phi Beta Kappa. Spot Hunt was another. The aptitude test at the University of Georgia rating me as marginally qualified for medical school didn't measure my determination.

Perhaps the most brilliant student during my years at the Medical College of Georgia was a fellow named Brantley Jenkins. I recall Brantley completing a physiology exam well ahead of everyone else in class without making a single mistake. He was far ahead of everyone. But he really wasn't too interested in medicine and he dropped out of medical school in his sophomore year to run a fishing camp. I applaud him for doing what he wanted to do in life. But I always wanted to be a medical doctor. For me, it took hard work. Based on my experience, I'm convinced passion and determination are the most important qualities in achieving one's goals.

To celebrate our graduation, a grand party was traditionally held at The Richmond Hotel in downtown Augusta. Before the celebration began, members of the senior class and their spouses or dates gathered anxiously to wait for a faculty member who would enter and announce who was graduating and who was not. Nobody could remember anyone failing to graduate after reaching this point. Nevertheless, we were a little nervous. When Peter B. Wright, professor of orthopedics, entered the room, he wasn't smiling. He named two members of our class who didn't make it. That killed the party and we quietly left. Fortunately, the two graduated a year later.

The ceremony for the graduating class of seventy-six men and two women was held at the Bell Auditorium in Augusta with Mama and Daddy looking on. Some years later I delivered the Medical College of Georgia commencement address. I was also the featured speaker at a ceremony for medical college students who were awarded their white coats. I was honored to participate in both of these ceremonies. I knew these milestones meant as much to those young medical students and graduates as they had to me.

Founded in 1828, Georgia's flagship public medical college is now part of a vast complex providing education in a wide range of disciplines, cutting-edge research, and state-of-the-art hospital and clinical services. As an appointee of two governors, I served from 2005 until 2015 on the board of directors of MCG Health System, the entity operating the hospital, clinics, faculty practice, and the Medical College of Georgia consisting of the medical college, nursing school, dental school, and allied sciences.

This was a period of great growth and change at the medical college. As one board member, my contribution was a small one. But I had a central role in one episode that might have had a damaging impact on the future of the medical college if it hadn't been resolved without breaking into an open political conflict.

My appointment came about in a circuitous way. In 2004, I asked a friend who was close to then-Gov. Sonny Perdue to approach the governor about an appointment to the Board of Regents, which oversees the university system. I thought a seat on the state board was opening up. A member was finishing his second term and members were traditionally limited to two terms. I had supported Sonny Perdue in his gubernatorial race, helping him raise $35,000 at a Dublin fund raiser. This wasn't a valid reason for awarding someone a seat on the Board of Regents. But it didn't hurt that he knew me personally, and I thought he would seriously consider adding someone to the board with a medical background.

But the member I sought to replace, Don Leeburn, Jr., a prominent businessman who was considered one of the state's most powerful movers and shakers, had served as chairman of the Board of Regents and on the board's strategic planning committee charged with mapping the future of higher education in Georgia. Citing his board experience in key roles, Gov. Perdue reappointed the incumbent. The governor appointed me to the MCG Health System board, which I greatly appreciated.

Several members of the Board of Regents also served on the MCG Health System board. Don Leeburn was one of them. In fact, Don became chairman of the MCG board. Although outwardly cordial, I felt Don did whatever he could to marginalize my influence. After all, I was the guy who had tried to interfere with his controversial appointment to a third term on the Board of Regents.

As I gradually learned, Don Leeburn and University System Chancellor Erroll B. Davis, Jr. strongly disagreed over the direction of the MCG Health System. Without re-litigating the issues, the chancellor had come to believe the system needed a change at the top. Some members allied themselves with the Don Leeburn. But I believe most, including me, sided with the chancellor.

My role in this unpleasant affair grew out of a board meeting where board members were asked to expel a young Asian resident at the hospital for a serious violation of protocol. When the expulsion was about to be routinely approved, I objected. This was excessive punishment. As we reviewed he facts, the chancellor, who also served on the MCG Health System board, and most of the other members agreed with me, and we voted to reprimand rather than expel the resident.

While talking about disciplinary policy, I commented on our goals for the system in a way that revealed my support for the chancellor's vision. I'm sure this is why he privately invited me to meet with him and another board member, Mansfield Jennings of Hawkinsville, for breakfast at the hotel where we were staying. This was where I joined in supporting their plan to engineer a change in leadership. This wouldn't be easy. Don had friends in high places. But we all did.

A situation that could have become an open controversy was resolved quietly. Although I wasn't there, I suspect the governor decided the chancellor's position should be upheld. Don Leeburn resigned as chairman in 2009 and was replaced by Mansfield. A new MCG Health System CEO was also named, Ricardo Azziz, a nationally-recognized figure.

While serving on the board was an honor, it was also hard and stressful work at times. But I was happy to make a contribution to a place where I spent four of the best years of my life and where the dream I had embraced at the age of twelve became a reality.

CHAPTER SEVEN

After passing the licensing exam administered by the Georgia Board of Medical Examiners in 1952, I served for two years at the Macon Hospital in an internship and a family practice residency.

The pay was minimal and the workload extreme. Interns remained on duty for thirty-six hours and were off for twelve. Every other weekend, we worked from noon on Saturday until 7 a.m. on Monday, forty-three continuous hours. After sleeping most of Monday, we returned early Tuesday morning to our thirty-six hour weekday schedule. We rarely had a moment of rest while on duty. One weekend I delivered fourteen babies, a mind-boggling number.

My salary started a $200 a month and peaked at $300. Considering the knowledge, experience, and skills I acquired, I was well compensated.

We moved into a low-rent apartment to make ends meet. I earned extra income by driving to Wrightsville on off weekends to help Dr. Harold Harrison, who was in general practice. Later, as a resident with more weekends off, I drove to Wrightsville more often to cover for Dr. Billy Dodd, who had succeeded Harold. By working at extra jobs, I not only gained more experience, we saved enough money to buy our first new car, a Chevrolet coupe for $1,700.

Meanwhile, our second child, Jane, was born. With the residency coming to an end, Luella and I were eager to settle down with our growing family in a permanent job at a permanent place.

While working as residents at the Macon Hospital, a classmate from the Medical College of Georgia, Herbert "Frosty" Frost, and I decided to open a practice together. We searched for a suitable community in middle Georgia needing more physicians. Swainsboro appeared to be a promising choice. When we introduced ourselves to some of the movers and shakers in the southeast Georgia community, we were warmly invited to settle there. So we did. A builder, R.J. Waller, constructed a house for Luella and me for a buyer-friendly cost of $7,000, the first home we owned. A prominent businessman, Frank Flanders, financed the construction of a small office building built near downtown Swainsboro just for Frosty and me to open our new practice.

Three medical doctors were practicing in Swainsboro when we arrived. One of them practiced at the Emanuel County Hospital and other two practiced at Smith's Hospital, a private facility. Frosty and I decided to practice at the Emanuel County Hospital. The physician who was already practicing there was a good doctor who was much loved by his patients. He had been exceptionally friendly to us. He and his wife, a gracious lady, had hosted Frosty and me and our wives at dinner. But on occasion he displayed a remarkable temper.

The three of us agreed to rotate calls at the Emanuel County Hospital emergency room. One night I was called to treat an emergency room patient injured in an auto accident. Believing I was on duty, I responded. Later that night, the physician called me at home and angrily told me he was scheduled to be on call to see ER patients that evening and if I knew what was good for me I better not answer emergency calls when it wasn't my turn. Although I didn't think he was really on duty that evening, I said I was sorry. I would be a lot sorrier if I wasn't careful, he responded. I asked if he was threatening me, and he said no. But, he added, "The next time you walk in front of me I'll stomp your ass into the ground."

That sounded like a threat to me. I called an attorney that night and he suggested I talk to the sheriff. The sheriff advised me there was nothing he could legally do but recommended I carry a pistol. Packing a pistol wasn't an option. Instead, I decided to try to resolve the situation peacefully.

The following morning I waited at the back of the hospital where our mercurial colleague parked. When he arrived, he climbed out of his car, walked up, put his arm around my shoulder, and asked me to accompany him to look at some X-rays. He wanted my opinion. That's what I did. His bizarre threat wasn't mentioned. A few weeks later he asked me to stop by his office. I was surprised when he urged me to ditch Frosty and join him as a partner in his practice. I turned him down, of course. I was happy partnering with Frosty and certainly didn't want to work more closely with someone with serious anger issues. Besides, by then I was thinking of moving to Dublin.

As we calculated, Swainsboro and the surrounding area needed a couple of more doctors. But soon after we established ourselves in Swainsboro two other physicians came to town. Four more medical doctors were too many. Frosty and I could barely earn a living. To expand our patient base, we arranged to see patients in nearby Kite two days a week at the town's pharmacy. Ellis Claxton, the pharmacist, was a cousin of a prominent Dublin physician who had recently died, Dr. E.B. Claxton, who owned the Claxton Hospital in Dublin. Ellis suggested I talk to Dr. Claxton's partner, Dr. John A. Bell, who was looking for a doctor to practice at the Claxton Hospital following the loss of Dr. Claxton.

When I met with Dr. Bell, he asked me to join him and I accepted. When I told Frosty, he planned to transfer to Dublin once I was established. This never occurred. When I left, Frosty did well financially after inheriting all my patients and he stayed in Swainsboro. At the time of our move to Dublin, Luella was pregnant. Frosty delivered our third child, Jim, and I later delivered his third child. We remained close friends for many years.

With my mother helping with much of the packing, Luella came straight to Dublin from the Swainsboro hospital when Jim was five days old. We were welcomed by a small army of family and friends. Several aunts and uncles lived in Dublin, including Aunt Ida who had moved from Douglas to Dublin after Uncle Emmett died. I renewed friendships with some of the Boy Scouts I knew when attending Scout meetings in Dublin and with some of the Dublin High football players I played against when the Wrightsville High and Dublin High teams met in 1941 and 1942. Wrightsville won both games, 7 to 6 in 1941 and 13 to 0 in 1942. The Dublin players jokingly insisted Wrightsville cheated. In fact, we did cheat in 1942, inadvertently playing an ineligible player. But I wouldn't admit it.

On December 14, 1954, Luella and I and our three children moved into a small rental home in Dublin. We were inundated with Christmas presents that year from family, friends, and new medical associates. I've never seen so many packages before or since.

John moved into Dr. Claxton's larger office and made his old office available to me rent-free. My space included two examining rooms and a small area to do my own lab work. John turned his overflow patients and house calls over to me, providing an instant practice that quickly grew. The Claxton Hospital received many emergency patients and John turned the night ER cases over to me.

Since I had recently completed my residency, John figured I was up to date on the latest medical practices and often consulted me. He asked my opinion in the puzzling case of a prominent Dublin citizen who was being treated for hypertension. The patient was taking a new medication for lowering blood pressure. It was working well until the patient almost passed out when he stood up. He told Dr. Bell the fainting spells were happening fairly frequently. When John asked me about it, it occurred to me the blood pressure medication was excreted from the body almost exclusively through the bowel. When the patient was constipated, the medication continued to be absorbed, lowering the blood pressure too much. By treating the underlying cause, the problem was essentially resolved.

John performed quite a few hysterectomies and I taught him the Torpin technique of ligating the uterine and ovarian arteries before beginning to dissect the uterus from the pelvis. I was responsible for bringing the Torpin pelvimetry to the X-ray department, a technique for measuring the mid-pelvis in first pregnancies. Dr. Richard Torpin, head of the OB/GYN Department at the Medical College of Georgia, invented the device and I was very familiar with it. When I assisted in the delivery of a baby for one of John's patients who had a very difficult and protracted labor, it helped make my case for the Torpin pelvimetry. His openness to new ways of doing things was one reason why it was rewarding to work with John.

Medicine was rapidly changing then just as it is now. As a board certified family practitioner, I could handle the diverse procedures competently with what we knew at the time and I could keep up with new diagnostic and treatment modalities with the help of continuing education courses. Many years later, when I retired from Congress after not practicing medicine for 12 years, I was astounded to discover how far I had been left behind even though I knew dramatic advances had continued to occur. It's not surprising physicians today limit their field of practice considering how much specialized knowledge is required. Once again I've immersed myself in continuing education courses to prepare myself for the work I'm now doing.

As my practice expanded, some of John's patients switched to me, perhaps preferring a younger doctor they perceived as more up-to-date on the latest medical advances. While I could contribute some knowledge about new medical developments, I certainly didn't have his years of experience. John was a fine doctor and I wasn't too comfortable when his patients switched. But he had a large practice and never seemed to mind.

Five years after settling in Dublin, my practice had continued to grow and I decided to seek a partner. John wasn't interested in partnering with anyone. If I recruited another doctor to join me at the Claxton Hospital, there wouldn't have been enough office space for the two of us. This is when I raised the idea of developing a new medical center. When I talked it over with John, he liked the idea and decided to help. He even planned to move his own independent practice to the proposed new facility.

We picked a downtown location because of my connection with two pharmacists, Louie Reynolds and Wendell Smith. I had known Louie during my freshman year in medical school. He transferred to pharmacy school after his freshman year in medical school and he and Wendell were now owners and operators of Dublin's Bellevue Pharmacy. They wanted to enlarge their drug store. Together we came up with a plan to purchase an adjacent house and vacant property contiguous to the pharmacy. We collectively borrowed the money to construct a medical complex with sufficient space to house the doctor's offices and the expanded pharmacy.

Following the headaches of any construction project, the work was completed and we moved into the facility, calling it the Medical Arts Center. We eventually added a new wing and a second story. The complex grew to include the pharmacy; Dr. Bell's practice; the second floor practice of Dr. Nelson Carswell, the only pediatrician in town; my partnership; and later a larger group practice I helped form. Now relocated, the group practice would eventually become one of the largest anywhere for a city the size of Dublin.

My first partner in Dublin was my old friend Spot Hunt. Spot had been practicing in the town of Mt. Vernon. We had stayed in touch, socially visiting one another from time to time. When I offered him a partnership in the growing city of Dublin with offices in a newly-built medical center, he accepted. I felt really fortunate. Spot was one of my most cherished friends and an outstanding young physician. We each had our own offices and we shared three examining rooms.

Our waiting rooms were racially segregated. At the time, we couldn't have sustained a practice with integrated waiting rooms. Segregation was still deeply rooted in society and it was never questioned by patients, white or black. When the center was expanded a few years later, we established one large waiting room for everyone.

Spot and I agreed he would receive thirty-five percent of the partnership's net income the first year, forty-five percent the second, and fifty percent after that. This was a generous proposal. It would give him time to become known in the community and grow his patient base in order to contribute an equal amount, more or less, to the practice's income. Our agreement was verbal. We didn't think a written contract was necessary, a serious mistake. While I worked hard to proactively expand the practice, Spot's patient base didn't grow as expected. After his first year, it was clear he wasn't seeing enough patients to earn nearly half of the partnership's income. When I talked to him about adjusting our agreement until he took on more patients, he adamantly refused. This created a rift. He soon left to go into practice in a community near Atlanta. I never saw Spot again, a sad ending to our long friendship.

After Spot left, the proposal to establish the group practice emerged. Such a practice, unusual for a community the size of Dublin and Laurens County at the time, promised advantages for both the physicians and the patients. It would enable the practice to employ a larger administrative and clerical staff to make the complicated management of a medical office more efficient. It would make it convenient for physicians with a variety of skills to consult one another on difficult cases. It would also make it easier to cover for a physician who was ill or temporarily away from the practice.

The idea sprang from a conversation at a motel in Atlanta between a fellow Dublin physician, Dr. Quentin Price, and myself. Quentin settled in Dublin about six years after I arrived and was practicing with Dr. Fred Chambliss. Quentin and I became close social friends, occasionally spending a few days of rest and relaxation with our wives at the Heart of Atlanta Motel near the center of Georgia's capital city. While sitting around the motel swimming pool one day, we idly speculated about merging our practices. The more we talked about the idea, the better it seemed. When our subsequent conversations about a merger became more serious, I decided to call an expert in medical office management for advice.

I had read articles in a magazine, *Medical Economics*, written by an authority on medical office management, an Englishman named Horace

Cotton. After obtaining his telephone number through the magazine, he enthusiastically offered to visit Dublin to help us get established. I couldn't have been more surprised and pleased. We agreed to a nominal fee for his services and he visited Dublin for three days, staying at our home. He was a fascinating conversationalist and we chatted every evening while he consumed exactly two drinks of scotch. He helped us develop a model for running a group practice that we followed all the years I was a part of it.

We formed the practice in 1964 with Quentin Price, Fred Chambliss, Jim Kibler, and myself as the four partners. Our wing included suites for each of the doctors; fifteen examining rooms; a laboratory staffed by a fulltime technician; and a waiting room with a seating capacity of about forty people. Almost always crowded, the waiting room resembled a bus station. To oversee the business end of the practice, the four of us rotated as the managing partner. We treated everything from colds and flu, other diseases, all kinds of injuries, and performed many surgical procedures. Starting in the 1970s, we developed a large OB/GYN practice. A highlight of my medical career was delivering more than 2,200 babies and watching many of those children grow to adulthood, and then delivering many of their children.

Although I felt a sense of loyalty to the Claxton Hospital which gave me my start in Dublin, many patients preferred the newer Laurens County Memorial Hospital. This was also where my partners maintained their hospital practice. Although I continued to steer patients to the Claxton Hospital when I could, it was difficult having patients at two hospitals and I gradually shifted my hospital practice to Laurens County Memorial Hospital. After I was elected to Congress, the Claxton Hospital closed. John continued his office practice into his nineties.

With few exceptions, every physician deals with stressful and tragic cases. When my father was injured in an auto accident while driving to Macon on business, and was brought to the Claxton Hospital where I had been practicing for two years, we called in a surgeon with extensive experience in dealing with the kind of severe trauma Daddy had suffered.

But we lost Daddy after fighting to save his life for several days. I can also never forget the day I was called on an emergency basis to see the wife of a good friend. Although the couple lived in Dublin, the woman, who was in near term pregnancy, was under the care of a Macon physician. When called and told she was bleeding profusely, I rushed to her home and drove her to Laurens Memorial Hospital myself. Contacting her physician in Macon, we did everything we could, but lost the mother and the baby, a tragedy that haunts me.

One rare case with a more fortunate outcome involved a 40-year-old woman who was pregnant for the first time. At her age, I wanted to be sure the size of her pelvis was normal. The pelvimetry and radiology report showed a borderline pelvis while a flat plate of the abdomen revealed a normal intrauterine pregnancy. Based on this information, I decided to do a cesarean section. When I opened the abdomen, I was shocked to see the fetus. I thought for a second I had cut through the abdominal wall and the uterine wall in one swoop. But this wasn't possible. I almost couldn't believe what I was looking at—a term fetus in the amniotic sac lying in the abdominal cavity.

An abdominal pregnancy going to term is very rare. If I had not done a C-section the baby would have died in the abdomen and there would have been major health complications for the mother. Fortunately, I delivered a healthy baby boy and the mother came through it just fine.

Although I wasn't thinking about politics at the time, joining with Quentin and others to form a group practice made it easier to run for the Georgia General Assembly in 1976. With more partners, I knew my patients would have access to capable care when I was on legislative leave.

CHAPTER EIGHT

When Congress passed the National Health Planning and Resources Act in 1974, I didn't pay close attention to the new federal law at first even though I knew from what little I had read it would impose an intrusive new level of federal control over state and community health care. My practice kept me extremely busy and sometimes I failed to stay fully informed about the latest political developments. When I eventually looked more carefully into what the new federal mandate would do, I couldn't understand why more medical professionals weren't speaking out against it. Those I knew were as fed up with burdensome and counterproductive government laws and regulations as I was.

What I learned touched off a sequence of changes in my life. It stirred me up enough to organize a statewide movement to resist bureaucratic excess. Political activism led me to run for political office. And running and serving in political office moderated my thinking about the government's role in a free enterprise system.

Although I never shared the extreme views of a few friends who belonged to the far-right John Birch Society, I stood well to the right of center when I entered politics. But my transformation to a more moderate conservative evolved rather quickly. As a doctor, my political views were influenced by government controls I believed interfered with good health care. While I had always supported a government role in areas like defense, law enforcement, education, and national security, I opposed government involvement in many other areas of life. My outlook changed as a candidate and officeholder who interacted more often with people struggling to survive. I soon saw the pragmatic need for government to play a more assertive role in areas like agriculture, social services, the environment, the economy, civil rights, and even health care.

I've always believed the free market should be kept as free as possible, fiscal responsibility should be at the top of government's priority list, and government, like a physician, should first do no harm. But when the private sector fails to address critical needs, government often has a responsibility to act. It's up to our elected representatives to decide when government involvement encroaches too much on a free society or weakens the economy. Throughout my eighteen years in political office, I often found myself squarely in the middle, advocating a balance between positions on the left and right and sometimes alienating both sides. I came to believe that a centrist position often served the best interests of the people I represented and the country at-large.

Back then, however, overbearing laws like the National Health Planning and Resources Act had pushed me well to the right of center. Under the law, the federal government could withhold millions of dollars in health care funding from states failing to comply. States complied by creating districts and forming appointed Health Planning Agencies (HPA's) to make decisions about where new health care facilities and services could be located within those districts. Overseeing the HPA's was a state Health Planning Review Board and overseeing the whole process was the U.S. Department of Health and Human Services.

The American Hospital Association supported the program. Hospital spokesmen argued that many hospitals were having trouble making a go of it and too much competition was a big part of the problem. They could point out, for example, that it might be economically unfeasible for a community hospital to provide costly emergency services if a competing medical facility took away some of the hospital's profitable surgical procedures. To the public at-large, preventing the expensive development of health care facilities and services where they weren't needed seemed to make sense.

The American Medical Association opposed the program. Creating a government bureaucracy to decide where health care facilities and services should go would inevitably delay and even deny communities the health care they needed, the AMA said. I wholeheartedly agreed. For the most part, I thought the free market controlled health care development reasonably well. I was convinced fewer miscalculations were occurring under the competitive system than would occur under a government-controlled system. Moreover, like the AMA, I took an apocalyptic view of the law, recognizing its bureaucratic infrastructure as something that could be used to implement a government-driven British or Canadian-style system.

Based on my experience with government medical programs, I felt a health care system totally under government control would lower the quality of health care and demoralize the country's community of health care professionals even more than it was already demoralized. Of course our concern about the certificate-of-need (CON) bureaucracy turning into a nationalized system never materialized. Before that could happen, the law became too controversial to survive nationally. After a few years, studies revealed CON decisions were often based on errors of fact or judgement. Even worse, in many cases political favoritism influenced the life-or-death decisions over a community's ability to provide quality health care. On the whole, the program's administrative costs were considerable and its overall savings appeared to be nil.

In 1987, Congress repealed the National Health Planning and Resources Act. Many states subsequently repealed the certificate-of-need programs they had adopted in compliance with the federal mandate. In most if not all of the few states where the law was retained, including Georgia, CON came under attack in the legislatures and courts.

When the federal mandate was passed by Congress in 1974, medical organizations provided information about it to their members. But information alone failed to arouse the medical community. As my concern grew, I asked other physicians what they thought about it and discovered they weren't focused on the law's implications any more than I had been. But they all emphasized how troubled and frustrated they were by government laws and regulations that interfered with their effort to provide the best medical care to their patients. "I object violently to cookbook medicine," one internist from Augusta told me. Every medical professional I contacted believed most lawmakers involved with health care legislation were only superficially knowledgeable about the delivery of health care and weren't listening to the concerns of professionals.

Somebody should do something, I decided. Joined by a few friends, I set out to organize health care professionals and other concerned citizens throughout Georgia. When we announced our new initiative to the media, one newspaper editorial called it a "crusade for free enterprise." My brother Joe came up with the name, Committee on National Trends, Ramifications and Origins of Legislation, Inc., or CONTROL. By the following year, I was devoting just about every minute of available time to CONTROL, calling and visiting as many medical professionals as possible in an energetic recruitment campaign.

During the summer of 1975, while involved in the organization of CONTROL, I joined a number of physicians in refusing to sign a Medicaid Provider Contract issued by the Georgia Department of Human Resources. The agency threatened to deny Medicaid payments to physicians who failed to sign the contract. I was prepared to treat Medicaid patients for free rather than comply. The agreement required physicians to "fully disclose" the nature of treatments given under Medicaid. Like many doctors, I felt such disclosure would put patients' privacy at risk. I didn't think the requirement would control costs and I was concerned Medicaid patients might avoid medical attention for conditions such as a venereal disease if that information was made part of the public record.

Eventually, most doctors signed, including me. A black minister of a Dublin church felt insulted by my stand. I had treated a Medicaid-eligible member of his family for years. I had always had a pleasant relationship with the minister and others in his family. But if I declined the government payment for the care his family member received, he thought I would be treating his family like a charity case. Even after carefully explaining my reasons for not signing, he remained irate. I finally complied with the new Medicaid requirement, hoping patients would trust the state agency to keep their records private. But I wasn't happy about it. In fact, I felt even more strongly about government excess. The government needed reasonable assurance Medicaid payments were made for legitimate Medicaid services. But I thought politicians were creative enough to devise a means for policing the system without jeopardizing patient privacy.

In a speech delivered in the fall of 1975 at the annual meeting of the Georgia Academy of Family Physicians, I explained why I started CONTROL. "Until several months ago," I began, "I had taken no real interest in politics or governmental affairs, except to vote and do my share of griping about taxes and the infringement of government on what I considered my personal prerogatives. I wasn't aware of it at the time, but I was living in a state of blissful ignorance while the foundations on which medical care and the other time-tested institutions of free enterprise in this country were methodically being chipped away beneath my feet and those of every other American."

Then I broadened my attack, declaring "...there is a force in this country... working diligently and methodically to convert our system of government from one that is a republic to one that is socialist. And they are making extensive and dangerous progress in their efforts." My rhetoric struck some people as extreme. But we were trying to stir people up enough to get them involved. Our goal was to convince politicians to try harder to avoid doing harm when enacting laws impacting the medical community.

In my talk, I cited Medicare and Medicaid as examples. On one hand, these programs made health care more affordable and accessible for many elderly and lower income citizens. On the other hand, the programs also had a negative impact. When patients realized they could receive care for little or no cost, visits to physician offices for minor complaints skyrocketed. The inflated workload inevitably limited the time physicians had to make a proper diagnosis and treatment plan. One way to mitigate this problem, for example, was to expand the country's network of federally-supported community health centers that provide free or low-cost primary care.

Referring to the certificate-of-need mandate, I told the Georgia Academy, "We cannot afford to let such a calamitous state of affairs come to pass again without our knowledge of it or our active participation against it."

The people who helped organize CONTROL were highly committed. Harry Powell, a far-right political activist who had published *The Laurens County News*, our community's weekly newspaper, was among the first to volunteer. He belonged to the John Birch Society, an organization founded in 1958 that believed a communist conspiracy threatened the free world and most of what the U.S. government did was a step toward communism. Although the society has faded from prominence, at the time it often made headlines and had a significant following in Georgia, especially south of Atlanta.

Visiting me at home, Harry did his best to sign me up for the John Birch Society. He persuaded me to accompany him to Cobb County near Atlanta to meet with U.S. Rep. Larry McDonald of Marietta, a fellow physician and a well-known John Bircher who later served as the organization's national president. I read material they provided including part, if not all, of the Communist Manifesto. I sympathized with much of what they advocated relating to governmental limits. But the John Birchers often went too far, overwhelming logic with paranoia. The organization and I weren't on the same wave length and I never joined.

Harry, an effective organizer, agreed to serve as CONTROL's Executive Director. My title was chairman of the board of directors. Also joining as board members were Dr. Hunter Rackley of Millen, a dentist; Dr.

Rex Parkerson of Eastman, a pharmacist; and my brother Joe, an attorney.

Forty one Georgia medical professionals joined as advisory members. One of the forty-one was the late Dr. James C. Dismuke, Jr. of Adel, then president of the Georgia Academy of Family Physicians. Jim and I were among a half dozen family physicians who worked together several years earlier to secure a charter for the state organization from the American Academy of Family Physicians. Once established, we were both active in the organization. It was Jim who arranged for me to speak about CONTROL at the state meeting. A national magazine for physicians, *Private Practice*, reported I had taken a closer look at the National Health Planning and Resources Act in preparation for a regional health care meeting that Jim had asked me to attend as a representative of Georgia's family physician association. Although my memory fails me on this point, I have no reason to doubt the article's accuracy. Apparently it was Jim who inadvertently started me on the path leading to politics.

Harry and I traveled to Washington, D.C., in September to meet with top officials at the Department of Health and Human Services and with a number of members of Congress including Rep. David Satterfield of Virginia, chairman of the House Ways and Means Health Subcommittee. Rep. Satterfield invited me to testify at a hearing on health care issues then being held by the Ways and Means Committee. In a statement Rep. McDonald published in the *Congressional Record*, I told the committee, "The relationship of the physician and patient would become totally impersonal under nationalized medical care. There are so many illnesses that have a psychogenic overlay which requires a very intimate and trusting relationship between physician and patient. This would be lost."

Late in the fall, I flew to cold and windy Chicago to attend a national conference of the American Academy of Family Physicians at McCormack Place. The academy's leadership let me host a booth in the foyer of the convention hall. I handed out material about CONTROL to members along with bags of roasted Georgia peanuts provided *gratis* by the Georgia Peanut Commission, telling the delegates, "Here are some Georgia peanuts and a Georgia idea." Whether or not I recruited any converts, I enjoyed talking to fellow physicians from around the country about issues of concern to us all.

While I had been asked to talk about CONTROL at a meeting of the Georgia academy, I didn't receive the same invitation from the national organization. Although my relationship with the American Academy's leaders was friendly, I suspect they considered me a little too radical for comfort.

On December 3 we held a statewide organizational rally, renting the spacious ballroom at the Hilton Hotel in Macon. We put a great deal of time and effort into the planning and it turned out to be a rousing event. More than 500 doctors and lay people from around the state attended. We attracted television, radio, and newspaper coverage. Our key speakers were two members of Congress, Rep. McDonald and Republican Rep. Phillip Crane of Illinois, a leading conservative who was then seen as a potential presidential candidate.

In a *Private Practice* article, the crowd response was described as "electric." The remarks of every speaker, including my own, drew enthusiastic cheers. CONTROL's future looked promising. The *Private Practice* article said, "The signers of the Declaration of Independence, including a number of physicians, were willing to commit everything they had to the service of freedom. J. Roy Rowland, Jr., MD, is in this tradition."

I appreciated the flattering comparison. But it was premature. The nation created by the country's founders has endured for nearly two and a half centuries. But the Macon rally turned out to be the high water mark for CONTROL. As we entered the New Year in 1976, financial support fell well below expectations. I put my own savings into it. But before too many months passed, it became apparent we couldn't sustain the staffing and travel necessary to be successful. We reluctantly agreed to disband. "There was (an) awakening," I told a reporter, "but still too much lethargy for sustained action."

With the demise of CONTROL, I could have given up part-time political activism and resumed my fulltime commitment to family practice.

But I was eager to continue in public life in some capacity. If anyone can say politics is in their blood, I qualify. I grew up in a politically-focused family whose dinner conversations often centered on politics and political issues. My family tree is full of elected officeholders starting with Papa Rowland's election as clerk of the Johnson County Superior Court early in the twentieth century. As a youngster I loved serving in the General Assembly as a page, and, as an adult, running for office had been in the back of my mind for years. I had urged medical professionals to run for public office when I was involved with CONTROL. Now I decided to practice what I preached.

Although my life as a family physician was highly satisfying, I was experiencing a degree of burnout. Many physicians put their emotions in check and treat patients in a clinical frame of mind. But my patients were like family to me and I maintained a very personal relationship with them. It was tough when modern medicine couldn't make some patients well. I was as dedicated to medicine as ever. But I was ready for a new direction. Many people turn midlife into rebirth, *The New York Times* columnist David Brooks has written. I can relate to this observation. Instead of experiencing a mid-life crisis, I was energized about a new future.

The first thing I did was take a course to improve as a speaker, and the lessons gave me greater confidence in public appearances. As luck would have it, an opportunity to run for an elected office opened up soon after I completed the course.

U.S. Rep. W.S. "Bill" Stuckey, Jr., of Eastman, former chairman of the famous Stuckey's roadside rest stops, announced he wouldn't run for reelection to the Eighth District seat in Congress he had held for eight years. Dublin was located in the Eighth District. When I learned of Rep. Stuckey's decision, I considered running for the open seat. Running in a widespread area of middle and South Georgia where I generally wasn't known would have been an ambitious step, especially for someone who had never run for political office. But I had created the nucleus of a campaign through my work with CONTROL.

W.W. "Wash" Larsen, a Dublin attorney, beat me to the punch. Wash disclosed he would run for the congressional seat after representing District 119 in the Georgia House for six years, a district covering the western half of Laurens County where Luella and I resided. My partner in CONTROL, Harry Powell, also entered the congressional race. But Harry didn't have sufficient financing or grass roots support and would finish far behind. Although I probably could have run a stronger race than Harry, I didn't have Wash's network of support through his contacts in the General Assembly.

Like me, Wash came from a politically-oriented family. His grandfather had served in the U.S. House during the first half of the twentieth century and had been close to former U.S. Rep. Carl Vinson, who was living in retirement in Milledgeville. Although Carl Vinson hadn't involved himself in a political campaign in years, he publicly endorsed the grandson of his old friend. Wash also had the support of Bill Stuckey. Although the retiring congressman didn't formally endorse Wash, he personally called politically-influential people throughout the Eighth District to urge them to help the state legislator from Dublin. Some of Stuckey's politically-experienced staff members served on Wash's campaign staff. Wash looked like a heavy favorite, and he might have securely held the seat for many years if elected.

Also entering the Democratic primary race was Billy Lee Evans, a thirty-five-year-old Macon trial attorney and a third-term member of the Georgia House. Billy originally served in the legislature as a Republican. But when reapportionment put him in a new legislative district with an apparent Democratic majority, he switched parties. Although Georgia would become a Republican state over the next couple of decades, this was a time when most Georgia voters voted Democratic, including most in the Eighth District. When he switched parties, Billy lost the backing of the Republican-leaning business leadership in Macon. It wasn't clear how Billy could raise enough money to overcome Wash's high-level support.

Impressively, however, Billy Evans pulled together a strong populist base of small businessmen, farmers, blacks, and lower income citizens, and raised sufficient campaign contributions without the help of most of the Macon business community. Playing off Wash's endorsement by Carl Vinson and support of Bill Stuckey, Billy Evans hammered away at his opponent as the hand-picked candidate of Washington insiders. Billy steadily gained ground on the frontrunner and captured the seat with fifty-four percent of the vote.

Meanwhile, I took the most realistic political course open to me and announced my candidacy to succeed Wash as the District 119 representative in the Georgia House. I was well-positioned to run a competitive local race. Luella and I had resided in Dublin for twenty-two years. We were active in our church and in civic activities. I knew many citizens from all walks of life as a family doctor. Luella was well-liked and respected and had many friends throughout the community. CONTROL had given me positive media coverage. A number of my fellow physicians were ready to contribute to whatever political campaign I entered. Most of all, I had the desire to run for office and Luella was ready to play an active role.

My partners in our medical practice agreed to see my patients when I was involved in legislative duties. If elected, I would be away from the practice for several months of the year when the General Assembly held its annual sessions in Atlanta. There would be other times when committee meetings or special sessions could require my presence. While the relatively-modest legislative pay wouldn't equal my income as a physician, which I would give up while away from my practice, I wanted to participate in the governmental process and income wasn't an issue. I publicly announced my candidacy in April 1976, at the age of fifty.

Leon Green, a friend and neighbor, had already entered the race. Leon, an attorney, had settled in Dublin four years before. He was one of the community's leading citizens, an able opponent. A third candidate also entered, Ralph Walke, 32, an attorney and businessman. Although it appeared Leon and I were pulling ahead as we campaigned that spring and summer, Ralph Walke attracted enough votes to prevent anyone from getting a majority and Leon and I ended up in a runoff. We campaigned hard with both of us seizing every chance to explain why we were the best choice and the other fellow wasn't. When I pulled it out in the late August election, Leon graciously called to congratulate me. We remained good friends.

According to *Private Practice*, I was one of thirty medical doctors serving in the fifty state legislatures and one of two in the Georgia legislature. I would focus on several big health care-related issues during my six years in the Georgia House. But I would also tackle a wide range of other issues and would learn about the legislative and political process from the inside.

The learning experience began before the General Assembly convened. A veteran legislator from Marietta, Al Burruss, was challenging incumbent Speaker Tom Murphy of Bremen for the top position in the Georgia House. Tom was a strong speaker, one of Georgia's most powerful political figures in modern times. But a speaker inevitably makes decisions that upset some members. By coalescing dissident members, Al believed he had a chance.

An ally of Murphy's from my area, Rep. Ben Jessup of Cochran, contacted me to twist my arm on behalf of Tom. Al Burruss had already called me twice to ask for my support and I had told him I would consider it. But I hadn't made a commitment. When Ben Jessup contacted me, I was ready to do some horse-trading. I told Ben I would commit to Tom and hoped the speaker would support me for assignment to the Health and Ecology Committee, the panel that dealt with health-related issues. The speaker would keep his unspoken end of the bargain by making sure I was approved for my top committee choice.

Although Tom and Al ran a hard-fought race, which Tom handily won, the speaker didn't hold grudges. The two forged a new alliance and Al worked his way into a leadership position as House whip. In the process, Tom solidified his position all the more, proving to me it's not smart politics to hold a grudge.

CHAPTER NINE

The 1977 session of the General Assembly began on the second Monday in January when Speaker Tom Murphy banged down his gavel and I recited the oath to officially become one of 180 members of the Georgia House of Representatives. Although the state constitution limited us to forty working days, weekend and other temporary adjournments could extend the annual sessions for up to several months. The session had unofficially begun the night before when Luella and I attended the General Assembly's traditional kick-off event, a wild hog barbecue dinner where we mingled with Gov. George Busbee, Lt. Gov. Zell Miller, Speaker Murphy, and other state officials; television, radio, and newspaper reporters; and fellow legislators and their families.

Many of the colleagues we met at the session-eve social gathering and would meet during my three terms in the Georgia House would become great friends and trusted allies.

Rep. L.L. "Pete" Phillips of Soperton was one of these. Pete and his wife Mary would become as close as any friends we ever had. Pete was a modest, well-liked, effective lawmaker, especially in the area of natural resources where he led the way in enacting many of Georgia's environmental safeguards. A farmer and surveyor, he had been elected to the Georgia House six years before. We were both from middle Georgia communities similar in size and interests, both Eagle Scouts, and we hit it off from the beginning.

During my eighteen years in political life, a few lawmakers with whom I served would prove to be less than trustworthy. But most had a real commitment to public service and tried to do what was best for their constituents. The close relationships based on respect and true friendship that would evolve between me and many of my colleagues would have a dramatic influence on my future. Without them, I couldn't have successfully run for Congress. Pete's guidance enabled me to function more effectively from the outset of my political career.

Politics can also take a toll on long-standing relationships. Quentin Price, the co-founder of our medical practice, a staunch Republican, would actively oppose me in my political campaigns. I was friendly with many people who didn't support me politically. But once I entered politics as a Democrat, Quentin's cool and distant demeanor made it clear we were no longer pals. Although Jim Dismuke supported me in earlier races for Congress, my fellow founding member of the Georgia Academy of Family Physicians and key supporter of CONTROL was unforgiving when I was unable to resolve a problem he was having with the federal government, opposing me in the next election.

Tom Murphy and I would remain on good terms even when we occasionally clashed over issues. Often chomping on an unlit cigar, the craggy-faced lawyer from the west Georgia town of Bremen was seen by many observers as a throwback to old-fashioned, smoke-filled-room Georgia politics. He played hardball politics and his manner could be tough and blunt. But I always found him to be truthful and fair and he used his power for the well-being of the state as he saw it.

The issue that drew me into politics is one that brought Tom and me into conflict. The speaker, Gov. Busbee, and Lt. Gov. Miller, the Senate's presiding officer, all supported the legislation to establish the certificate-of-need (CON) program in Georgia, a program states had to adopt under the National Health Planning and Resources Act or risk losing federal health care funding. Most of the media portrayed the program as a progressive step in controlling wasteful spending and insisted failure to enact the bill would be a backward step that would cost Georgia an estimated $65 million in federal aid. Although the law authorized the U.S. Department of Health and Human Services to withhold funding from states failing to comply, I didn't believe the federal government would deny states the fair share of tax revenue their citizens paid for federal health care programs. But supporters of the CON program and much of the media were sure non-compliance would result in the loss of funding, a difficult argument to counter.

"Every time I look at this bill I get nauseated," I told *The Atlanta Journal*, expressing my frustration at the one-sided way the issue was generally presented.

Because of my medical background, opposition forces in the House looked to me as the leader. As a member of the Health and Ecology Committee where the bill was referred, I unsuccessfully attempted to prevent the panel from reporting the measure to the House floor. When the bill came to the floor, I organized the opposition. Some legislators opposed anything they perceived as a federal intrusion on state and local jurisdiction. My opposition was based on the damage I believed the program would do. Several allies with influence among our colleagues, like Benson Ham, a studious lawmaker from Monroe County, joined me in arguing that the program would seriously interfere with community efforts to correct deficiencies in local health care services and facilities.

The House approved the measure 98-61, a remarkably-close margin considering that it had the solid support of the state's top government leadership. Rep. Sidney Marcus of Atlanta, chairman of the House Health and Ecology Committee, a principal supporter, acknowledged proponents had to wage a "bitter struggle."

The Senate had already passed its version of the bill. Under the Senate version, a health care facility or service would have been approved if the issuing CON authority didn't take formal action to reject it in a timely manner. The House version didn't include this provision. Under the House version, a health care facility or service couldn't ever be added in a community without the approval of a certificate of need, no matter how long the issuing authority waited to act on it. At the urging of Gov. Busbee's House floor leader, Rep. Roy Lambert of Madison, a Senate-House conference committee agreed to the House version, making the proposed program even worse in my view.

It wasn't until the final night of the final day of the 1977 session that the final CON bill, as agreed upon by the joint conference committee, came before the full House for a vote. Under the Georgia constitution, the House and Senate cannot waive the requirement to adjourn sine die at the end of their allotted forty working days. The governor and speaker must have thought the debate had run its course and the bill would pass without significant resistance. The CON conference agreement was called up for a House vote less than an hour before the midnight deadline.

They didn't count on my stubbornness. When it was my turn to address the House on the CON bill from the front podium, or well, I decided to conduct a solo filibuster to prevent the House from voting on the measure before the legislature was forced to adjourn for the year. Normally I would have made my points as succinctly as possible and yielded the floor. This time I kept chattering while watching the minutes tick away on the chamber's large overhead wall clock. The CON bill was one of several issues of critical importance to the leadership still pending. I believed killing the CON bill was more important than passing the remaining measures on the calendar.

As I talked about anything that came to mind, I noticed Al Burruss walking toward the podium. As he passed by, he slipped a note in front of me. It was signed by the speaker, Tom Murphy. "Get out of the damn well," the note said. It didn't say "please" get out of the damn well.

I could either get out or become a martyr. I got out. If I had refused to relinquish the well, the governor could have called a costly special session to deal with the issue. While this would have made me a newsworthy figure statewide, it would have also made me an outcast in the eyes of the speaker and governor and probably condemned me to a lonely and unproductive legislative future. My best strategy was to retreat and fight another day. If reelected, I planned to do everything possible to eliminate the program during my second term.

As the election approached, it looked like I might face the toughest possible challenge. Wash Larsen considered running against me. For several weeks, stories appeared in our local media speculating about whether he would try to reclaim the Georgia House seat he had held for six years. When Wash didn't deny the speculation, I was concerned. He had a proven record as an experienced and effective candidate in past state legislative races and he had a strong community following.

But I had worked hard to stay in touch with the voters. I wrote a regular column on legislative affairs in *The Dublin Courier Herald*, made frequent appearances before community groups, and spent as much time as possible greeting people everywhere I went in Dublin and Laurens County. Jet Toney, a young staff member with the House communications office under the speaker's supervision, tape recorded a statement on current issues every morning in back of the House chamber to send to my local radio stations. A few other House members were invited to record such feeds. But not many.

When asked by *The Courier Herald* whether I spent much time politicking, I said I politicked all the time. In fact, I enjoyed "politicking" and I found people appreciated being "politicked."

It was a relief when Wash, an attorney, announced he was too busy with his professional life and wouldn't run. I believe he realized it would have been a difficult test. I ran without opposition in both of my two races for reelection to the Georgia House.

With the state's top leadership still strongly backing the CON program, the odds were stacked against me when I returned the following term. But those of us opposing the program had one thing going for us.

The powers-that-be couldn't avoid another showdown by keeping a bill to repeal it bottled up in committee. Congress had amended the CON guidelines and the legislature had to approve the changes to be in compliance with the federal mandate. When the measure to adopt the new guidelines came to the House floor, I introduced an amendment calling for repeal. This gave us another chance to make our case. But we lost again even though the CON process was beginning to cause problems.

In time, the Center for Studying Health System Change documented rulings on certificate-of-need applications that were highly subjective and strongly influenced by political ties rather than policy objectives. The Federal Trade Commission and the U.S. Justice Department criticized the program for contributing to rising health care costs. The Goldwater Institute in Phoenix, AR, a free market advocacy organization, produced data indicating health care costs were higher in states with CON programs. But these findings weren't available at CON's inception, and our objections weren't persuasive enough to stop Georgia's CON program from becoming law in Georgia.

A bill to legalize the sale of mixed drinks in private clubs in communities where liquor sales were prohibited and another bill to lift the prohibition against the transportation of oversized fourteen-foot-wide mobile homes on Georgia highways and roads were among the most controversial issues to arise during my state legislative years.

When local reporters asked how I stood on the mobile home issue, I said I would vote "nay." No one in public life wants to waffle on the issues. But this was an instance when I should have waffled. The media was mostly critical of the proposal. If you believed what you read in most Georgia newspapers, allowing these trailers on the roads wouldn't only be a nuisance for other motorists, it would be extremely dangerous. It was assumed frustrated drivers would take chances to pass the wide, slow-moving mobile homes as they were towed to their destinations, creating hazardous situations.

We didn't have a mobile home industry in my district and no one had given me industry's side of the story. I accepted the commonly-held point of view that anyone who supported legalizing fourteen-foot-wide mobile homes on Georgia roads was putting the interests of a big business over the safety of the people at-large. But I wasn't aware of all the facts. As I later learned, several states had voted to allow them on their roads and the statistical evidence indicated the wider loads hadn't increased the overall accident rate. And lifting the ban against them would benefit working families, providing much-needed jobs by making it possible for the mobile home industry to locate in Georgia. The availability of mobile homes also would provide affordable housing for lower-income families, some of whom might otherwise not be able to own a residence.

When I reversed my position and cast a "yea" vote, I was criticized for flip-flopping. "My mind can be changed if I have enough evidence to convince me, and that's what happened concerning the mobile home bill," I explained to *The Courier Herald*. The General Assembly prudently included a sunset clause to require the law to be renewed the following year, guaranteeing lawmakers an opportunity to overturn the law if statistics proved the oversized mobile homes were dangerous. But Georgia's experience with the mobile homes would be positive. Most people came to see the mobile home industry as a good thing and my flip-flop didn't cause a long-term political problem.

An even more controversial issue involved the state's alcoholic beverage laws. During my first years as a legislator, a bill was introduced in the House with the support of the governor to authorize the state tax commissioner to override local "blue laws" by licensing and regulating the sale of mixed drinks in private clubs. Private clubs were widely ignoring the law and serving liquor, beer and wine even in dry counties. The proposed "pouring" bill would establish state controls over alcohol sales and provide revenue through licensing fees. But much of the religious community opposed any relaxation of laws restricting alcohol sales and many Georgians didn't like the idea of legalizing something for members of private clubs that was prohibited to the public at-large.

The bill failed to pass. I voted against it because it gave the state the power to approve pouring licenses in a community rather than local voters or local officials.

It was a different story the next year. Following a heated debate, a statewide pouring bill was passed on the final day of the session that allowed alcoholic drinks to be served at private clubs if approved in a referendum called by local governing bodies or by a petition signed by thirty-five percent or more of the local voters. I not only voted for this bill, I was included on the six-member House-Senate conference committee that worked out the final version. In addition, I succeeded in passing a separate pouring bill that applied only to my community. It gave the Dublin and Laurens County governing bodies more flexibility. Under my local "population" bill, the governing officials could approve pouring licenses without a referendum or petition. If locally-elected officials were willing to take the responsibility, voters were still in control through the ballot box.

A Baptist minister who opposed the sale of alcoholic beverages in Laurens County accused me of "cronyism" in a newspaper letter-to-the-editor for joining with local officials in supporting the local population bill. He had every right to express his point of view. But I really wasn't just yielding to the bidding of local officials. I believed it was appropriate government policy to place the authority with locally-elected officials.

Two health care-related bills were perhaps the most notable measures I introduced as a state legislator. One bill would have required insurers to provide catastrophic long-term care. The other would have legalized "living wills." Although I preferred to call it a "living will" bill, the media and most of my legislative colleagues called it the "right-to-die" bill, a tag that stuck. A living will, or "end of life directive," is now known in Georgia as a "Georgia Advance Medical Directive for Health Care," a document accompanied by a "Durable Power of Attorney."

When I introduced the first bill to legalize living wills, it touched off one of Georgia's most emotional debates. The legislation would have enabled a mentally competent person who was eighteen years of age or older to sign a "directive," or "living will," to allow artificial means for sustaining life to be withheld or withdrawn if he or she was in a vegetative state without any hope of recovery as determined by multiple physicians. The measure would have authorized a spouse, children, parents, or siblings to invoke a living will for a patient who was irreversibly unconscious. A number of safeguards were written into the measure. One required non-family witnesses with nothing to gain from a patient's death to sign off on the decision to comply with the terms of a living will.

Today the right to a living will is recognized just about everywhere. But it was a disturbing idea for many people in the 1970s. Only eight states had enacted "right-to-die" laws when I came to the legislature in 1977. But the tragic case of Karen Ann Quinlan, who suffered irreversible brain damage in 1975, had made it an issue of nationwide concern.

She was the twenty-one-year-old daughter of devoutly Catholic parents in New Jersey who fell into a deep coma after taking valium and consuming alcohol at a birthday party. Her parents asked for life-support measures to be discontinued when she remained in a coma for months and was given no chance of recovery by attending physicians. The request was denied. A prolonged court case brought by her parents received national and even international coverage. After losing in a lower court, the New Jersey Supreme Court finally ruled in favor of the parents.

In states without a clarifying "right-to-die" law, like Georgia, physicians were reluctant to discontinue or withhold artificial life-sustaining procedures. As a result, families were left without recourse while loved ones suffered with terminally-comatose conditions, sometimes for years. While Medicare and Medicaid could offset some of the horrendous cost of care for patients in a vegetative state, families suffered extreme prolonged stress and even financial ruin. When I entered the medical profession in the 1950s, physicians generally followed the wishes of the closest family members in deciding whether to artificially sustain life in irreversible situations. By the 1970s, the changing political climate left physicians no choice but to use every possible means to artificially sustain life.

Much of the senior population and medical community supported the "right-to-die" bill as a fundamental right. But some opponents, including some religious leaders, insisted it would amount to "playing God" by deciding when or when not to sustain life. Some critics compared the denial of artificial means for sustaining life under the terms of a living will with the practice of euthanizing "undesirables" in Nazi Germany. Catholic leaders like Archbishop Thomas A. Donnellan of Atlanta and Bishop Raymond W. Lessard of Savannah waged a vigorous campaign against the bill. Bishop Lessard called me at home one evening for no other purpose than to heatedly scold me. I have great respect for the Catholic Church. But I thought these religious leaders were terribly misguided on this issue.

During my second year in the legislature, the proposal picked up the support of Gov. Busbee. At a Capitol news conference, the governor endorsed the concept by stating he would want a living will for himself if given the opportunity, adding he would have to look at the details of any specific "right-to-die" bill. Considering the emotional intensity of the opposition, it was a courageous position. We also had the support of Speaker Murphy.

With the speaker's approval and the governor's backing of the concept, the bill was favorably reported to the House floor in mid-February and passed by a vote of 98-63. Then it went to the Senate where highly-respected Sen. Beverly Langford of Calhoun sponsored the bill. If the proposal reached the Senate floor, its chances of passing and being signed into law by the governor looked good. But first it had to be reported out by the Senate Human Resources Committee.

That's when I discovered how powerful one lobbyist can be. Cheatham Hodges, a personable and energetic lobbyist for the Georgia Catholic Conference, had wined and dined a number of influential state legislators, including members of the Senate Human Resources Committee. When the panel held a hearing on the measure, Hodges testified a "right-to-die" law could lead to killing minorities. A natural-death law was adopted in Germany when the Nazis were in power, he said. A supporter of the living will bill on the committee, Sen. Richard Green of Macon, shot back, "Isn't it true that the Third Reich also had traffic laws?" His comment pointed out how illogical it was to compare a living will with Nazi euthanasia.

I'm convinced Hodges swayed committee votes. And every vote counted. When the Senate Human Resources Committee deadlocked over the issue, Sen. Pierre Howard of DeKalb County, the committee's chairman, kept the bill bottled up in committee by not casting a tie-breaking vote to send the bill to the floor for consideration by the full Senate.

I had met with Pierre earlier and he had promised to help move the bill to the Senate floor if it passed in the House. Not long after his committee failed to report the bill, I ran into him while I was walking up a Capitol stairway and he was coming down. "You didn't keep your word," I bluntly told him. "I changed my mind," he answered. "But you didn't tell me," I responded, as we turned to go in separate directions. Pierre later ran for lieutenant governor and won. When the "right-to-die" issue fell in his lap, it was evidently too hot for him to handle.

In subsequent terms, I resumed the fight. There was reason for hope. The bill received widespread newspaper editorial support. It also had considerable backing from many families who had gone through terrible experiences. But it also continued to be attacked. Although I was open to revisions to deal with as many concerns as possible, the bill continued to be held captive by Senate committees. The highly-publicized debate over my bill made Georgians more aware of the issue, and growing public pressure eventually led to the approval of a living will a few years after I left the legislature. Now referred to as an End of Life Directive and accompanied with a durable power of attorney, it is advised for everyone.

I also introduced a catastrophic insurance bill during my first term and reintroduced it in later terms. The measure would have required insurance companies to provide coverage for the kind of long-term major illnesses that can financially destroy families. It guaranteed coverage even for people with pre-existing conditions. The bill originally would have provided up to $250,000 for out-of-pocket medical expenses after paying a deductible ranging from $3,000 to $7,500 a year.

Included in the bill was a provision to provide tax credits to offset losses insurers might incur for writing the high-risk policies. But I didn't think insurance companies had anything to worry about. Three other states had adopted similar catastrophic coverage laws, Minnesota, Connecticut, and Rhode Island, and insurers in those states hadn't lost money on catastrophic policies. Although the state laws were fairly new and the statistical evidence might not have been conclusive, I thought the bill's tax credit offset provision adequately protected insurers.

After debating the bill for several years and revising it to meet various objections, the House passed a version early in 1980. Among the compromises I accepted was one capping coverage for the uninsured with existing medical conditions at $100,000. But the House also deleted the crucial tax credit offset.

Without an offset provision, the bill was doomed in the Senate. It was deleted by an amendment offered by Rep. Marcus Collins of Cotton. Marcus wasn't trying to kill the bill. He was concerned the tax credit could result in a serious loss of revenue for state and local governments. The state comptroller's office had estimated the tax credit would cost government $400,000 and $500,000 in the first year. This was a small amount of money for sparing families the loss of homes, businesses, and life savings because of a medical catastrophe. But, as Marcus pointed out, no one could know if the state comptroller's projection was accurate.

The chairman had an idea for a state funding pool that would better protect government while still protecting insurers. We both thought there was time to study the idea and to get it inserted into the bill when the Senate took it up. But this didn't happen. When the bill was referred to the Senate Banking, Finance and Insurance Committee, the panel quickly voted to put the measure on hold "for further study" without considering an offset provision. I knew the "delay" was intended to kill the bill for the remainder of the session. If insurers wouldn't accept the proposal, neither would most of the committee's members.

Representatives of the Georgia Association of Life Insurance Companies testified the costs of catastrophic coverage could be ruinous to insurers and requiring companies to provide such coverage conflicted with free enterprise. I didn't fault the industry for doing what it felt was necessary to protect its financial security. But I believed the Senate committee could have fully protected insurers while providing at least some help for people facing a health care crisis. The Medical Association of Georgia, traditionally an advocate of market solutions, endorsed the bill on the grounds that the proposed government program was necessary to meet a desperate need not being fulfilled by the market.

While I lost my two biggest health care battles, I succeeded on some other big issues. One of them, a ban on Quaaludes, saved many lives. Teaming up with the Georgia secretary of state's office, the agency that administered the state medical licensing board, I introduced legislation early in my third term to impose a prohibition on methaqualone, commonly known by its brand name, Quaalude, as a prescribed drug. Rep. Bobby Parham of Milledgeville, a pharmacist, cosponsored the bill.

Quaaludes were introduced in the United States in 1965 as a sleeping aid. The new drug was supposed to be a safer option to barbiturates, which could be as addictive as heroin and deadly when taken in excessive quantities. But Quaaludes were far from safe. People took the drug for non-medical reasons because it could induce a feeling of euphoria. Like heroin, a methaqualone overdose could have fatal results. When mixed with alcohol, the danger increased. By the mid-1970s, hundreds of deaths were being reported nationally from Quaalude overdoses. By 1980, Quaalude-related deaths had soared to more than 2,300 a year.

So-called "stress clinics" had opened in many communities around the country where unethical doctors dispensed Quaaludes to anyone who entered the door, including teenagers, whether or not there was medical justification for such a prescription. Nothing like these "stress clinics" has existed before or since. But in the 1970s, they were an open scandal. A Chicago television newsman, Rich Samuels, reported that patients, or customers, paid $250 for each prescription and the prescribing doctors were paid $80 of the $250. The clinics, he said, were profiting by many thousands of dollars a month.

A number of pharmacies stopped selling Quaaludes because of their record of abuse. But a few sold the drug in extraordinary quantities. One Atlanta pharmacy sold a mind-boggling 155,000 Quaalude pills in one year. In just a few years Quaalude abuse had become the fastest growing drug problem in the country, especially among adolescents.

Georgia was among the leading states in the amount of Quaaludes distributed to the public, not far below states like New York and California with much larger populations. Most of Georgia's trafficking emanated from a downtown Atlanta area where "stress clinics" were mainly located. People from throughout the state and even from other nearby states patronized the "clinics," which in reality were nothing less than candy stores openly peddling a dangerous substance.

Secretary of State David Poythress was the first to do something decisive about the rapidly-growing problem. He contacted me and asked if I would take the lead in a legislative effort to shift methaqualone from the Schedule II category of drugs to Schedule I. Schedule II drugs can be prescribed by physicians. But heroin and other Schedule I drugs, while available for research, cannot be prescribed at all to the general public. Reclassifying Quaaludes as a Schedule I drug would shut down the "stress clinics" overnight.

I eagerly took on the task. In my own practice, I had discontinued prescribing Quaaludes less than six months after the drug became available. Patients returned for refills much more frequently than needed and I determined on my own the drug had a high potential for abuse. Some pharmaceutical representatives didn't like the idea of politicians outlawing a drug with a medical use. But many people within the industry welcomed a ban. "I'll be glad not to have to deal with it," said Jane Dukes, president of the Middle Georgia Pharmaceutical Association.

After hearings were held, Georgia became the first state to ban Quaaludes when our bill swept through the House and Senate with little opposition and was signed into law by Gov. Busbee. Within a year, law enforcement statistics showed Quaalude overdose cases in Georgia had dropped sixty to seventy percent. Florida soon followed Georgia's lead in prohibiting Quaalude prescriptions. But "stress clinics" still operated in other states and methaqualone users and dealers could still travel elsewhere and bring back large quantities. A nationwide ban was needed. That would come later.

I served on three committees during my initial term in the Georgia House, Health and Ecology, State of the Republic, and Judiciary committees. Although I felt I served a special role as the only non-lawyer serving on the Judiciary Committee, I gave up that seat at the start of my second term to accept a seat on the Ways and Means Committee, the powerful panel that shaped the state's tax structure. Ways and Means Committee Chairman Marcus Collins appointed me as secretary of a key subcommittee, Taxes and Tax Revision, and named me chairman of a newly-created ad hoc subcommittee to study proposed technical changes that were eventually approved to make the state tax system more efficient and fair.

Membership on the Ways and Means Committee put me in a position to sponsor a state constitutional amendment imposing a tighter limit on state spending. Under Article VII, Section III of the constitution, the state was prohibited from incurring debt service of more than fifteen percent of the state's revenue. Under the fifteen percent cap, the state could have then borrowed nearly $3 billion, incurring an annual debt service of about $450 million a year. This level of indebtedness would have placed an excessive burden on taxpayers and potentially crippled the economy. My proposal called for a debt service ceiling of five percent.

This concerned some government and business leaders who feared a strict limit on bond financing would make it more difficult to improve Georgia's infrastructure including the state's principal port in Savannah. While I certainly didn't want to interfere with critically-needed projects that would serve a public need, I was conservative enough to believe the state could address its needs within fiscally-secure budgetary limits. Eventually, a compromise was reached. Under the amendment passed by the General Assembly in 1982, and later approved by the Georgia voters, the debt service was capped at seven percent. The amendment included a contingency provision making it possible for the General Assembly to raise the cap to ten percent with a vote of at least two-thirds of both houses.

During my second term, I joined Pete Phillips in speaking out about what we saw as a growing bias in legislative funding for urban areas, especially for the metropolitan Atlanta area. Not only was this an unfair trend for the less populated areas, we thought, it was an unhealthy trend for the whole state. When the old "county unit" system was in effect, urban areas received less than their fair share of state revenue. But with the federal court-mandated one person, one vote principle long in place, the balance of state spending had shifted to facilities and programs in the metro Atlanta area with, in my words, "little or no regard for the rural areas."

Pete started the discussion about "two Georgia's," the urban "haves" and the rural "have-nots." In a letter sent to the governor and released to reporters, I sided with Pete by saying, "at the end of the 1979 session of the General Assembly, I thought the urban areas of the state had done quite well from a fiscal standpoint (and) in some instances that occurred at the expense of the less urban areas." Moreover, under the projected 1980 census, it was certain the number of legislators from urban areas would substantially increase and the number from rural areas would decline. I pointed this out, adding that "the probability of a snowball effect becomes evident with the increasing enhancement of urban prospects and economic strangulation of the more rural areas to the detriment of our state as a whole."

I cited several examples of state funding for projects in metro Atlanta that were difficult to justify by population alone.

One example was brought to my attention by Rep. Terry Coleman of Eastman, who sat next to me on the House floor. Terry had learned the state Department of Education planned to build four new vocational education schools and all of them were to be located somewhere in the greater Atlanta area. This was the recommendation of a consulting firm. Although a few vocational educational schools already existed in metro Atlanta, I'm sure more were needed in this rapidly-growing area of the state. But none were located in the middle Georgia area Terry and I represented. When we looked into the situation, we learned that the data used by the consulting firm to make its recommendation was outdated, a 1967 population growth study.

While agreeing the schools should be located in areas with the greatest need, Terry and I were convinced accurate, updated data would support our contention that one of the four schools should be placed in the nine-county middle Georgia area known as the "Heart of Georgia." We talked to our two close allies from the nearby town of Soperton, Pete Phillips and Sen. Hugh Gillis, the politically-shrewd son of longtime State Highway Director Jim L. Gillis, Sr. The four of us decided to work together to try to land one of the four schools for our area. When we conferred with Gov. Busbee and state School Supt. Charles McDaniel, they were sympathetic to middle Georgia's needs but made it clear they weren't prepared to support vo-tech funding outside the Atlanta area in the foreseeable future.

I called on the Dublin-Laurens Industrial Development Authority to help with research. The authority's staff came through, producing a report that compared the number of potential vo-tech students from our area who didn't have reasonable access to a vocational education facility with the number from metro Atlanta; presented updated population growth projections; and cited the lower cost of construction in middle Georgia.

A breakthrough occurred just before a new legislative session convened. The General Assembly and the governor traditionally gathered for a forum at the Continuing Education Center on the University of Georgia campus in Athens to study current issues in advance of the annual legislative terms. The four of us arranged a private meeting with Gov. Busbee while we were attending the forum. When we presented our data, the governor appeared to be impressed. He indicated at our private get-together, and later confirmed it in statements to the media, that consideration should be given to the Heart of Georgia area as a vo-tech priority. Supt. McDaniel, a separately elected state official, also concluded we were right.

The state board of education would propose where the schools should be built. But it would be up to Gov. Busbee and the General Assembly to make the final decision in the authorization and appropriations process. Soon after our meeting, the state board approved a planning budget request of $60,000 for a middle Georgia vo-tech school. The House Appropriations Committee upped that amount to $100,000 with the support of the superintendent. Although it earlier looked like our chances were in the slim-to-none range, we had succeeded in securing approval for the "Heart of Georgia Vocational-Technical School," a major asset for our area and the specific community where it would be located.

Once the funding was approved, the exact site had to be selected. All of the nine "Heart of Georgia" counties wanted the facility. This included the counties represented by the four of us who had doggedly sought the school. The chances of getting a vo-tech school would have been jeopardized if we had clashed over the site selection. So we made a pact not to engage in a turf war and Laurens County was selected without political interference for several reasons. It was centrally located in the nine-county area, an ideal site was available at West Laurens Comprehensive High School, and Interstate 16 had recently opened through Laurens County, enhancing accessibility to everyone who would be served by the school.

One other responsibility of a state legislator should be mentioned. Local legislation (measures affecting local governance that require the approval of the General Assembly) is often one of a state legislator's most controversial and challenging responsibilities. My relationship with city and county governing officials generally remained very positive during my years in the legislature, facilitating the passage of a number of important local bills. One that particularly stands out was an historic redistricting bill for the election of members of the Laurens County Commission. Working with local officials and many diverse citizens in the community, we developed and passed a bill that made the election of the first black representatives on the country's governing body possible.

CHAPTER TEN

I was a rookie state legislator when my name surfaced as a possible candidate to represent Georgia's Eighth District in the U.S. House, a seat held by Rep. Billy Lee Evans of Macon. Although I wasn't really ready to run for another political office, I had idly chatted with a few General Assembly colleagues about the possibility of running for Congress someday. These conversations led to rumors and rumors spread quickly at the state Capitol. When a reporter covering the legislature for *The Macon Telegraph and News* asked if I was thinking about such a race, I acknowledged I had given it some thought.

The story saying I was thinking of running for Congress concerned me. On one hand, I knew the people I represented wouldn't be happy if they thought I was more interested in seeking another political job than concentrating on the job they elected me to do. On the other hand, the story gave me recognition with the media as a potential candidate for higher office. From this moment on, my name would often be among those mentioned in speculative news stories about future races.

In a talk to the Dublin Rotary Club at the beginning of my second year in the Georgia House, I mentioned I planned to run for another state legislative term. Doug Hall, editor of *The Dublin Courier Herald*, noting I had been "widely mentioned" as a possible opponent of Rep. Evans, wrote that I had "all but dismissed any chance" I would run for a seat in Congress that year. If Evans had stumbled badly, I might have seriously considered challenging him. But at the time he looked politically secure. Lately he had stepped-up appearances at home. He had just completed a fourteen-day tour of the Eighth District and was scheduled to speak to the Dublin Rotary Club the following week. He had also recently sent 150,000 newsletters under the congressional franking privilege to district residents, bolstering his already-substantial name recognition.

I also wanted to deal with unfulfilled state legislative goals. I had won some legislative battles like the Quaalude ban and the cap on state borrowing and was confident I could win some more. I was on good terms with the speaker and most of my colleagues. My committee assignments couldn't have been better. The Ways and Means Committee appointment showed my influence was growing. I would also be named to the Rules Committee during my final term, an influential panel that decides which measures go to the House floor for a vote during the final ten days of the session and which ones get left behind.

Considering the good things that were happening, I might have remained in the Georgia House for the duration of my political career. But as I began my third term, my medical partners had a different idea about my future. They had talked among themselves and agreed they would no longer cover for me during my absences from the practice. I could either leave the partnership or return to the medical practice fulltime. Under our agreement, a partner who left the practice was barred from opening a competing practice in Dublin and Laurens County. If I continued serving in the General Assembly, I could no longer practice medicine in my home town.

Maybe this was fate giving me a kick in the backside. Now I knew it was time to seek higher office. As a state legislator, I continued to practice medicine when not involved in legislative duties. But serving in a statewide or congressional office would be a fulltime job.

Although I had considered running for Congress off and on since entering politics, I first set my sight even higher. I decided to run for governor. As Georgia's chief executive, I figured I would have a chance to accomplish all my state legislative goals. Under the state constitution, Gov. Busbee couldn't serve another term after serving two. There would be no incumbent to run against. Although better-known candidates were likely to enter the governor's race, I was confident I had a chance. I could raise seed money for an expensive statewide campaign from my contacts within the medical community and I was counting on my friendships with legislative colleagues to give me an instant political base.

In mid-January 1981 I told friends and reporters I was contemplating a gubernatorial race. In July, *Courier Herald* editor Doug Hall wrote a column in which he asked, "What are Rowland's chances? Better than you might think, but still a long shot.

"His worst problem is identification," Doug said. "Though he has been in the state House for five years, he is not in the leadership (nor) a headline grabber. To compensate for this shortcoming, Rowland is pushing hard for campaign funds to buy advertising and he is seeking free publicity across the state. Another drawback could be his record. The twin mantle pieces of his legislative career—'right to die' and catastrophic health insurance—have yet to be passed by both houses. But Rowland is an impressive campaigner. He has television looks, he is well-educated, well-read, articulate-- one of the best speech-givers of the mentioned candidates-- and intelligent. He is also conservative… which is no handicap in these times. He handles his media relations well and is popular with the House leadership."

But, he added, "if Rowland was to take a shorter leap—say from the state House to Congress—he might stand a better chance than he does of being governor."

A month later, Christopher Bonner, a Washington, D.C.-based reporter for *The Macon Telegraph and News*, included me among prospective candidates for governor, saying, "The Dublin physician… should be able to tap the money necessary to run a sophisticated campaign, but politicians here feel he has only an outside chance."

These were encouraging comments. At least I was viewed as a serious if longshot gubernatorial prospect. Longshots had won before by running better campaigns than their opponents. Jimmy Carter, then a state senator, was widely considered a hopeless underdog when he ran for governor against former Gov. Carl Sanders of Augusta. But the future president out-campaigned Sanders, ultimately winning the race that propelled him to the presidency. With a burst of energy, I was able to raise $25,000 for a gubernatorial campaign, mainly from fellow doctors and other friends.

Two people, in particular, influenced my decision to withdraw from the governor's race and run for Congress instead.

One was Tom Murphy. When I visited the speaker in his Capitol office just off the House chamber to fill him in on my plans and solicit support, he told me, "You're wasting your time. Joe Frank Harris is going to be the next governor." The speaker had successfully backed the previous governor, George Busbee, who had risen from the position of House Democratic majority leader. If the speaker was now backing Joe Frank Harris, the chairman of the House Appropriations Committee, I knew I would have little chance. Most state legislators who might have supported me were loyal to the speaker and would have supported the speaker's choice for governor. It wasn't a popularity contest. It was practical politics. The speaker controlled House committee assignments and the fate of most legislation. As it turned out, Joe Frank did become the next governor.

Another influence was Billy Evans himself. Billy was elected to Congress the year I came to the General Assembly. We had met occasionally when we attended the same functions. When Luella and I travelled to Washington, D.C. to attend a barbecue on the White House lawn held by President and Mrs. Carter for several hundred Georgians, we spent much of the evening socializing with Billy. We enjoyed his company. He had a sense of humor and interesting things to say about his experiences on Capitol Hill. Although not close friends, we had always been friendly in spite of the speculation about my running against him.

Then came an encounter that wasn't exactly chummy. Following my brief meeting with Tom Murphy, I hadn't completely given up on the idea of running for governor even if it meant going against a much stronger opponent like Joe Frank Harris. But I was wavering. When a reporter with *The Courier Herald* questioned me about my political plans I admitted I wasn't dismissing the possibility of switching races. Billy would have seen the story about my possible switch. When he ran into me on a visit to the state Capitol, he greeted me with these words, "Roy, you can't beat me."

The words "you can't" got my dander up a little. "We'll see," I responded. The Eighth District congressman's dismissive remark helped firm up my decision to challenge him.

Congressional redistricting, a responsibility of the General Assembly, was also a factor. The U.S. Justice Department had approved a new congressional reapportionment plan reuniting a number of whole counties in the same district that previously had been split into separate districts. Two previously-split counties, Johnson County, my birthplace, and Washington County, where I had many connections, were both placed entirely in the new Eighth District. My home county, Laurens, was located just about in the middle of the new Eighth. As realigned, it was a significantly improved district for a candidate from Laurens.

When I arrived to give a talk at the Mercer University School of Medicine in Macon one day late in September, a reporter with *The Telegraph and News* asked about my political plans in a brief interview. I had made up my mind. For the first time I publicly acknowledged I was dropping out of the gubernatorial race and challenging Billy Evans in the upcoming congressional Democratic primary. "Things just didn't work out for me in the governor's race and I've been very seriously thinking about Congress for a while now," I explained. "I'm running for the office and not against Evans," I added, avoiding any criticism of the incumbent for the moment.

When reporters asked Evans to comment, he replied, "I think Roy Rowland is a very competent legislator. He is a good man and... what can

I say? If he wants to be in Congress, I think he ought to run." Our race began on a polite note. It wouldn't remain that way for long.

Billy told the reporter this would be his "toughest" race since defeating Wash Larsen. But he hadn't faced a strong challenge since waging his energetic and effective campaign to win the Eighth District seat six years earlier. He was reelected to a second term in 1978 without any opposition and to a third term in 1980 with only token Republican opposition.

We were hearing several negative things about Billy's political standing from people involved in politics. They said Billy had failed to stay in close touch with constituents lately; he had alienated Democratic activists by voting more with Republicans than Democrats; and his support of President Reagan's so-called "trickle-down" economic policy hadn't played well with many constituents at a time when the country was experiencing a prolonged economic downturn. Although there was nothing in the rules to prevent it, the media was questioning why he hired his ex-wife for his congressional staff rather than someone with more staff experience. He had also come under attack for voting for a tax benefit for members of Congress.

While I knew Billy Evans faced some problems, I didn't really have any idea how vulnerable he might be. With few exceptions, the media and most other political observers thought he would surely be reelected. His greater name recognition and the advantage of an incumbent in raising campaign funds appeared to give him an overwhelming edge. Since I wasn't well-known outside of my own community, I generally wasn't considered a serious challenger.

My first task after announcing my candidacy was organizing a campaign from scratch. State legislative races didn't cost much, didn't require a fulltime campaign staff, and my political instincts could carry me through. But running in the thirty counties that made up the newly-reapportioned Eighth Congressional District presented a huge fund raising and organizational challenge. I could shift most of the $25,000 in campaign contributions I had received when gearing up to run for governor to the congressional race with the approval of the contributors, providing seed money to get a campaign started.

I called together a group of friends in Dublin to ask their advice about organizing a congressional campaign. Someone suggested contacting Ron Payne. Ron had recently settled in Dublin as president of a large furniture company. I hadn't met him, but he was described as a nice guy with experience as a campaign activist. An Alabama native who had played football at the University of Alabama under Bear Bryant, he was outgoing, good-natured and, as reported, well-versed in politics.

When we met in his office, Ron offered to design a "Rowland for Congress" bumper sticker. Before the end of the week, it was ready. He located vacant space at a Dublin shopping center for our campaign headquarters. He donated furniture and loaned the campaign a computer, a new and baffling gadget in 1982. Ron came to the campaign headquarters in the evenings after work to enter data in the computer on campaign contacts, scheduling, and other useful information. His wife Karen joined as a volunteer, answering phones and helping with many campaign chores. Their contribution of time and expertise, without any personal gain, was crucial in getting the campaign off the ground. Although Ron's role diminished somewhat after we were fully organized, Ron and Karen continued to assist in the trenches until it was over.

Tom Murphy quietly helped. He was interested in many races, including the gubernatorial race of Joe Frank Harris and those of the House members loyal to him. Although my race may have been of marginal concern to him, he supported me because we had a good personal relationship and I'm sure he saw Billy more as a Republican than a Democrat. Republicans in the General Assembly gave Tom a hard time and he really didn't care for them as a class. When I was looking for someone to join my campaign as a fulltime aide, a job involving grueling hours with token pay, Tom recommended Keith Perdue, a young man who had served five years as a House aide during legislative sessions. A Decatur resident, he was a graduate of Georgia State University and a student at Emory University where his father was a neuro-surgeon at Emory University Hospital.

Keith became the campaign's "logistics coordinator," moving into a rented room in Dublin. Although few people were optimistic about my chances, I suspect Keith signed on because he believed the speaker's support made an upset possible. Keith was smart and hard-working. Throughout the many months of hard campaigning, he served as my principal driver and sidekick, often working seven days a week, rising before dawn and staying on the go into the night.

Shirley Nowell, a mother of three who had worked for many years at a Dublin bank, took the key position of manager of the Dublin campaign headquarters. We had known Shirley and her husband Robert for some time. She handled the job requiring non-stop multi-tasking with dedication.

Our first campaign manager, who shall go nameless, didn't work out. Like Keith, he came to my attention through legislative contacts as someone with political experience who might be available. When I contacted him, he agreed to join the campaign, moving into a rented place in Dublin that I arranged for him. He wasn't happy from the get-go. He found a lot to complain about, including his room. Too often he dealt with people in a brusque manner, offending supporters. Perhaps he was put off by the fact that our campaign was basically an amateur operation. It was clear Dublin wasn't where he wanted to be. After a brief period we told him his services were no longer needed and he packed and left town.

Luck was with me. A first-year University of Georgia law student from the Atlanta area, Jim Comerford, called out of the blue and offered to join the campaign. With summer vacation approaching, he was prepared to take time off from studies and campaign fulltime as a volunteer. I didn't know Jim or his family. As someone who was avidly interested in politics and as the step-son of a medical doctor, he wanted to help get a physician elected to Congress. Like me, Jim was raised in a political environment. A number of leading political figures were among his parents' friends and he had campaigned door-to-door for one of them, state Sen. Paul Coverdell, who was later elected to the U.S. Senate.

I soon discovered Jim had encyclopedic knowledge of politics and qualified as a bona fide expert on campaigning. His self-assurance was advanced beyond his years. We developed a close rapport and he was a natural choice to fill the vacancy of campaign manager. He became a strategy planner, fund raiser, message shaper, and grass roots' support builder. He wrote and designed TV, radio and newspaper ads. Sometimes he accompanied me on the road. Although scheduled to return to law school in the fall, he stayed with the campaign until its conclusion.

Many people advised me to solicit the support of Gus Kaufman, a Macon businessman. Gus was a highly-committed Democrat who had helped scores of Democratic candidates he perceived as having values similar to his get elected to local, state, and federal offices. He was noted for supporting humanitarian causes. A life member of the NAACP, Gus was in the forefront of the civil rights movement in middle Georgia. His wife Miriam was also politically influential as a leader in the Girl Scouts, League of Women Voters, Georgia Democratic Party, and as a board member of the Middle Georgia Community Food Bank. Gus and Miriam were prominent in the Jewish community.

After introducing myself to Gus on the phone, we met for coffee at a place in downtown Macon. As we discussed politics, Gus commended President Reagan for doing "a pretty good job" and asked how I felt about it. I realized Gus, a liberal who wouldn't likely be fond of Reagan's politics, was testing me. I told him I thought the president was a good person but I didn't agree with him much of the time. My answer was exactly how I felt. I didn't think President Reagan was doing enough to bring deficit spending under control. Although I supported a strong defense, I thought the president was contributing to the out-of-control deficits by inflating a defense budget that included too much wasteful spending. Two other things helped me connect with Gus. The NAACP had given me a high rating for my voting record on issues of particular concern to minorities during the previous legislative term. I'm also sure Gus wanted to support me in order to help oust Billy Evans, whose Republican-oriented voting record was making my primary opponent *persona non grata* among many Democrats.

Gus stayed in contact with the reporters and editorial writers of *The Macon Telegraph and News* and he was well-liked and respected by them. He undoubtedly talked to them about my candidacy. I've always believed he was responsible for the newspaper's early endorsement that gave our campaign a big boost, convincing many people I had a fighting chance. Gus and Miriam's support would continue throughout the campaign against Evans and in future races even after I sometimes voted more conservatively than they would have liked. They became dear personal friends.

Starting with a handful of family members and friendly acquaintances, the number of volunteers who actively worked in the campaign rapidly proliferated. We eventually could turn to volunteers for help in every county in the Eighth District. In Macon and Bibb County, Billy Evans' home area and the most populous in the district, a small army of volunteers joined the campaign. Among them were Hale Almand, a cousin and a former U.S. attorney. Another cousin residing in Macon, Winifred Jackson, worked virtually fulltime in the campaign. She arranged meetings between me and people from blue collar backgrounds in Macon and Bibb County, expanding my support among working families. Winifred helped organize the active support of a large contingent of Johnson County natives who had settled in the Macon. She also introduced me to a close friend, Dot Green, who agreed to run a second campaign office we opened in Macon and did a great job.

The state legislators from the Eighth District that I had served with provided a crucial base of support. Their advice about how to make inroads in their communities was invaluable. A number of state legislators promoted my candidacy as they participated in their own campaigns. While several state lawmakers from Macon endorsed Billy Evans as a home town candidate, several others like Rep. Frank Horne campaigned openly for me. These supportive legislators were all friends of mine. But the widely-held perception that Tom Murphy favored me didn't hurt.

No one was a more effective campaigner than Luella. She helped make decisions and campaigned exhaustively. She would often go in one direction to fulfill a separate schedule of campaign activities while I would go in another direction. In a newspaper feature story, a reporter described Luella's role as attending teas and talking about family values. She really participated in all kinds of campaign events and talked about many issues including the economy. We were pictured together in many of our newspaper and television campaign ads. This prompted Billy to suggest we were subtly trying to turn a personal matter, divorce—which, in fact, we never mentioned-- into a campaign issue. In reality, our campaign was a partnership and the ads picturing us together were entirely fitting.

Following the campaign, I attended a civic event in the southern end of the district. When introduced as J. Roy Rowland to someone I hadn't met before, the individual said, "Oh, you're Luella's husband." If that's how I'm remembered, I'll be happy.

Dr. George T. Anderson, a clinical psychologist in Dublin and a friend, made an unexpected contribution that gave early momentum to the campaign. George had started a cottage industry-type polling operation, Anderson Research. I didn't know he conducted public opinion surveys on the side until he called me one day while I was still wavering between running for governor or Congress and said he had some interesting information to share with me. He had just completed a poll for someone in Macon. While I don't recall the main purpose of the survey, George had piggy-backed questions to evaluate Billy Evans' standing with his home constituents. I don't even recall the numbers, but they reflected deep dissatisfaction with the incumbent congressman.

Several months later, as the campaign was getting fully underway, George again polled prospective Macon voters, asking them which candidate they favored for the Eighth District congressional seat. The results showed Billy Evans with twenty-seven percent; myself with twenty-six percent; Edd Wheeler, an attorney and Bibb County commissioner who had also entered the race, with twelve percent, and thirty-five percent undecided. When asked to rate Billy's job performance, seventeen percent said "good" or "very good;" thirty percent said "poor" or "very poor;" and thirty-three percent said "average." These were devastating numbers for an incumbent. I was in a virtual dead heat with Billy in his own home town even though the campaign had hardly begun. Pollsters generally agree a negative rating of thirty percent or more is the threshold which a candidate has trouble overcoming.

Polls are expensive. George didn't charge the campaign a dime. His polling results energized Luella and me, our campaign staff, and many hard-working volunteers, one of whom was George's wife, Nanette. When we released the results to the media, it helped us attract supporters including financial contributors. Apparently Billy Evans didn't take George's polling seriously. After the election, he said his own polling showed he would win without a runoff. Such an optimistic outlook did him a disservice. As the outcome would confirm, George's polling was as accurate as it was surprising.

The editors at *The Macon Telegraph and News* confessed after the election they thought endorsing me was a futile gesture because Billy Evans was better positioned to raise campaign money and was much better known to voters across the vast Eighth District. A prestigious Washington-based publication, *Congressional Quarterly*, published an article about members of Congress who might be at risk. Billy Evans wasn't mentioned. Billy was obviously confident. Until he unexpectedly found himself in a runoff, he responded to opponents' criticisms and made occasional campaign appearances. But he avoided the all-out campaigning that I was doing. Although he had some negative things to say about Edd Wheeler and me, he didn't really go into an all-out attack mode until the runoff.

When Billy did take shots at me, he contradicted his earlier comment about my legislative competence by portraying me as a "do-nothing" legislator who lacked his depth of understanding of the issues. He called me a "silk stocking" doctor with no feeling for the common man, even though I treated about as many low-income patients as affluent ones. He also needled me for flip-flopping from the governor's race to the congressional race. But mostly his campaign rhetoric and advertising emphasized his seniority and experience and his record fighting crime and helping farmers. It was my impression he embraced the theory of U.S. Sen. Herman Talmadge who famously wouldn't actively campaign against lesser-known opponents. Sen. Talmadge was convinced his campaigning would only help such opponents gain greater name recognition. This theory may work, but only for candidates in good standing with constituents.

Billy ran TV ads contending I accomplished little other than the Quaalude bill. *The Telegraph and News* assigned reporter Janet Groat to interview my colleagues in the General Assembly about what kind of legislator I had been. Fortunately, everyone she questioned was complimentary. Bobby Parham of Milledgeville, my partner on the Quaalude bill, rated me in the "top ten percent" in effectiveness, saying, "He seemed to do his homework a little better than a lot of others." Sidney Marcus of Atlanta, the liberal chairman on the Health and Ecology Committee, said, "He and I didn't always agree, but I was impressed with his depth of knowledge." Marcus Collins of Cotton, the Ways and Means Committee chairman, said, "He's one of the hardest-working members we have." The article helped counter Billy's "do-nothing" accusation.

I turned on the heat from the start, relentlessly hammering Billy in campaign speeches, media interviews, face-to-face campaign appearances, and television, radio, and newspaper advertising. I criticized him for losing touch with the people he represented; voting for benefits for members of Congress at a time of economic hardship; embracing an economic policy that contributed to a prolonged recession, and his inconsistency in party affiliation. We also questioned putting his former wife on the payroll if people with more staff experience were available.

"J. Roy Rowland, A Congressman You Can Be Proud Of," became our campaign slogan.

On February 6, 1982, Luella and I hosted a campaign kick-off barbecue in Dublin that drew an estimated 650 friends and supporters, an encouraging start. Beginning just after the legislative session ended, we campaigned constantly, covering thousands of miles on the highways and back roads of the Eighth District. We arose at 5 a.m. or even earlier and typically returned home late at night. We randomly greeted people on the streets and shopping centers of towns and cities. We talked to civic organizations, appeared at political rallies, and organized many chicken and barbecue dinner fund raisers, usually charging $10 or less, some attracting hundreds of people and others only a handful.

Everywhere we talked about Billy's problems, stressed the need for change, and pledged to be a "congressman you can be proud of."

When I was running out of energy toward the end of a long day on the road, we searched for the local Dairy Queen and an ice cream cone would revive me for the remaining hours of campaigning. We learned where every Dairy Queen was located in the Eighth District.

Midway through the primary, Billy and I participated in a political forum for local candidates sponsored by a group of private citizens at the Laurens County Agricultural Center. Candidates in each of the races were invited to give a brief talk about why voters should support them. When it was the turn for the congressional candidates, Billy, as the incumbent, was introduced first. In an oblique reference to my attacks on him, he said, "I left my horns and tail at home because I wanted to make a good impression." That drew some laughter. When I stepped to the podium, I said, "He may have left his horns and tail at home but he sure wears them in Washington." That prompted a bigger outburst of laughter.

Although I, too, would make some serious missteps during the campaign, the breaks mostly fell my way.

CHAPTER ELEVEN

"We haven't seen you," a secretary curtly told Billy Evans as he circulated at the Jones County Courthouse on a campaign visit.

According to the *Telegraph and News* reporter covering Billy, "her voice suggested a congressman should be seen and heard from, and not just at election time. As Evans shakes hands and asks for votes, it is with the knowledge that his opponent for the Eighth District congressional seat, state Rep. J. Roy Rowland, has probably shaken the same hands three or four times to his one while he was hundreds of miles away in Washington, D.C. The courthouse regulars remember seeing Rowland who has campaigned fulltime for months," the story said. Nothing hurt Billy Evans' chances more than the perception he had lost touch with the people he represented.

The economy was another major problem for the incumbent. Public anxiety over income and jobs was high. Although President Reagan would become a popular figure in Georgia, his popularity was then at a low ebb. The Reagan administration believed supply-side economics featuring relief for high income taxpayers would stimulate economic benefits for everyone. Billy was one of the so-called Democratic "boll weevils" who supported President Reagan's budget and economic proposals. This was "in line with the conservative beliefs of the people of this district," he explained to reporters, predicting it would have a "positive effect" on his reelection. He was wrong.

According to news reports, Billy was among a group of boll weevils who met with the president's budget director, David Stockman, to express concern about supporting the administration's supply side policy in the face of a political backlash over the sluggish economy. Stockman urged them to stay the course, insisting an economic recovery would soon come. Earlier Billy had publicly predicted the recovery would begin by the spring of 1982. But the recession would continue well past the 1982 Democratic primary.

In June 1982, in the midst of our race, Billy Evans voted for a Republican-sponsored budget that passed by a razor-thin margin of 210-208. The bill's tax cuts were not fully offset by spending cuts, contributing to a national debt exceeding $1 trillion. On the campaign trail, Billy criticized the Reagan administration and Democratic congressional leaders for not having the "intestinal fortitude" to reduce entitlements in an election year in order to bring deficit spending under better control. But, he added, "this was about the best we could do. It's a budget we can live with." When we portrayed him as a supporter of policies contributing to deficit spending and the weak economy, he didn't have a convincing response.

As a U.S. House member, I would consistently oppose cutting taxes or increasing spending without a matching revenue offset. But I would also vote for federal budgets I didn't particularly like because they were the best of the bad choices, belatedly making me more sympathetic to Billy's position.

Billy Evans' shaky party affiliation also created a political problem. As an up-and-coming Macon trial attorney from Tifton, he ran as a Republican for the Macon city council and lost. He won his next race for a seat in the Georgia House as a Republican representing a Republican-majority district. When state legislative reapportionment placed him in a Democratic-majority district, he switched to the Democratic Party and won again. This switch made it possible for him to run a successful congressional race in 1976. Except for pockets of Republican strength, the Democratic Party then held a commanding advantage in most of Georgia including most of the Eighth Congressional District.

A third candidate in the Eighth District Congressional race, Bibb County Commissioner Edd Wheeler, attacked Billy's "chameleon-like tactics," saying, "he likes to represent himself as a Republican at times but wants to pass himself off as a Democrat when it's advantageous to do so." I referred to Billy as my "sometimes Democratic, sometimes Republican opponent."

According to a voting survey by *The Chicago Sun Times*, Billy voted with Republicans in the U.S. House fifty-eight percent of the time during the previous term. Although my career voting record in Congress would turn out to be about 50-50 I never leaned to the Republican side to the degree that Billy did in his final years in Congress. I also maintained much closer ties to Democratic Party activists in Georgia than Billy. "I didn't let blind party loyalty control my votes," he explained. But on one occasion he called the Democratic Party in Georgia "irrelevant," convincing many Democratic regulars he was really a Republican in Democratic clothing. This impression was reinforced when Macon's Republican Mayor George Israel gave him a highly-publicized endorsement.

Eighth District Democratic Chairman Ben Dixon and Bibb County Democratic Chairman Charles Mobley were among the Georgia Democratic Party leaders who supported me over their party's incumbent. Ben was a pharmacist who operated a Macon drug store where many local politicians and community leaders regularly gathered. His vocal support of my candidacy rippled through the community.

Although he originally won the congressional seat by building a populist base, Billy Evans moved away from that base as he gained the support of much of the Republican-oriented business leadership. As reported by

Christopher Bonner in *The Telegraph and News,* "The chill between Evans and the business community persisted during his early years in the (U.S.) House. But after aligning himself more with the Republicans than with the Democratic majority in Congress, especially on economic issues, Billy gained the backing of elite business leaders who earlier had not supported him, especially in Macon." As our race would show, this move cost him grass roots support.

Billy's vote for a $75-a-day tax deduction for members of Congress was difficult for him to explain. Congress passed the tax break in December and repealed it six months later in the face of strong public and media criticism. Like most other House members who voted for the tax break, Billy voted to repeal it. He told a reporter he was unaware the tax relief was part of the bill he supported in December, saying he thought he was voting for black lung benefits and later found out the congressional tax break was included in the bill. However, he had earlier gone on record as favoring the tax deduction, comparing it to business-related deductions in the private sector. If this was his belief, he was asked by a reporter, why did he vote to repeal the deduction? He said members of Congress should make a sacrifice when times were hard.

"There was a great deal more optimism about the economy in December," he explained. "Then we thought the economy would improve by spring, then late spring, and now late summer." But when late summer came, it still hadn't noticeably improved.

Possibly his most perplexing problem was the widespread talk about the hiring of his ex-wife. *The Telegraph and News* first reported he put his former wife on the Congressional payroll as a legislative assistant to temporarily fill an unexpected staff vacancy. Although it's unlawful for members of Congress to employ family members, there's no prohibition against hiring an ex-spouse. But it apparently seemed close to nepotism to some constituents. It was something people talked about everywhere we went. His former wife was undoubtedly a capable person. But if he could have hired someone with more congressional staff experience, I considered it a fair campaign issue. Whether fair or not, the incident raised questions that plagued him until the end.

One big advantage Billy had was financing. He could raise more campaign money than we could because of the support a sitting member of Congress receives from lobbyists and Political Action Committees (PAC's), the political contribution entities connected to businesses and other special interest organizations. By the August 31 primary, he reportedly collected nearly $150,000 in contributions, more than half from PAC's. Our campaign raised about $40,000 in pre-runoff contributions, mostly from small contributors including those attending our barbecue and chicken dinners. My campaign received $2,200 in PAC donations prior to the runoff, including one from the Georgia Medical PAC which gave a like amount to Billy's campaign. After promising Luella I wouldn't spend our savings on the campaign, we eventually put $100,000 of our own money into the race, seriously depleting our savings but enabling us to remain competitive.

With more money at his disposal, we were concerned Billy Evans might dominate the airwaves with ads to repair his wounded image and injure mine. He ran a substantial advertising campaign and, in the final weeks, saturated TV, radio, and newspapers with campaign ads. But we didn't think his ads emphasizing his efforts to support agriculture and fight crime were especially hard-hitting. We managed our resources well enough to maintain an aggressive self-produced advertising campaign all along and were able to match, or nearly match, Billy's advertising surge during the campaign's homestretch.

Billy's name recognition was another big advantage for the six-year incumbent. Although reapportionment brought new areas into the district, Billy was well-known in most of the district as a result of the publicity he received as a member of Congress, personal appearances, and the newsletters on congressional issues which he and his staff periodically prepared and mailed to residents throughout the district under the free franking privilege. As historic voting trends demonstrate, people often vote for the incumbent because it's the candidate they recognize.

When the campaign began, I was unknown to most Eighth District voters. But something clicked in our campaign that isn't easy to explain. Certainly the support of many state legislators throughout the district made a huge difference. The grueling campaign schedule maintained by Luella and myself was a factor. An anti-government mood had taken hold in the country, and I suppose this worked in our favor as the non-incumbent. But whatever the reasons, we began attracting larger and larger crowds and attracting widespread volunteer help. Although Billy was making a number of campaign appearances, we felt we were out-working him.

As the campaign progressed, the Anderson Research polls and the encouraging words we heard throughout the district made us feel pretty good about our chances. We felt even better during the final ten days or so when we were greeted at every campaign appearance with increased fervor. Even when Billy stepped-up his campaigning and increased his campaign advertising, our momentum as reflected in the enthusiasm of our supporters grew stronger.

Nevertheless, most onlookers thought Billy would finish in front. But would he draw more than fifty percent of the vote to win without a runoff? Our hope was pinned on the underfunded third candidate in the race, Edd Wheeler. If Wheeler pulled enough votes away from Evans to prevent the incumbent from getting a majority, we believed most of the Wheeler votes would be anti-Evans votes that would shift to me in a runoff. If I could get into a runoff with Billy, my chance of overcoming any lead he might hold looked good.

Although Luella and I were feeling positive, we never felt overconfident. There were too many uncertainties.

We were particularly concerned when we learned an eleventh hour debate between the three Eighth District congressional candidates would be held in Macon. It would be televised and, considering the interest our race had generated, it was expected to attract a large audience. Billy and I had appeared on the same platform at a number of campaign events. But we had engaged in only one debate held early in the campaign in the town of Blackshear, and that one wasn't televised. As usual, I went on the attack. I vividly remember Billy's mother sitting directly in front of the podium. She was holding an umbrella in her lap and looking daggers at me. While I didn't really think she would hit me with the umbrella, I have to admit the idea occurred to me. Although her presence was a little discomforting, I got through that first debate okay as did the other two candidates. I thought the debate was a draw.

But we knew the second debate, sponsored by the Student Bar Association at the Mercer University Law School, could have a decisive impact. First, it was to be aired by WMAZ-TV, a Macon-based network affiliate that covered most of the Eighth District. Second, it was scheduled just five days before voters would go to the polls. Third, we would be asked unpredictable questions by a panel that included news reporters and a Mercer law professor. If Billy performed well and I performed poorly, it could potentially reverse our perceived momentum with little time left to recover.

When invited to the August 26 debate, I was scheduled to speak to the Exchange Club in Alma on the same evening. We discussed whether it would be safer to stick to our schedule and skip the debate. But Billy had accepted and we decided it wouldn't be in our best interests to try to duck the showdown. Edd Wheeler had prodded Billy to agree to a series of debates earlier in the campaign. Although Billy denied he was avoiding debates, the media jumped on him for not rearranging his schedule to make them possible. I suspect Billy agreed to the second debate because he had begun to doubt the outcome was as secure as he had expected. I agreed because I didn't want to be the candidate accused of avoiding the challenge.

It was a different Billy Evans at the Mercer Law School debate. This time he came out swinging, accusing me of violating federal election law by accepting corporate contributions while planning to run for governor and transferring these funds to my campaign for Congress. Corporate contributions are allowed in state races but not in races for federal office. It's true I received $7,000 in corporate contributions for the governor's race. The contributors gave me permission to shift the money from the gubernatorial campaign to my personal account. When the $7,000 became personal income, I paid taxes on it. This was perfectly legal. I had sufficient savings without the $7,000 to cover the personal income I later contributed to my own congressional campaign.

Federal campaign financing laws can be confusing. As Billy was well aware, it would take a somewhat lengthy explanation to respond to the charge. While I responded as briefly and carefully as I could, it was an accusation that could leave doubts in the minds of viewers no matter how I responded. In the news stories the next day, the headlines and leads focused on the charge and the explanation appeared down in the body of the stories. This was a punch Billy evidently landed.

Billy also tried to pin me down on whether a television ad we had run asking voters to elect an "honest person" wasn't just "campaign rhetoric" to suggest that he, Billy Evans, wasn't honest. I agreed it was campaign rhetoric. Any campaign statement could be defined as campaign rhetoric. It was also fair, in my opinion, because some of Billy's campaign attacks were wrong. I wasn't really a "silk stocking" doctor, for example. But when I agreed our ads could be described as campaign rhetoric, it gave Billy an opening to insist I was deliberately misleading voters by questioning his honesty, possibly landing another punch.

One of the panelists, a Mercer Law School faculty member, persistently fired questions at me about my position on abortion. Although I thought I answered clearly, he used his lawyer skills in a way that apparently made me look uncertain and uninformed to some viewers. I had expressed my position on this issue many times. While I didn't support abortion as a method of birth control, I believed the decision should be between the patient, her physician, and her faith when a woman's health was at risk. But if anyone was left with the impression my position wasn't clear, it was another punch that landed.

For much of the debate I sat and listened as Billy Evans and Edd Wheeler exchanged barbs. I answered any criticisms aimed at me and fielded my share of questions from the panel. But I stayed out of it when Wheeler's feisty style drew Billy into extended attacks and counter-attacks. For much of the time, I saw no reason to get involved and I let them pummel each other. I was surprised when some supporters suggested afterward my silence made me seem passive and disengaged.

When the debate ended, I joined a few supporters who accompanied me. They were concerned I had come across as weak and indecisive and Billy's accusation about campaign financing might have left doubts about my integrity. In a post-debate interview, Billy was buoyant. He said I had "definitely" lost ground while he had gained ground by clearing-up misleading attacks. *The Telegraph and News* described my performance the next morning as "disastrous."

If there was a lower moment during this or in any later campaign, I don't remember it.

When I arrived at the Macon campaign headquarters the next morning, I felt apprehensive. But I would soon feel better. Telephone calls were coming in from all over the district. And they were sympathetic. Many viewers were incensed by what they considered unfair questioning on abortion. For days people would tell me I had come across as thoughtful and dignified while my opponents appeared to be angry and strident.

While I had taken some hard punches, I hadn't suffered a knockout.

On election night, many friends and family members gathered at our Dublin headquarters. We tallied returns as they were reported on television and called in by supporters. The news was promising from the get-go and got better as the evening wore on. When the results were finally counted, I was not only in a runoff with Billy, I held a surprising lead. We thought Edd Wheeler might help us get into a runoff. Instead, we would have likely won without a runoff if he hadn't been in the race.

I polled forty-eight percent of the vote, Billy forty-two percent, and Edd ten percent. I carried Macon and Bibb County with 13,426 votes to Billy's 11,024 votes and Dublin and Laurens County with 5,995 votes to Billy's 2,061 votes. I swept most of the middle Georgia counties covered by the Macon television market where we concentrated much of our advertising. Billy ran stronger in the northern end of the district covered by the Augusta television market and the southern and eastern edge covered by the Savannah and Jacksonville television markets, but not nearly strong enough.

Interviewed at his campaign center in Macon late in the evening, Billy let it be known it was going to be a different kind of runoff. "It's frustrating that lies can elect people," *The Telegraph and News* reported him as saying. "Now we're taking the gloves off and running the same kind of campaign he is. If he has any skeletons in the closet, he better get out of this race now. I'm tired of rumors about me and my (former) wife. We're going to be asking the questions now. I'm going to ask how much of that money he has down there in that bank did he get doing abortions, killing babies."

Abortion became the main focus of Billy Evans' comeback effort during the three-week runoff. He repeatedly accused me of performing abortions for profit, sometimes citing my sponsorship of the right-to-die bill as an indication I lacked sensitivity to life. To reinforce his accusations, he came out in support of a constitutional amendment to ban abortions. He told the media it would have to be a "properly constructed" amendment so a mother's life wouldn't be endangered, but declined to say how a properly constructed amendment should be worded.

Billy also called me a liar for running a TV ad featuring a supporter who said she had supported Billy Evans in the past but was now voting for me. Although the supporter we asked to appear in the ad was really a supporter, we didn't know she lived in Houston County outside the Eighth District and couldn't vote for either one of us. When Billy Evans discovered this fact, he used it as the basis for accusing me of lying. Many residents of the Eighth District had previously voted for Billy and were now supporting me, and any of them could have served as a spokesperson in the ad. This was an unforced error on our part. But it was a mistake that would be neutralized by deceptive campaign advertising Billy was running.

His campaign TV spots made it appear as if average citizens were randomly stopped in their daily routine and gave unrehearsed laudatory testimonials about the Macon congressman. But when questioned by reporters, Billy admitted the people in the ads were invited to participate and were coached on what to say. Although the vignettes were made to look spontaneous, they were not.

Moreover, a four-page flier that looked like a tabloid newspaper was placed on the windshields of parked vehicles at campaign events that included "stories" claiming I performed abortions as a means of birth control while Billy Evans was working against legalized abortions. Under federal law, material promoting or opposing candidates must identify who authorized it. The flier was, in fact, a political publication that failed to carry the required identification. When the media wrote stories about it, the flier disappeared. While the source was never disclosed, I thought media stories about it hurt Billy more than the flier hurt me.

When asked about the abortion charges, I explained I had performed two abortions during my medical career. In both cases, I consulted with other physicians and only proceeded after it was determined the pregnancies endangered the women's health. That had been years ago. For a long time I had referred such cases to other physicians.

Billy also accused me of having "John Birch sympathies." As a general principle, I think the least government possible is the best government. But I supported many social programs the John Birch Society opposed.

In addition to his personal attacks, Billy called on Republican supporters in his crucial home territory of Macon and Bibb County to help turn things around. A group of Macon citizens led by Carr Dodson, a former GOP Georgia House member, formed a "Committee to Re-Elect Our Congressman" with the avowed purpose of retaining the Eighth District seat in Congress for someone from Macon. Said Dodson, "We've got a congressman from our hometown. We want to make sure that continues. We in Macon and Bibb County can't let Dublin and Laurens County take advantage of us." I'm not sure this favorite son appeal influenced many people from Macon and we used it against Billy in other areas of the district.

Two days before the runoff an *Atlanta Journal-Constitution* reporter wrote that Billy and I were "exchanging low blows that make Rocky Balboa and Apollo Creed look like a Sunday afternoon tea dance," calling our campaign "one of Georgia's liveliest blood baths." But this wasn't quite correct. At this point in the campaign the "low blows" were really one-sided. By then we were running a positive campaign. Some supporters urged me to counter Evans' accusations, especially the one about killing babies, by firing back at him with everything we had. But Jim Comerford thought we should keep our cool. We were now the favorite and Jim believed the best strategy was to build a positive image during the final weeks of the campaign.

Keeping cool is what we did. My only response was that the Evans' campaign was practicing the "politics of desperation." When Billy tried to goad us into another debate, I pointed out we had debated twice, and another one just to stir up more mudslinging would benefit no one. We kept extremely busy staging rallies, organizing a long motorcade that wove through the district from Dublin to McRae, and doing everything we could think of to keep our grass roots support active. Luella and I talked about the need to create jobs, stabilize the economy, and establish effective leadership in Washington, D.C. Our advertising stuck to the "congressman you can be proud of" theme.

On the eve of the runoff election, we hosted one last rally in Laurens County's Stubbs Park. Hundreds of people turned out, many wearing "Rowland for Congress" T-shirts and eating free hot dogs. As I moved from person to person, shaking hands and hugging, supporters chanted "Rowland, Rowland, Rowland." Television cameras panned the scene and reporters interviewed people in the crowd.

"Looks mighty good for Roy," said Twiggs County Sheriff Earl Hamrick. "With his character, you can't make mud stick," said my legislative pal from Soperton, Pete Phillips, adding "I have a feeling he's going to win and be the next congressman." I appreciated every chant and every reassuring word. But nothing could convince me the outcome was a sure thing. Unexpected things happen in politics and I wasn't about to count my chickens prematurely.

On election morning, September 21, Luella and I, holding umbrellas, arrived at our polling place in a light rain to vote. We were smiling broadly, obviously in good humor as a newspaper photographer snapped our picture. Later we drove to Macon where we stood on the side of busy Georgia Highway 247. Luella held a "Rowland for Congress" sign up high and I waved to passing motorists. By 7 p.m., we arrived at the Dublin headquarters decorated with red, white, and blue balloons and crepe paper, where our children, my mother, campaign workers, and an estimated 600 to 700 supporters gathered to watch the returns. The crowd spilled over into the shopping center parking lot where Civil Defense workers had set up outside lights.

With Atkinson, Coffee and Telfair counties reporting first, Evans took a slight lead. Jim Comerford recognized these early votes as positive. In the first primary vote, Billy carried Atkinson County by 374 votes, Coffee County by 465 votes, and Telfair County by thirty-nine votes. This time Billy carried Atkinson County by sixty votes, Coffee County by eighteen votes, and lost Telfair County by thirty-four votes. Billy's intensified campaigning paid off in a few places. He carried Dodge and Jeff Davis counties by higher percentages. But we ran even stronger in most areas, carrying twenty of the thirty counties. Our share of the vote increased from thirty-two to fifty percent in Bacon County; twenty-eight to fifty-eight in Charlton; thirty-four to sixty-three in Glascock; thirty to fifty-four in Hancock; thirty-one to sixty-five in Jasper; thirty-eight to fifty-four in Putnam; twenty-seven to sixty-three in Taliaferro; and forty-two to fifty-two in Ware. We carried Bibb County 13,027 votes to 10,680 and Laurens County 6,746 to 1,827.

When all the votes were tallied, we won by an astounding margin of fifty-eight to forty-two percent.

At 8:20 p.m., we received a call from Macon. Although I'm not sure who it was, I remember a voice calling out, "Evans conceded! He's conceded!" Billy Evans had delivered a statement at his Macon campaign center a little more than an hour after the polls closed acknowledging he had lost. He thanked his supporters and graciously called on them to "move behind Dr. Rowland." People noisily hugged me. A reporter wrote that I appeared "slightly dazed" as I threaded my way to the front of the crowd to face the TV cameras. "Slightly" might have been an understatement. "I'm so grateful," I said. "I asked the people of this district for this responsibility. And I'm going to work very hard to fulfill that responsibility."

Later, I told a reporter, "We had a campaign held together with baling wire. We just had a whole lot of people who worked awfully hard."

Billy called to congratulate me and offer help in the office transition. I appreciated that. He told news people that evening he might be back in a couple of years to run again. We didn't know for quite a while if the next election would be deja vu all over again. It had been a grueling race and the idea of going through it all over again wasn't a happy thought. As it turned out, Billy didn't run for Congress again until I retired from Congress. When I stepped down in 1994, he entered the Democratic primary race for the seat I was vacating but lost to a younger opponent. I never doubted he was an able person and wasn't surprised when he became a successful governmental affairs adviser for a Washington consulting firm following his service in the U.S. House.

The celebration at our Dublin headquarters continued into the early morning hours. Keith stayed up until 5:15 a.m., keeping a few lingering supporters company. Luella and I broke away at midnight. Tired but happy, we sat up talking with our children at home until we finally collapsed at about 2 a.m.

When Jim Comerford returned for his second year of law school at the University of Georgia campus in Athens, he spotted former U.S. Secretary of State Dean Rusk, who taught international law, standing with a couple of people outside the law school. Rusk called him over. Jim first thought the renowned statesman might give him a scolding for skipping the first couple of weeks of classes. Instead, Rusk smiled and said, "Jim, you're probably the only law student in the country who spent the summer unseating an incumbent who served on the Judiciary Committee in Congress."

Like many politically-knowledgeable people throughout the country, Dean Rusk had taken notice of the upset in Georgia's Eighth District.

Following the election we ran an ad in newspapers throughout the district. Under a photo of Luella and me, we said, "Words cannot express our gratitude and deep affection for those of you who made our victory on September 21 possible. As supporters, your tireless effort and brave initiative made it all happen. We are grateful. As voters, your message was Loud & Clear! I pledge to keep my promise to be a congressman you'll be proud of."

CHAPTER TWELVE

Now that the emotionally and physically challenging congressional race was over, we could relax a little. But not a lot. Our schedule didn't ease up much at all between the runoff election on September 21, 1982, and the day I took the oath of office as a member of the U.S. House on January 3, 1983.

We made several trips to Washington, D.C., flying from the Atlanta airport to National Airport (now Reagan National Airport) and back, a flight we would take hundreds of times over the next twelve years. We found a place to live, attended a blur of social and orientation activities for incoming members of Congress, and employed a staff, a vitally-important process that took place both in Georgia and the nation's capital. At home, we had civic events to attend and media interviews to do. We also held several fund-raisers to cover campaign costs that soared during the campaign's final weeks, including a $10 buffet at the Greene County Country Club that drew close to 200 people, an indication of the enthusiasm and high expectations our campaign had generated.

Something unexpected happened when we ran into people we had known for years. They congratulated us warmly. But we detected an awkward reserve that hadn't existed before, leaving us feeling a little lonely.

Although winning the election was a significant accomplishment, and we now had a difficult and important job ahead of us, we knew very well we were the same people we had always been. But now we were about to serve on the national level, many friends regarded us in a different light. Luella and I would get used to our new role. But our lives had changed.

Our busy schedule began at noon on the day following the election when Keith Perdue and I climbed into a four-seat prop plane at the Dublin airport piloted by a friend, Dr. Eugene McNatt. We had planned to fly to communities around the district to thank supporters whether we won or lost. We took off on a blustery day and, in spite of the buffeting, made stops at Macon, Milledgeville, Eatonton, Greensboro, and Louisville on time or close to it. We flew for three consecutive days from Dublin to as many other communities as we could fit in to tell supporters who turned out at the airports they were the reason we won.

In late September we took our first trip to the nation's capital as a congressman-elect to go house hunting. Finding the cost of property in D.C. sky high compared to Georgia, Luella redefined Washington real estate as "unreal estate." After searching for several days, we settled on a relatively-affordable, attractive two-story townhouse in a small complex called Justice Court behind the U.S. Supreme Court building, located a few blocks from the U.S. Capitol and the Cannon House Office Building where my office would be.

We were staying in a motel and decided to rent a roll-way bed, purchase sheets and towels, and move into our own place while we shopped for the furniture. This was before cell phones and we arranged to have our home telephone connected before moving in. When we arrived at the townhouse, the phone was still disconnected. When we looked in the packages we thought contained the sheets and towels and a few other necessities, we discovered the sales lady had failed to put the sheets in the bag. Things weren't getting off to a very smooth start. But the phone company soon had our telephone working and a Justice Court neighbor welcomed us and loaned us sheets, making us feel more at home.

When we saw the prices of furniture in the Washington area, we figured we could make the purchases in Georgia and ship them by van to Capitol Hill. An ex-Marine-turned-reporter, Bill Boyd, who penned a popular column for *The Telegraph and News*, wrote that our furniture-buying decision demonstrated we were "close with a buck," adding this was good news for taxpayers. Although the political honeymoon wouldn't last long, the media was extraordinarily nice to us during the early months. "The Rowlands Take Their Charm to Washington," proclaimed a feature story headline in *The Courier Herald*.

We were often treated like royalty. When our moving van arrived, the driver couldn't pull his cumbersome truck into the long, narrow townhouse driveway and he had to park on busy Maryland Avenue, a thoroughfare leading to the U.S. Capitol. A policeman showed up and threatened to give the driver a ticket, ordering him to move on. When I came out and explained I had just been elected to Congress and we couldn't figure out where to park so we could get moved in, the officer let the van stay where it was. He also remained on the scene for more than an hour to direct traffic. We appreciated his help and thanked him profusely.

In mid-November we came to Washington to participate in a whirlwind of activities that continued until just before Christmas. Along with the other seventy-nine Democratic and Republican freshmen members of the U.S. House, I attended briefings sponsored by House leaders on congressional rules and procedures, office administration, current issues, and ethics. I also joined most of the freshmen on a three-day side trip for a seminar sponsored for new members of Congress by the John F. Kennedy School of Government at Harvard to study the economy, tax issues, agriculture, health care, energy, defense, foreign affairs, and proposals for stabilizing Social Security, attending classes from 8:30 a.m. into the evening.

We attended a bewildering series of breakfasts, brunches, lunches, dinners and receptions. President and Mrs. Reagan held a White House reception for the freshman class where we chatted with the First Couple and administration officials. The speaker, Thomas R. "Tip" O'Neill, Jr. of Massachusetts, hosted incoming House members at a dinner in Statuary Hall in the Capitol and a future speaker, Democratic Majority Leader Jim Wright of Texas, held a dinner for incoming House Democrats in the Cannon House Office Building, an event featuring the Air Force Strolling Strings who played while circulating among the tables. We met Walter and Mrs. Mondale at a reception they held, and the former vice president kidded us about how he fought off the Georgia gnats while visiting Jimmy Carter in Plains.

During the orientation process we regularly hung out with two other first-termers from Georgia, Lindsay Thomas from Screven and Richard Ray from Perry. As fate would have it, the first Republican we got to know well in the freshmen class was Mike Bilirakis from Florida, my future partner in efforts to overhaul the health care system. Mike and his wife Evelyn also moved into Justice Court.

Several of the fifty-seven Democratic freshmen, including myself, decided to form our own caucus to do research on issues, calling it the Legislative Action Group. Most of the new Democratic members subsequently joined. We organized subcommittees on defense, budgeting, social security, and health care, and I was elected chairman of the health care panel. The relationships I established with members of my large freshmen class enabled me to become an active player on a number of issues from the beginning, especially efforts to reduce the deficit.

Members of Congress are given a budget to hire a staff, open district offices, and cover expenses. Within that budgetary limit, I needed to employ a staff with the skills and experience to efficiently run a congressional office. I wanted a diverse staff in terms of race, gender, and geographical distribution. Two key members of our campaign staff accepted positions, Shirley Nowell as manager of the three district offices we opened in Dublin, Macon, and Waycross, and Keith Perdue as a legislative aide on the Washington staff. With Jim Comerford resuming his law studies and Dot Green returning to private life, I needed to recruit personnel from outside the campaign to fill the remaining positions in the district and Washington offices.

Two outgoing Georgia members of the U.S. House, Bo Ginn of Millen and Jack Brinkley of Columbus, recommended several of their staff members who became mainstays on the Eighth District staff. Barbara McElveen, from Bulloch County, now Barbara Schlein, who had served nearly ten years in Bo Ginn's Washington office, signed on as executive assistant and manager of office operations in the Washington office. Becki Brady, from Augusta, also from Bo Ginn's Washington staff, became legislative director. Kathy Bryant, from Pine Mountain, now Kathy Hennemuth, came from Jack Brinkley's Washington staff to serve as a legislative aide.

No one on Capitol Hill was more skillful and knowledgeable than Barbara in dealing with the many tasks facing a congressional office including budgeting, ethics, and personnel management. She worked incredibly-long hours, as did others on the staff, often picking us up or delivering us to the airport and other places we needed to be at all hours. Becki oversaw the legislative staff and handled the especially-challenging issues of appropriations and budgeting herself. Kathy, raised on a dairy farm, dealt with a variety of key issues including health care and agriculture and would play an important role in the 1993-94 effort to restructure the health care system.

Selby McCash, from Decatur, called to express interest in a staff position. Selby was serving as communications director for David Poythress, appointed Georgia's Secretary of State following the death of longtime Secretary of State Ben Fortson. In his bid to be elected to the post, David had just lost a close race to former U.S. Veterans Affairs Secretary Max Cleland. Having served as state Capitol correspondent for *The Telegraph and News*, political editor of *The Atlanta Journal*, columnist for *The Journal and Constitution*, and as a commentator for Georgia Public Television, Selby was known in Georgia politics. Although he served as the Washington-based administrative assistant with a supervisory role, he focused on communications.

We produced a newspaper column carried by weeklies and some dailies; a television program produced in the U.S. House studio and regularly run on several of Georgia's local TV stations; statements and speeches; and periodical newsletters, all focusing on what I was doing in office and how I stood on the issues.

Barbara, Kathy and Selby remained on the staff for all twelve years I served in the U.S. House. Becki stayed for most of my congressional tenure, leaving when she and her husband Chris decided to put their professional lives on hold and see the world. Keith and Shirley would go on to other opportunities after a few years. Many others served with me during those twelve years who made a real contribution and deserve recognition. Several years later, Bill Stembridge of Macon came from an administrative staff position at Mercer University to serve for nine years as our district representative and director after Shirley left. Bill's skill at building bridges to the district's diverse constituencies and his knowledge of what the district's movers and shakers were doing was extraordinary.

During orientation activities in December, Jim Comerford suggested I meet with Al Gore, then a U.S. House member from Tennessee. Gore had established a particularly-effective model for staying in touch with constituents, one we wanted to emulate.

Casually sitting back in a leather easy chair with his feet propped on a coffee table, Gore spent more than an hour in his office explaining in detail how he crammed multiple town hall meetings into his district schedule on weekends and other times when Congress was in recess. Some members never held town hall-style meetings. Others held one or two town hall meetings when they were at home. But Gore held three or four in a single day to report on current issues and answer questions from the audience. Sometimes the turnouts were bigger in the smaller communities than in the larger ones, he said. Whether or not people in a community attended, most were aware their representative in Congress had visited their community through word of mouth and stories in the local media, he explained.

I followed the Gore plan throughout my years in Congress. We held four or even as many as five meetings a day the first few years, later cutting back to a more manageable schedule of three or four a day. Starting in the morning and ending in the evening, we held the hour-and-a-half sessions at county courthouses, city and town halls, and other community gathering places. We held sixty-nine of the meetings during the first term, including a number at nursing and assisted care facilities for people who couldn't get out. We never failed to meet our goal of holding a town hall meeting in every one of the Eighth District's counties at least once a year.

In addition to notices we sent to local newspapers and radio stations, we mailed cards to every resident under the franking privilege notifying them of the upcoming meetings. The turnouts averaged about a dozen or so people and some fewer than that. When people were concerned about an issue, we occasionally drew much bigger crowds. Several hundred people turned out for a series of town hall meetings in middle Georgia I held jointly with U.S. Sen. Wyche Fowler of Georgia. Regardless of the crowd's size, I spent the same amount of time in every community, giving briefings on current issues and discussing any issue anyone wanted to raise.

We drew an audience of 100 or more when Sen. Ted Kennedy of Massachusetts joined me at a town meeting in Sparta, the county seat of Hancock County, one of Georgia's poorest counties. The senator, a leader in health care issues, had contacted me to arrange a public event together in order for him to become acquainted with a poor area where a federally-funded community health center was planned. The joint town meeting with Sen. Kennedy in Sparta established a friendly relationship that later played a key part in getting two major bills I authored through the Senate.

At almost every meeting, people with personal problems relating to the federal government appealed for help. A staff aide who accompanied me would take the information from the person seeking assistance and we would do whatever we could appropriately do to help. We also established a mobile case work program in the district. Staff members from our district offices visited communities in every Eighth District county to meet with constituents in need of assistance. But most case work was handled in the Washington office.

Much of the public isn't aware of how important this congressional responsibility has become. Getting the attention of the massive federal bureaucracy can be difficult and many people don't know where to turn when they need help on a personal matter connected with the federal government. Case work issues are wide-ranging. They involve Social Security and veterans' benefits, federal aid to small businesses and farms, tax and civil service issues, and problems relating to many other areas of the federal government. When natural disasters and violent events occurred around the world, we were often called upon to find out if loved ones were safe, including U.S. tourists, military personnel, and government employees.

Sometimes a constituent is wrong and a congressional office can't help. But sometimes a constituent is right and the bureaucracy is stubbornly resistant to the facts. A congressman can always get the immediate attention of a federal agency through the agency's congressional liaison office, and a fairly high percentage of our cases were resolved in favor of the constituent. But sometimes it took persistence and good argumentative skills by staff members and sometimes my own intervention to secure a ruling we considered fair.

One example involved a federally-funded program called Upward Bound. For 20 years, Mercer University in Macon had sponsored the program to help low-income middle Georgia high school students who had worked hard at their studies prepare for college. Upward Bound programs were required to periodically submit detailed applications to the U.S. Department of Education to requalify for funding. If an application failed to score high enough, that program's federal funding would go to a proposed program with a higher-rated application.

In 1986, the director of Mercer's Upward Bound program, Samuel Hart, was notified his application had received 96.66 points out of 100, a fraction of a point below the cutoff of 97.17. Mercer had lost its projected $240,000 Upward Bound grant, leaving 145 youngsters who were slated to take part in the program out in the cold. Sam Hart couldn't believe it. His program had always easily made the grade and this application was no different. When he looked into it, he discovered the Education Department had failed to give his application points for listing the qualifications of instructors and staff. In fact, the qualifications were included in the application. He also found his application had been penalized for omitting student-to-counselor ratios. But, in fact, student-to-counselor ratios were included. It looked like an entire section of Mercer's application had been overlooked in the Education Department's evaluation, costing more than enough points to bring Mercer's score into the approval range.

When he filed an appeal, it was rejected without explanation. No errors were admitted and no corrections would be made. That's when Sam contacted our office.

When we inquired about the situation, we were told the process was completed and nothing could be done to reevaluate the Mercer application. We pressed the Education Department's Upward Bound acting director, Walter Lewis, for a better explanation. But all he told us was that the Mercer application couldn't be reconsidered. I have no reason to believe politics was involved. I think it was probably just a careless mistake and the agency didn't want to own up to it. Perhaps the agency feared there were mistakes in other applications and if it reversed itself on the Mercer application it would open up a can of worms.

We knew it wouldn't be easy for the Education Department to either overturn an application that had already been approved in order to accommodate the Mercer program or to find extra funds for an additional program. But we believed it would be possible, even if difficult, for the agency to come up with the relatively-modest amount of money in its massive budget to correct a gross injustice.

In June 1986 I spoke from the well of the House. "The Upward Bound program has been administered in an unfair and irresponsible manner by the U.S. Department of Education," I said. Based on our own probing, I pointed out problems in the review of Upward Bound programs had existed for some years and little or nothing had been done to correct the situation, adding, "This may be the worst year ever." Noting we had hit a stone wall in trying to get it corrected, I called for the creation of an effective Upward Bound application appeals' system.

At this point, it looked like the Educational Department would stand firm on its rejection of the Mercer application no matter what was said in Congress.

Following my floor remarks, Georgia reporters and then the national media picked up on the story, one that revealed how mistake-prone and indifferent a bureaucracy could become. Once the fate of the Mercer University Upward Bound application began to be widely publicized, something happened at the top echelons of the Education Department. The Mercer application was quietly reconsidered. As an agency under a Republican administration, the announcement that the Mercer program would be reinstated was released through the office of a Republican senator from Georgia, Mack Mattingly. Although our office had frequently been in touch with the Education Department over the issue, the agency was probably steamed over my critical comments and didn't bother to notify us.

Case work was seldom this acrimonious. But it was often difficult and time-consuming work.

Answering mail was another challenging congressional responsibility. Once our office was up and running, we received 1,000 or more letters a week. It was our policy to respond to every one within two or three days. We prepared issue briefs on just about every issue we could think of and used these briefs to write individualized replies. From the beginning, we set up a system that enabled the staff to meet our quick turnaround policy most of the time. I reviewed every letter, made changes in many, and signed them all.

The assignment of member offices took place in December just before the new congressional term began in January. Returning members were given the first choice of offices from among those vacated by members who had retired or lost in the election. What was left was available to the seventy-nine freshmen. Numbers were picked out of a hat with the member picking number one getting the first choice and the member picking number seventy-nine getting the last. Becki Brady was given the honor of selecting the number for our office. She selected number seventy-nine. She later told me she was "mortified" when she picked the highest number. At the time, she took a lot of good-natured ribbing from her fellow staffers.

The Cannon House Office Building is the oldest of the three U.S. House office buildings, all located across Independence Avenue from the Capitol. Our office, 513, was on the top floor, which originally served as an attic but had been converted to offices many years before and was now commonly called the "penthouse." The fifth floor offices had lower ceilings and somewhat smaller rooms. Although we moved into more spacious quarters after a couple of terms, the penthouse remained our most memorable accommodation.

In addition to the study caucus formed by the Democratic freshmen, I joined a coalition of moderate-to-conservative Democrats called the Conservative Democratic Forum (CDF), an organization founded by Texan Charles Stenholm in 1980. The CDF would morph into the so-called Blue Dog Coalition years later. Although its membership fluctuated, it stood in the mid-to-high thirties when I became a member. Although I don't recall the details, I was among the new Democrats Charlie and others with the CDF would have recruited. With many more Democrats than Republicans serving in the House, the CDF couldn't tilt the balance of power on its own. But it commanded enough votes to get the attention of the party's more liberal leadership and on occasions persuade the leadership to moderate its positions. Acting almost like a third party at times, the CDF would serve as a base for me throughout my years in Congress.

On January 3, 1983, a Monday, the day I was scheduled to take the oath as Georgia's Eighth District congressman, Barbara opened the office at 8:30 a.m. Other staff members and I arrived shortly thereafter. I had started jogging in the morning, something I would do regularly on Capitol Hill throughout my years in Congress, often with other House members. But this morning I arose at 7 a.m., consumed a light breakfast and a cup of decaffeinated coffee, and headed straight to the Cannon building. Staffers had tacked a hand-made banner on one wall, "Congratulations, Congressman Rowland." The House office of administration had delivered our furniture. But desks, chairs, and bookcases were still scattered in an unarranged fashion around the office's four rooms. Nails where the previous occupant had hung art work were sticking out of the walls. But it wasn't long before the staff placed the furniture in functioning order and hung pictures of Georgia scenes on the walls.

A couple of reporters stopped by. They were covering the swearing-in ceremonies scheduled to take place that afternoon in the House and Senate chambers. One was Bill Boyd, the pleasantly gruff ex-Marine who was visiting Washington to write about the opening day as a reporter and columnist in Macon. A couple of dozen well-wishers from Georgia came by to say hello before heading to the House gallery to watch the opening proceedings. Two of our grown children, Jane and Jim, and our grandson Robb, were there. At noon, Robb joined me on the House floor while Luella and other family members took their assigned seats in the gallery.

First on the agenda was electing a speaker. Since Democrats were in control, the election of Tip O'Neill to his fourth term as speaker was automatic. After his election, O'Neill administered the oath of office to the 435 members of the U.S. House of Representatives for the 98th term.

At exactly 1:33 p.m., I officially became one of three physicians serving in Congress. The other two were returning House members, the only two physicians serving in the House or the Senate during the previous term. I only temporarily brought the ranks of medical doctors in Congress up to three. Before the year ended, a tragedy reduced the number to two again. After the next election, political fate left me as the lone physician in Congress.

Of the three who took the oath on January 3, 1983, I was closest to the political mainstream. The other two were definitely on the ideological edge. One was the congressman from Georgia who had supported my ill-fated attempt to organize CONTROL, Larry McDonald, an urologist from Marietta, who had just become national chairman of the John Birch Society. He was serving his fifth term in the U.S. House. He ran as a Democrat because this was still the era when the Democratic Party dominated politics in Georgia and the South and, in many districts, only Democrats could win. The other physician was Republican Ron Paul, an OB/GYN from Texas, a libertarian thinker who would later become the Libertarian Party's presidential candidate. He was serving his fourth term.

McDonald rarely voted with the Democratic majority and was the only Democrat to vote against the party's candidate for speaker, Tip O'Neill. Larry was shunned by the party's leaders who passed him over for choice committee assignments. Maybe it didn't matter all that much to Larry. Congress served primarily as his base for anti-communist activities, a forum for hailing Sen. Joseph McCarthy as a hero and assailing Dr. Martin Luther King as a communist sympathizer. From promoting the use of nuclear weapons in Vietnam to attacking virtually every government program except defense as unconstitutional, McDonald thrived on endless controversy.

Larry had the pugnacious image of a far-right activist. But I knew him as a thoughtful person who went out of his way to help me and other newcomers get settled in Congress. His office was noted for maintaining an effective case work program to help constituents in need. At the same time, he didn't hesitate to scold me on the House floor for the way I voted. His manner was never hostile. He was just disappointed we weren't on the same wavelength.

On September 1, 1983, eight months after the session had convened, Larry lost his life along with 268 other passengers when a Soviet fighter downed Korean Air Lines Flight 007. Larry was en route to a ceremony commemorating the U.S.-South Korea Defense Pact. The passenger airliner had accidently strayed over Soviet territory and was shot down by an air-to-air missile. Although Flight 007 evidently flew near a militarily-sensitive area, the attack on a defenseless passenger plane was a barbaric act that created a greater strain in U.S.-Soviet relations. In the spring, a white dogwood tree from Georgia was planted on the U.S. Capitol grounds in Larry's memory with Rep. Elliott Levitas of DeKalb County, dean of the Georgia House delegation, presiding over the short ceremony.

Ron Paul, a Texan originally from Pennsylvania, also marched resolutely to his own drummer. Although he didn't officially affiliate himself with organized libertarians until he became the Libertarian Party's presidential candidate in 1988, he always espoused the libertarian blend of conservative and liberal views. In 1984, he ran for the U.S. Senate and was defeated, leaving me as the only physician in the U.S. House for two terms, from 1985 to 1989.

Rep. Jim McDermott, a psychiatrist, joined me as the second MD in the House in 1990. Jim was a traditional liberal. A hefty, bearded, genial individual, he was born in a working class neighborhood of Chicago and paid his way through college by loading coal and ore boats on the Great Lakes. Moving to Washington State after serving in the Navy, he ran for Congress after serving in the state legislature and unsuccessfully running for governor. Larry McDonald and Ron Paul both wanted to disengage government from the health care system. Jim advocated a single-payer, government-controlled system. I was somewhere in between.

The medical doctors I knew who served in Congress were as far apart philosophically as it gets. But they had one thing in common. They were all fighters. They believed with all their heart they were fighting to make the country better. We need more health care professionals serving in public office because the government needs people with expertise in the delivery of health care to help make health care policy. But we also need more health care professionals in public office because they tend to be people who are more interested in making the country better, as they see it, than in perpetuating themselves in office.

On January 25, 1983, members of the House and Senate gathered in the House chamber to hear President Reagan deliver the 196th State of the Union address. George Washington established the traditional presidential address which is now delivered before a prime time national television audience. On the evening of the president's presentation, Luella and I came to the Capitol early to observe the scene as it unfolded. Nolan Walters, the Washington correspondent for *The Telegraph and News*, asked me when I arrived whether I was awed to be in the midst of history. I was prepared for the challenges and was confident I was up to the job. But, yes, I was truly awed by the surroundings and opportunity.

Luella took her assigned gallery seat and I sat on the Democratic side of the aisle on the House floor. There was a buzz of excitement as the members gradually filled the chamber and visitors, dignitaries, and the media settled into the gallery.

The speaker of the House entered and took his seat at the dais. The sergeant of arms appeared in the center aisle and announced the arrival of the vice president who took his seat next to the speaker while everyone stood and applauded. The Supreme Court justices, cabinet members, diplomatic corps, and Joint Chiefs of Staff filed in, all announced and greeted with standing applause. Then the sergeant of arms reappeared in the center aisle and declared, "Mr. Speaker, the President of the United States."

President Reagan, accompanied by a bipartisan congressional escort group, emerged from the back of the chamber and made his way down the aisle, stopping every few feet to shake hands with members of Congress sitting along the aisle. Everyone stood and the applause was thunderous. Onlookers applauded either as supporters of the president or out of respect for the office. President Reagan took his place at the podium with the speaker and vice president sitting above him as the applause continued. A U.S. flag was displayed above all of them and inscribed in gold letters above the flag were the words, "In God We Trust."

I remember thinking, *All of us sitting in this historic room really aren't Democrats or Republicans, black or white, Christian or Jews, or anyone with antagonistic differences—just Americans who are proud of their country.* As he began speaking, the president reinforced this thought. "I would like to talk to you this evening about what we can do together," he said, "not as Republicans and Democrats, but as Americans to make tomorrow's American happy and prosperous at home, strong and respected abroad, and at peace in the world."

Since that evening I've wondered whether we've abandoned the unifying principles that made the country great. Our representative government thrives on free speech and diverse opinions and can never be free of political disputes. But throughout most of the country's history, our leaders have ultimately resolved differences, no matter how deeply felt, to advance vital national interests. This was true when I arrived in Congress. But the longer I stayed, the more difficult it became to bridge the widening political and ideological gulf.

CHAPTER THIRTEEN

The task of appointing committees in the U.S. House of Representatives takes place at the start of each new two-year term. For most members it's a routine process. But as I would sadly discover, sometimes it can be a disheartening struggle.

My top two choices as I began my twelve years in Congress were the Veterans' Affairs Committee and the Energy and Commerce Committee, one of several House committees with jurisdiction over civilian health care issues. I would have no trouble securing a seat on the VA committee. Although I hadn't met the chairman, G.V. "Sonny" Montgomery of Mississippi, he had reached out to recruit me shortly after my election to Congress. He wanted a physician to join his committee to help him improve the veterans' health care system. Connecting with Sonny would be about the best thing that happened to me during my congressional career. But pursuing a seat on the Energy and Commerce Committee would be one of the most difficult and trying things I would ever undertake.

As I quickly learned, the two major parties were apportioned a certain number of seats on each of the twenty-two standing House committees. For Democrats, the party's thirty-member Steering and Policy Committee made the appointments. If more Democratic members sought a seat on a particular committee than the number allotted to the party, it would be up to the Steering and Policy Committee to decide who was seated and who was turned down.

Although Democratic leaders in the House didn't entirely control the party's committee appointments, they strongly influenced them. The speaker, Tip O'Neill, chaired the Steering and Policy Committee. Others in Democratic leadership positions automatically served on the committee as did the Democratic chairmen of major committees including those chairing the Appropriations, Ways and Means, Budget, Rules, and Energy and Commerce committees. Most of the other seats were held by regionally-elected members. States were grouped into regions and members from those regions elected colleagues to represent them on the panel. One seat was reserved for a member elected by the freshman class.

For my final term in Congress, I would be elected to the Steering and Policy Committee to represent a region that included Georgia and several other Southern states even though I probably wasn't the first choice of the House Democratic leadership. I had a close working relationship and friendship with many colleagues from my region and was able to overcome the lack of leadership support. But as a freshman, I had few contacts other than the members of my state's delegation. My fate in the committee selecting process would undoubtedly be in the hands of the Democratic House leadership.

Going in, I thought my party's leaders would see the wisdom of appointing the only physician in good standing with the party to a committee dealing with general health care issues. I didn't understand the dynamics. In fact, I was downright naïve. What really mattered to the leadership was party "loyalty." Would a Democratic member tend to support the generally left-leaning party leadership position or stand more with Republicans? During the previous term, House Democrats had engaged in a vigorous discussion over the question of party discipline. With some fifty Democratic members in the liberal wing calling for some kind of action, the speaker and Democratic Majority Leader Jim Wright held a meeting called a "harmony caucus" to work out disciplinary guidelines. One idea, for example, was to designate certain votes as key votes and those votes would be a factor in rewarding committee appointments and other leadership benefits. But if any specific sanctions were adopted, I wasn't aware of it.

The Democratic leadership was walking on a fine line. On one hand, Tip O'Neill and Jim Wright didn't want to reward members like Georgian Larry McDonald and Texan Phil Gramm who voted overwhelming with the Republican majority. On the other hand, the party's leaders didn't want to banish all conservatives and moderates from the Democratic tent. While Republicans had steadily become a more ideologically uniform party, the Democratic ranks were still ideologically more diverse. Without the conservative wing, Democrats in the House would be at risk of losing their majority advantage. Democratic leaders had sanctioned McDonald by denying him his preferred committee assignments. They had considered punishing my congressional opponent, Billy Evans, and Charles Stenholm of Texas, the 1980 founder of the Conservative Democratic Forum, the main moderate-to-conservative House coalition. But they had stopped short of sanctioning those whose Republican-leaning voting records weren't as extreme as Larry's.

At the start of the next term of Congress, Tip O'Neill would form a "Speaker's Cabinet" that included some notable moderate conservatives in the House, including my Georgia colleague, Ed Jenkins of Young Harris, to advise Democratic House leaders and the Democratic Steering and Policy Committee on party policy. But the issue of party discipline would remain unsettled. For the most part, so would the relationship between Democratic House members on the right of center and the Democratic leadership on the left.

When I consulted Ed Jenkins about my chances of landing a seat on the Energy and Commerce Committee, he warned me I would face stiff competition. With some forty percent of all measures considered in the House referred to the Energy and Commerce Committee, it rivaled the Appropriations and Ways and Means committees as the most coveted House committee. But he also believed I might have a reasonable chance if I could convince the Steering and Policy Committee members of the importance of including a medical professional on a committee with health care jurisdiction.

Lobbying for the committee seat was a lot like running for office again. It involved hard campaigning. During the orientation process, I called on all thirty members of the Steering and Policy Committee to tell them of my interest in the Energy and Commerce Committee and the reasons why I should be a high-priority choice. I met with John Dingell of Michigan, the committee's powerful chairman. He was cordial, advising me "not to worry." I also met with Henry Waxman of California, chairman of the Energy and Commerce Committee's Health and the Environment Subcommittee, a power in his own right. Henry was polite, but his demeanor was somewhat cool and noncommittal.

Ed Jenkins, one of the moderate conservatives held in high regard by Democratic leaders, did all he could to help me. But his support wouldn't be enough. Ed delivered the bad news after the vote was held behind closed doors. There were five openings for Democrats on the Energy and Commerce Committee that year. It was decided one of those five seats would be given to a freshman. He told me it came down to a tie between me and Jim Slattery of Kansas. The tie-breaking vote was cast for Jim by the one freshman who had been elected to the Steering and Policy Committee by his fellow freshmen, Buddy MacKay of Florida.

As a consolation, I was named to the Public Works and Transportation Committee, an assignment I would find rewarding. It would give me an opportunity to negotiate an agreement leading to the passage of a landmark Clean Water Act and to try to get a better deal for rural areas in the allocation of federal highway funds. But no goal was more important to me than helping improve the health care system, and membership on the Energy and Commerce Committee would give me a better opportunity to achieve that goal.

Buddy MacKay, who served three terms in the U.S. House and would later serve as Florida's lieutenant governor and briefly as governor following the death of former U.S. Senator and then Gov. Lawton Chiles, soon became a friend and ally on a number of issues, particularly deficit reduction. We jogged together on Capitol Hill occasionally. Later in our first term, he and Rep. Tim Penny of Minnesota co-organized the Democratic Budget Study Group which met weekly, often hearing from top budget officials and leading economists. I regularly attended the study group's get-togethers, finding them most helpful in understanding budgetary issues.

Although I never held any ill feelings toward Buddy, the outcome of the vote on committee assignments was tough to swallow. I was reminded of this setback whenever I saw my new Republican friend and Justice Court neighbor, Mike Bilirakis. Mike, an attorney and municipal judge from Tarpon Springs, Florida, had also asked for a seat on the Energy and Commerce Committee. Although his party was allotted fewer seats as the minority party in the House, Mike was selected for one of them. Not only that, he was picked to serve on the committee's Health and the Environment Subcommittee.

The Steering and Policy Committee did discipline Phil Gramm, kicking him off the Budget Committee. He switched parties and was reelected as a Republican. An effort was also made to remove Sonny Montgomery as chairman of the Veterans' Affairs Committee. Although all of the other returning Democratic committee chairmen were easily reappointed, the Steering and Policy Committee allowed Sonny to retain his chairmanship only after sharp discussion and a surprisingly-close vote of 16-11. While Sonny voted with the Republican majority more often than the Democratic leadership liked, his voting record was hardly comparable to the Republican-oriented records of Phil Gramm or Larry McDonald. Nevertheless, a few Democrats on the left wanted him punished. But Sonny lobbied to keep his chairmanship, making it clear he was a Democrat, and he received the crucial backing of the speaker. If he had been booted, my career in Congress would have been far different.

A couple of reporters suggested Democratic House leaders must have had a higher regard for the other freshmen members of the Georgia delegation than they did for me because I was the only one denied a committee preference. But none of the other Georgia freshmen sought a seat on such a highly-coveted committee as Energy and Commerce. I'm sure Democratic House leaders wondered if I would side with the Republicans more than the Democrats like my predecessor, Billy Evans, and they must have viewed Jim Slattery as less of an unknown quantity. But I didn't think the leadership had anything against me. I thought I would have an excellent chance of securing a seat on the Energy and Commerce Committee if elected to a second term.

When I again sought a seat on the committee two years later, however, I was definitely out of favor with the two most powerful Democrats on the Energy and Commerce Committee.

During my first term, a bill to legalize heroin as a painkiller for terminal cancer patients was sponsored by Energy and Commerce Health and the Environment Subcommittee Chairman Henry Waxman and supported by the committee's chairman, John Dingell. I understand one of John's parents had died of cancer. It was an emotional issue for him. But less dangerous painkillers were available that were just as effective if managed correctly. Heroin would have inevitably spread to a broader patient community if legalized as a prescribed drug in terminal cases, resulting in even more widespread addiction and unnecessary deaths. Today, opiates prescribed for pain have become an out-of-control national problem.

As a physician, my outspoken opposition helped kill the heroin bill. It also antagonized John Dingell and Henry Waxman. When I decided to actively oppose the measure, I hoped I wouldn't be blackballed because of my stand on one issue. But this was wishful thinking. When I applied for an appointment to the Energy and Commerce Committee for the 1985-86 term, I was rejected again. Two years after that I would be passed over for a third time. Most members of the Steering and Policy Committee weren't willing to override the wishes of two powerful lawmakers like

Dingell and Waxman. It looked like I would never be allowed to serve on a committee dealing with civilian health care issues.

By the start of my fourth term, however, my standing with the Democratic leadership, including Dingell and Waxman, had undergone a startling transformation. What brought about this change was my work on two issues, HIV-AIDS and a revolution in Nicaragua.

From the day I entered the U.S. House, military aid to the Contras in their fight to overturn the Marxist Sandinista regime in Nicaragua was a hotly-debated issue. The Reagan administration and Republican leadership in Congress were waging a vigorous campaign to provide military as well as other forms of aid to the Contra revolution. Democratic leaders supported only humanitarian aid such as food and medicine for the Contras and opposed providing weapons to a guerrilla force at war with a foreign government. While I supported military assistance for the Contras for several years, I became one of the few moderate and conservative Democrats in the House to vote against additional military aid at a time when it threatened to upset a peace process leading to a free, internationally-monitored election in Nicaragua.

Although I got in hot water with some constituents and conservative media commentators who thought I had gone "liberal," my vote proved to be the right one when a free election subsequently took place and the Sandinista regime was ousted. The intent of President Reagan's Nicaraguan policy was supposedly to coerce the Sandinistas into submitting to a free and fair election and I didn't think it made sense for Congress to do something that would have given the Sandinistas the excuse they needed to call off the election. Several swing votes of moderate conservatives, including mine, made it possible for the Democratic leadership position against more military aid to prevail.

I authored a bill to create a National Commission on AIDS in an effort to bring better coordination and more efficiency to the federal fight against the disease. Henry Waxman strongly supported a pro-active federal role in trying to bring HIV-AIDS under control. Once I emerged as a leader in shaping HIV-AIDS policy, my relationship with Henry improved. I took some political heat for my work on AIDS from opponents who criticized me for promoting the "homosexual agenda," a ridiculous accusation based on the fact that gay rights' organizations supported the same AIDS policies as leading health authorities. Henry Waxman was aware my leadership in the fight against AIDS came at a political price. His support was a key factor in my finally gaining a seat on the committee and his health subcommittee.

A number of factors converged in my favor. House Democratic Whip Tony Coehlo of California agreed to support me. Although I sometimes supported Republican and bipartisan positions, Tony recognized I supported the Democratic majority when I believed the Democratic position was right and he knew I had sometimes taken political flak at home for doing so. I hadn't joined some conservative Democrats who had supported Rep. Charles Stenholm when he temporarily challenged Tip O'Neill for House speaker in 1985, withdrawing before the election for speaker was held. Although a member of the Conservative Democratic Forum then headed by Charlie, I chose not to isolate myself from the party mainstream by supporting a symbolic challenge to the incumbent speaker. Tony recognized it would be unfair and strategically unwise for the House Democratic leadership to exclude moderate conservatives.

Another key factor was the support of Georgia's Democratic House delegation. No Georgian had served on the Energy and Commerce Committee since Bill Stuckey left Congress. Every member of the delegation agreed to make my appointment to the Energy and Commerce Committee the delegation's top priority in committee recommendations that year.

Two seats were available to Democrats and up to 20 Democratic members were seeking those seats. In spite of the strong competition, I felt better about my chances.

When I sat next to John Dingell on the House floor and asked him if I had a chance shortly before the Steering and Policy Committee voted on committee assignments, he assured me I now had his essential support. Rep.

Beryl Anthony of Arkansas, a close friend of O'Neill's successor as speaker, Jim Wright, indicated the speaker supported me. Rep. Steny Hoyer of Maryland, who had served as past co-chairman of the Steering and Policy Committee, and who would become chairman of the House Democratic Caucus that year, a rising Democratic leader who had worked with me to create the AIDS commission, told me I had "nothing to worry about."

It was a relief when I was finally told the assignment I had sought for six years was mine. If I had received the appointment earlier, I might have achieved more in health care. But with six years left in my congressional tenure, the belated appointment would enable me to achieve a number of health care goals. I told Associated Press reporter David Pace that "members have been coming to me for the past couple of years asking about health legislation and I think several of them voted the way they did because of information I provided them. Certainly I'm more knowledgeable than anyone else (in the House) in treating sick people, and that's what we're talking about."

Failure certainly isn't fun, but it can be an effective teacher. While my six-year struggle to join the Energy and Commerce Committee was frustrating, it sharpened my legislative negotiating skills, giving me a better sense of when to be assertive and when to be patient. It taught me about colleagues who were trustworthy and about some who weren't. What I learned not only helped me finally secure a seat on the Energy and Commerce Committee, it helped lead to leadership roles such as election to the Steering and Policy Committee for my final term by fellow House members from Georgia, North and South Carolina, Tennessee and Alabama.

Sonny Montgomery wrote me a letter after my win over Billy Evans asking me to join the VA committee. He had just completed his first term as chairman of the Veterans' Affairs Committee and was eager to get a team in place that could make the kind of changes he envisioned. Like me, Sonny was a World War II veteran who had fought in Europe, a second lieutenant who became a major general in the Mississippi National Guard. He would serve twenty-four years in Congress, sixteen years as

VA committee chairman, shaping many of the veteran programs existing today. He was primarily responsible for the "Montgomery GI Bill" that continued educational benefits to veterans begun during World War II.

Later on, Sonny would make a personal sacrifice so I could chair the VA Committee's Hospitals and Healthcare Subcommittee. He was serving as chairman of both the full committee and the Investigations and Oversight Subcommittee. Although the investigations' role was important to him, he stepped down after convincing Rep. Lane Evans of Illinois to switch from chairman of the health subcommittee to chairman of investigations so I could move up to the health subcommittee chairmanship during my last two years in Congress.

I credit Sonny with making major advances at the Carl Vinson Veterans' Administration Medical Center in Dublin. He may well have saved the hospital. The medical center, constructed in 1943 at Carl Vinson's instigation, was named in honor of the longtime Georgia congressman under a bill I introduced during my first term. The center provides care for a veterans' population of more than 100,000 in middle and south Georgia. It's the only veterans' medical center between Atlanta and Lake City, FL, providing services both at the main facility in Dublin and five outreach clinics around the area. The number of outpatient visits at the Dublin hospital and the satellite clinics exceeds 320,000.

While mainly important for the care it provides, it's also as a major economic asset for our entire region. Playing a leading part in preserving and expanding the hospital of such crucial importance to Georgia's veteran population and the community at-large would be one of the most important tasks I would undertake during my legislative years.

Two VA health subcommittee hearings were held at the Dublin center at my request. At a hearing held in May 1985, chaired by Sonny, a record of need was established for enlarging and modernizing the hospital's aging outpatient clinic. This factual base of information eventually helped make it possible for proposed improvements to rise on the priority list. In December 1988, I chaired two days of hearings by the subcommittee at the hospital. Out of these hearings came a $9.5 million authorization for a new outpatient clinic. Funding for the clinic was eventually included in President George H. W. Bush's 1990 budget and approved by Congress.

At the 1988 hearings, a case was also made for saving the center's threatened surgical unit. A Veterans Administration task force studying excess capacity throughout the vast VA health care system had recommended closing the surgical facility. According to the center's director, William O. Edgar, the subcommittee hearings were a "catalyst" that "kept our surgery open." A few months after the hearing, VA Secretary Ed Derwinski disclosed the Dublin surgical unit had been removed from the list of VA health care facilities to be shut down. According to a House VA Committee staff member who had inside knowledge, the Veterans Administration had previously viewed the closing of the surgical unit as a step toward converting the hospital into a long-term assisted care facility. With the need for veterans' care rapidly growing in our area of Georgia, closing the hospital would have had tragic consequences.

Sonny pro-actively took my side. He was one of President Bush's closest personal buddies. Armed with facts and figures produced at the hearings, I'm certain he talked to the president about the critical need to preserve the surgical unit and to upgrade the whole medical center to accommodate the area's expanding veterans' population. I'm convinced my friendship with Sonny and Sonny's friendship with President Bush made all the difference in the Bush administration's support of the retention of the surgical unit and expansion and modernization of the hospital.

I travelled with Sonny a lot. The VA Committee held many field hearings around the country to give veterans an opportunity to speak out on veterans' issues. Sonny also included me in delegations that traveled abroad when issues of concern to veterans arose in far-away places like the Philippines. He named me to the congressional delegation that attended the fiftieth anniversary of the D Day landing in Normandy, France. He also asked me to accompany him on a special mission to Central America at the request of the elder President Bush to look into the Contra situation and a crisis in Panama, a trip I believe had an immediate impact on U.S. policy.

A co-founder of the Congressional Prayer Breakfast, Sonny urged me to attend the weekly Thursday morning gatherings and I did so throughout my years in Congress. Although primarily a spiritual experience, the fellowship also proved to be beneficial from a practical standpoint. The close friendships I developed with other regulars at the breakfasts proved to be significantly helpful on any number of issues.

Once, when flying home from field hearings in a large, gleaming Air Force jet, the chairman asked the pilot to land in Dublin to let me off. This was the largest plane to ever land at the small Dublin air field. When I disembarked, several Dublin residents who happened to be at the airport were watching with interest. "I like your plane," one of them said as I came over to say hello. I liked it myself, and I never forgot it was Sonny Montgomery who made so many opportunities possible.

CHAPTER FOURTEEN

As a new congressman, I cited deficit reduction as the most critical issue facing Congress. If we couldn't balance the federal budget, I told the media, at least we should reduce deficit spending as much as possible. Reducing the amount of money the federal government borrowed to pay interest on the growing national debt would help revive the country's long-sluggish economy and give Americans greater long-term economic security, I maintained.

At the time, high interest rates were restricting business growth. Considerable research suggests a connection has traditionally existed between high government debt relative to the size of the economy and high interest rates that deter domestic investment. Servicing the debt also diverts income needed for other purposes. Everyone knows excessive debt can devastate families and businesses. It can also have a devastating impact on nations and their citizens.

My position on deficit spending would lead me to oppose budgets proposed by the top leadership of both parties. Republican budgets featured tax cuts and increases in defense spending that were funded with big budget deficits in spite of cuts in social programs. Democratic budgets featured increases in social programs that were funded with big deficits in spite of cuts in defense and either tax hikes or smaller tax cuts than the Republicans proposed.

From the outset I aligned myself with centrist factions advocating alternative budgets calling for balanced levels of tax cuts and defense and domestic spending and smaller deficits than the Democratic and Republican budgets. Deficit reduction was a primary goal of the moderate-to-conservative coalition of Democratic House members I had joined, the Conservative Democratic Forum. I also belonged to a coalition of freshmen Democrats led by Florida's Buddy MacKay pushing a centrist budget.

In the middle was exactly where I stood in the 1983 budget battle in the House, a stance that would put me in an uncomfortable position with my party's leadership.

Democrats and Republicans always introduce clashing budgets. The two parties were certainly divided over a budget resolution in 1983 to establish a budgetary blueprint for the coming fiscal year. The federal budgetary process is complex and confusing and seldom works as designed. Congress had failed to agree on a new budget the previous year and the federal government was operating under a continuing resolution that extended the old budget enacted the year before. Under the old budget, the deficit threatened to bust the $200 billion mark, exceeding five percent of the Gross Domestic Product (GDP). Unless Congress enacted a new and improved budget, I was sure this level of deficit spending would slow the recovery and make it more difficult to reduce unemployment, then exceeding ten percent.

The Democratic majority under fiscally-liberal Speaker Tip O'Neill proposed a budget resolution with a projected long-range deficit of $174 billion. President Reagan and the Republican minority proposed a budget resolution with a projected deficit of $188 billion over the same period. With House committees under Democratic majority control, the Budget Committee approved the Democratic leadership-backed resolution for a vote on the House floor and the Rules Committee adopted a rule that disallowed amendments but did allow Republicans to offer their proposal as a substitute.

If the Republican proposal failed, as it surely would, the House would vote up or down on the whole Democratic resolution.

A total of 269 Democrats and 166 Republicans were serving in the U.S. House during the 1983-84 term. The Republican substitute didn't stand a chance. Under a less restrictive rule, Republicans could have potentially attracted bipartisan support for amendments to specific provisions in the Democratic version that could have altered it more to their liking and less to the liking of the Democratic leadership. Even if both sides wanted to manipulate the rules to their advantage, Republicans were understandably angry over the partisan rule. They protested by refusing to even offer their proposal.

But could the Democratic leadership plan pass? Republicans would vote against it as a bloc, and a substantial number of Democrats weren't pleased with it either. Charles Stenholm and some members of the Conservative Democratic Forum vocally opposed it because they felt its level of defense funding was too low and its projected deficit too high. So were a number of the freshmen aligned with Buddy MacKay. Members representing districts with defense installations and large military-connected constituencies were sure to face criticism at home for supporting the Democratic budget plan.

Although I hadn't yet shared my feelings with the Democratic leadership, I had decided to oppose both the Democratic and Republican budget proposals. I considered domestic spending too high in the Democratic version, defense spending too high in the Republican version, and the deficit projections too high in both. I would support the more balanced options proposed by the CDF and the coalition of freshmen.

I was concerned about my party's resolution on its merits. I was also concerned about the political ramifications. This would be my first vote on a federal budget and the way I voted would likely set in stone the way many constituents perceived me. Robins Air Force Base in Warner

Robins and Moody Air Force Base in Valdosta were crucial to the economic well-being of my area and my entire state. Would I vote the way my party's "bosses" wanted me to vote? Or would I stand up for the best interests of Georgia?

At this point, Speaker O'Neill, Majority Leader Jim Wright of Texas, Budget Committee Chairman Jim Jones of Oklahoma, and other top House leaders sponsoring the Democratic resolution didn't know how a number of rank-and-file Democrats would vote. The speaker and other Democratic leaders needed to secure as many Democratic commitments as possible or risk an embarrassing loss. In mid-March, a letter signed by the speaker, the majority leader, the Budget Committee chairman, and other Democratic leaders was sent to Democratic House members stating the Democratic budget resolution and the amendment-restricting rule were "matters of party policy."

The meaning was clear. Anyone who voted against the Democratic leadership position on the Democratic budget resolution would risk becoming a party outcast.

On March 23, a Wednesday, Tip O'Neill asked the first-term Democratic House members—all 57 of us—to meet with him for a briefing on the budget. I remember filing into the Capitol meeting room with other freshmen members, bantering pleasantly with them as we took our seats, expecting a friendly sales pitch on the positive features of the Democratic leadership proposal. All I would have to do, I thought, was sit and listen.

The speaker welcomed us. He noted Congress had been unable to pass any budget the year before and the federal government was operating under the old outdated budget that fell far short of meeting current needs in many areas. The vote on the Democratic resolution would be a litmus test of whether the Democratic majority was strong enough to pass a budget, he said. If the Democratic resolution was defeated, he suggested, the federal government might again be left without a budget to meet the needs of many important programs. He denounced President Reagan's plan, saying it called for draconian cuts in social programs in order to fund deep tax cuts and a huge increase in defense spending.

Like others advocating a bipartisan middle ground, I wanted both the Democratic and Republican proposals to be rejected and for Congress to ultimately reach agreement over a compromise with balanced levels of spending for defense and domestic programs and a lower projected deficit. Such an alternative had been worked out by our freshmen Democratic coalition, but was barred from consideration by the restrictive rule.

One thing I wouldn't do was buckle under to a party position I believed would be bad for my district and the whole country, not to mention my political well-being. Although I wasn't sure how to avoid it, I also didn't want to be ostracized by my party's leadership. Considering Billy's history in Congress, it was understandable if Democratic leaders were already uncertain about my relationship with the party. I could only hope to be accepted as a loyal Democrat by supporting the Democratic position whenever I could, the Republican position when I thought it was right, and working for a bipartisan option when I thought both party leadership positions missed the target.

Suddenly Tip O'Neill asked anyone in the room who didn't intend to vote for the Democratic resolution to stand up, catching me by surprise. This was pure intimidation. I had no choice but to rise. I was sitting near the front row and didn't see anyone else standing. I felt absolutely alone with every eye in the room staring at me, and I had a sinking feeling I was fated to be a party pariah.

"I'm not a Republican and I'm not a boll weevil," I assured the speaker. "I'm a Southern Democrat. I believe the best way to change the party is from inside the party, not outside the party." Then I quickly sat down.

Later, I learned several others were on their feet behind me. I knew I wasn't the only Democratic freshman who didn't favor the Democratic leadership's position on the budget and it was good to belatedly learn I had company that day. Within a day or so, I was relieved to receive a letter from Budget Committee Chairman Jim Jones commending me for explaining my vote. The Democratic leadership was making it clear it wanted to keep moderate-to-conservative House Democrats within the party fold. For now, at least, the leadership had decided to be tolerant of my independent stand.

The vote on the rule was fairly close. But it passed by a vote of 230-187. The Democratic resolution then swept through the House. The Democratic leadership's arm-twisting tactics worked. Twenty CDF members voted against it, but 15 followed the party line and voted for it. The Senate passed a resolution resembling the Republican House proposal and a Senate-House conference committee subsequently approved a compromise with a projected deficit that fell between the Democratic and Republican proposals, and the compromise was enacted.

It wasn't much of a compromise as far as I was concerned. But it was the best we could get.

The following year the Democratic House leadership changed tactics. Instead of an extremely restrictive rule resulting in an up-or-down House vote on only one partisan plan, a rule was adopted allowing a wide range of budget resolutions to be considered. A plan was sponsored by the Conservative Democratic Forum, but it attracted few votes outside of its membership. The coalition of freshmen again introduced a deficit- cutting plan, and it drew fairly strong support, losing 310-108. The Congressional Black Caucus and a liberal House faction presented plans that would have cut the deficit even more than the CDF and freshmen coalition plans. But their plans slashed defense spending too severely to have a chance. Once again, the plan sponsored by the majority leadership was passed and the process proceeded much as it had the year before.

Over the coming years, I believe bipartisan deficit reduction efforts pushed leaders of both parties to trim the deficits in their proposals more than they might have otherwise done. But with other priorities like tax cuts and defense and domestic promises tugging at party leaders, it was always an uphill struggle. The anti-deficit forces made some difference, but never won a truly decisive victory.

Economists now say the deficit left by the 1983-84 federal budget actually reached $208 billion, 5.6 percent of the Gross Domestic Product

(GDP). This would be the highest percentage of deficit spending relative to GDP during my twelve years in Congress. During my remaining years, the deficit percentages would run as high as 4.8 percent and as low as 2.7 percent until the Clinton years when a booming economy would give us historic budget surpluses.

The federal budget deficits and the rising national debt continue to threaten the country's economic well-being. At the start of President Trump's administration, long-term projections indicated the deficits would continue to rise to alarming new levels in the years ahead unless the president and Congress took meaningful steps to enable the federal government to live within its means.

The Committee for a Responsible Federal Budget correctly points out the country should pay attention to long-term solutions and not be lulled into a false sense of complacency by short-term trends. This private bipartisan organization is co-led by distinguished figures on both the left and right, including Tim Penny, the former congressman with whom I worked on deficit-reduction efforts during my years in Congress, and Leon Panetta, President Clinton's budget director.

Congress has adopted a variety of budgetary disciplines over the years. An example is the pay-as-you-go provision, or "paygo" for short, to require spending increases above inflation to be matched by a tax cut or spending cut. But the "paygo" rule was often evaded. A constitutional amendment to require balanced federal budgets was repeatedly introduced, and I signed on as a cosponsor. Critics said such an amendment would tie Congress' hands in times of war or other national emergencies. Although the proposed amendment always included a provision for waiving the balanced budget requirement to meet an emergency, it was never passed by Congress and sent to the voters for ratification.

I supported the Grace Commission, officially the Private Sector Survey on Cost Control, created by President Reagan in 1982 to eliminate waste and inefficiency in the federal government. Headed by businessman J. Peter Grace, the citizens' group made 2,478 recommendations, claiming they would save $424 billion. While this wouldn't have wiped out the huge budget deficits, it was enough to make a significant difference. Moreover, getting rid of inefficient and downright foolish spending was just a good thing to do.

The Reagan administration implemented several hundred of the recommendations administratively. But most of them required congressional action. By 1985, it was apparent Congress wouldn't act on the remaining recommendations. Critics said the commission was biased against social programs. But many of the recommendations identified examples of pure waste. For example, the Environmental Protection Agency was renting the same trailers for $100 a day that the Coast Guard rented for $100 a week and the Transportation Department was contracting for additional computer services when eighty percent of the agency's computers were sitting idle.

When a group of anti-deficit congressmen organized the Grace Caucus to seek enactment of the commission's recommendations in May 1985, I joined as one of about fifty House members. The group was divided into twelve task forces and I was named chairman of the one to deal with waste and inefficiency in federal health care programs. Along with other task force chairmen, I met with President Reagan in the Oval Office and discussed how to proceed with the administration's support. We passed many of the recommendations over the next few years. I don't know how many millions of dollars we saved, but it was a quite a few.

I didn't support every proposal to reduce the deficit. The year before I arrived, Congress had enacted a new tax withholding requirement that infuriated many Americans, swamping congressional offices with irate protest letters and calls. Our office received more than 5,000 calls and letters angrily opposing the requirement in the first few weeks of the 1983 session.

A provision in the lengthy 1982 Tax Equity and Fiscal Responsibility Act would have required 10 percent of the income from interest and dividends earned on savings and investments to be withheld by the Internal

Revenue Service. The federal government could collect an additional $4 billion a year by capturing unreported and underreported earnings on financial assets such as bank accounts, savings and loan accounts, bonds, stocks, and money market certificates. Aimed mainly at tax cheaters, the withholding requirement appeared to be politically benign when passed with the bipartisan support of President Regan, Speaker O'Neill, and most members of Congress.

But when the newly-elected Congress convened in January 1983, the requirement had gone viral. Citizens' tax watchdog organizations were attacking the provision as an example of Uncle Sam's greediness. With the quiet support of the president and speaker, a bill to repeal the requirement was quickly introduced and passed. If the government kept income Americans planned to invest, maybe it would have had a negative influence on the economy as many people claimed, I figured. But aside from the merits of the issue, the overwhelming constituent backlash convinced me it wasn't a good idea.

A similar public outcry would occur two years later when the Internal Revenue Service adopted a rule requiring extensive record-keeping to qualify for a tax deduction in the use of vehicles for business purposes. Many people who depended on the deduction couldn't keep up with the paperwork. When complaints from affected taxpayers reached a fever pitch, Congress didn't waste time passing a bill to overturn the rule. I voted with the majority.

Americans believe special interests exert too much influence over the governmental process. Too often they do. But when the public expresses its feelings loudly and clearly on an issue, it's likely the public voice will overwhelm any conflicting special interest. Someone once said our governmental process runs about as smoothly as a car with square wheels. Maybe so. But it has essentially worked as the founders envisioned it. At least it has so far.

Let's hope the public speaks out decisively on federal spending in the near future. A financial crisis looms ahead in a number of federal programs including government health care costs. Aside from the interest on the national debt, health care costs were projected to be the most rapidly soaring part of the federal budget during the coming years.

CHAPTER FIFTEEN

The bill to create a national holiday commemorating the birthday of Martin Luther King, Jr., the debate over U.S. involvement in a Nicaraguan revolution, and the controversy over the federal tobacco program and other programs to keep family farming alive were among the issues of historical significance to arise during my first term.

A King national holiday bill was first introduced in Congress in 1968 following Dr. King's assassination and was reintroduced every term thereafter. For ten years, the measure remained buried in committee. Congress avoided a tough vote by keeping it bottled up. With the Martin Luther King, Jr. Center in Atlanta aggressively campaigning for the proposal, popular momentum for the holiday honoring the non-violent civil rights movement had grown progressively stronger over the years. At the same time, passionate opposition to the proposal had also persisted.

When the measure was finally reported out of committee and called up for a vote in the House in 1979, it failed to pass by a five-vote margin.

For the next couple of years, the King Center did everything conceivable to promote the holiday. The center collected more than six million signatures on a petition, the largest petition on any issue in U.S. history, and mobilized celebrity support. Stevie Wonder released a hit song in honor of Dr. King, "Happy Birthday," helping attract wider support across the country. The Congressional Black Caucus worked overtime to get white colleagues behind the bill. When the center presented the massive petition to Tip O'Neill in 1982, it was certain the King holiday bill would be brought to the House floor the following year to be debated in the glare of intense national publicity.

To the political discomfort of many members, including me, this is exactly what happened. The legislation was reported out of committee as expected and the speaker scheduled a vote before the full House in August of 1983.

As the showdown approached, the debate escalated and the pressure on many members increased, especially on many of us from the South. Many people in the white community who had resisted racial integration were up in arms over the bill. Even some whites who favored racial reconciliation weren't happy about honoring Dr. King because they believed their communities would have made racial progress without the turmoil caused by his confrontational strategy. Some people were convinced Dr. King had communist ties and setting aside a day in his honor would be unpatriotic. Others opposed the bill because it would cost taxpayers' money, an estimated $18 million a year in overtime pay and lost work by governmental employees.

For most of the black community, the issue was sharply drawn. You were either for racial justice and equality under the law or you weren't. The vote for or against the King bill would be a defining moment.

At the time, I remember thinking a vote either way could lead to my defeat in the next election. One summer evening I was relaxing over a drink at the Washington residence of a Georgia House colleague, Rep. Charles Hatcher, after the House had adjourned for the day. Charlie was from Albany in southwest Georgia, the scene of one of Dr. King's major protest campaigns. Protestors were beaten and arrested during the Albany movement and it had made unpleasant headlines for the city throughout the country and even the world. The King bill was su-per-controversial just about everywhere in Georgia and it certainly was in Charlie's district.

We discussed the bill's pros and cons at length. The bill's passage would certainly make many of our constituents angry. But it would celebrate human rights for everyone, honor the principle of nonviolence in seeking political change, and help bring the racially-divided country together as a nation unified over justice and freedom. No one had produced any real evidence connecting Dr. King to communism. And the cost of adding an additional national holiday was questionable. We suspected most of the workload not handled on the holiday could be compressed into other work days and wouldn't require overtime pay. We were also well aware that the petition demonstrated that the national holiday had overwhelming national backing.

Charlie and I concluded voting for the King holiday bill was the right thing to do regardless of the political repercussions.

The measure swept through the House 338 to 90 and through the Senate 78 to 22. President Reagan, who originally opposed the bill, citing costs, signed it into law. The bill had bipartisan support. It was cosponsored by Rep. Katie Hall, a Democrat from Indiana, and Rep. Jack Kemp, a Republican from New York. Georgia's Newt Gingrich, a future Republican House whip and speaker, voted and spoke for the bill in the well of the House.

Although the political backlash was softened to some degree by the fact that members of both parties and those from conservative as well as liberal ranks voted for the bill, Charlie and I took some lumps at home. Bo Whaley, a former FBI agent who wrote for *The Dublin Courier Herald*, scorched me in a column for honoring someone he believed was tainted with communist sympathies.

While at home in Dublin, my cousin, Joe Harry Rowland, who had paid my qualifying fee to run for Congress, asked me to take a ride with him to discuss my vote on the King bill. He lectured me about why my vote was wrong as we rode around for two and a half hours. My brother Joe was a little disgruntled. Although the calls and letters I received on the issue were mixed, more were against my vote than for it. I calmly explained my point of view in media interviews and public appearances. But it took a while for it to blow over.

Most Georgians came to recognize the King holiday as a positive observance. For the most part, people who weren't pleased with the King holiday vote eventually shrugged it off. Surprisingly, it never became a major political problem for me or for Charlie. But the black community would never forgive those who voted against it. Rep. Richard Ray of Perry, who represented the Third Congressional District next door to the Eighth District, voted against the King bill, expressing concern about the expense. A few years later, this vote contributed to his loss to a Republican challenger when he was unable to energize a bigger black voter turnout on his behalf.

On other measures of particular concern to minorities, I helped secure the renewal of a grant for the Comprehensive Sickle Cell Center at the Medical College of Georgia to provide services to families in middle and south Georgia affected by the disease and worked for an increase in minority participation in federal contracts at a time when minority firms were receiving less than three percent of the federal procurement budget. Although I would be accused of turning against it, I supported the Civil Rights Restoration Act.

While the King holiday bill was a symbolic step in making the country's promise a reality for everyone, the 1988 restoration bill made civil rights history by dealing with the nuts and bolts of federal law. In 1984, the U.S. Supreme Court narrowed the scope of anti-discrimination laws by ruling that federal funds could only be withheld from a particular program or activity in non-compliance with such laws and not from an entire institution. The restoration bill would have restored congressional intent by allowing federal funds to be denied to a whole institution if any division within that institution failed to comply with fair employment practices. According to civil rights' advocates, the Supreme Court ruling had made it more difficult to take action against discriminatory practices.

When the bill first came before the House, I voted for it. I supported the principle of requiring institutions receiving federal funding to treat everyone equally regardless of race, religion, gender, or disability. But when President Reagan vetoed the bill, pointing to language he believed could give the federal government excessively-invasive power over private institutions, I took a new look at it. After consulting with legal advisers in Congress, I agreed some key provisions were vaguely written and could potentially be misused. My experience as a physician who had to cope with unnecessarily-burdensome federal oversight in medicine influenced my reading of the Civil Rights Restoration Act.

I was among the members urging House Democratic leaders to return the bill to committee, tighten up the language, and send an improved version back to the president.

There was never any doubt the legislation would pass. It had far more support on both sides of the aisle than needed to override the veto. But I voted to sustain the veto to express my conviction the bill would substantially benefit from a few revisions. I wasn't entirely alone. Nine other Democratic House members who voted for the bill the first time voted against overriding the veto. Although still supportive of the bill's goal of upholding anti-discrimination laws, I considered it careless for Congress not to improve the bill's language when it had an opportunity to do so. But I understood the politics. It would have been politically risky for the leadership to uphold the veto for any reason. The veto was overridden by a vote of 292 to 133 in the House and 73 to 24 in the Senate.

Not long after the vote, Bill Stembridge and I attended a gathering of middle Georgia civil rights leaders and supporters in Macon. The guest of honor was the Rev. Joseph E. Lowery, a nationally-known civil rights leader who succeeded Dr. King and Dr. Ralph Abernathy as the third president of the Southern Christian Leadership Conference. When Dr.

Lowery rose to make a few remarks, he let me have it, accusing me of voting against a bill to ensure fair treatment for minorities in the workplace. He failed to mention that I originally voted for the bill or that sustaining the veto would have only temporarily delayed passage and, in my opinion, would have enabled Congress to make it a better bill.

I was more than a little peeved when I left the event. If Dr. Lowery's sharp criticism of me had been factual, I wouldn't have had anything to complain about. But he didn't tell the whole truth and I wasn't given an opportunity to respond. Fortunately, I continued to have a good relationship with leaders in black communities throughout in the Eighth District.

U.S. resistance to the Marxist Sandinista regime in Nicaragua was another super-controversial issue that confronted Congress during my first term and would annually reemerge for the next seven years. During my first few years, I had no special involvement in the issue other than to vote for or against the measures that came before the House to provide assistance to the anti-Sandinista insurgents, called the Contras. But I was eventually drawn into a central role in the issue, one that would make me a target of attacks by political activists and media commentators on the right.

In mid-May 1983, President Reagan proclaimed the Reagan Doctrine at a joint session of Congress, a commitment to support political and military movements in Latin America to counter the spread of Soviet-influenced regimes. The president described the communist threat in Nicaragua and other areas of Central and South America as the gravest crisis in the region's history. In Nicaragua, he said, the Sandinistas were building military bases, airstrips, and ports with Soviet and Cuban assistance. He accused the Sandinistas of supplying arms to Marxist guerrillas in El Salvador and Honduras. He justified Contra support by saying it was aimed at preventing the Sandinistas from threatening democratic movements in neighboring countries, thereby protecting our own national security.

The Sandinistas had overthrown the repressive Somoza dictatorship in 1979. Although the Sandinistas never defined themselves as communists, former President Carter noted they "flirted" with communism as a governing philosophy and formed close ties to pro-Soviet Cuba. Before I came to Congress, President Reagan had issued a secret national security directive authorizing the CIA to provide weapons, food, clothing, medicine, and training to the Contra forces based primarily in Honduras. It later came to light CIA personnel were involved in Contra guerilla operations in Nicaragua. When I first arrived as a U.S. House member in 1983, President Reagan's clandestine campaign in Nicaragua became an open political issue when he asked Congress to provide military and other forms of aid to the Contras.

Tip O'Neill opposed U.S. military aid to a guerilla force trying to overturn a foreign government. A State Department report acknowledged there was little evidence of direct Soviet influence in the Sandinista regime and the speaker questioned whether the Sandinistas were really helping Marxist movements in other countries. He also questioned whether the Contras were committed to democracy. Members of Somoza's oppressive National Guard were among the insurgents who came together to form the Contra coalition, and, in time, we would learn both sides were guilty of human rights' abuses.

Influenced by post-World War II Soviet expansionism, I supported President Reagan's policy in Nicaragua. Most people in Georgia's Eighth District supported U.S. resistance to the expansion of communist-leaning regimes on our doorstep. When the president proposed a $24 million military and humanitarian aid package for the Contras, I was called by Richard Stone, the president's Special Envoy to Central America, who asked me not to "cut the rug out from under me down here." Although I assured him I would vote for the package, I wasn't entirely convinced the money the U.S. was spending in Nicaragua would produce positive results. Following the president's address, I told reporters, "We should take a hard look at whether an escalating role in Nicaragua would be helpful or counterproductive to the cause of democracy."

The Reagan-backed package passed over the speaker's objections with bipartisan support, including mine.

J.Roy Aug. 1944, Camp Blanding, Florida.

J.Roy & Luella Aug. 3, 1945 on their wedding day.

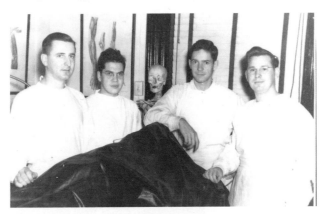

Anatomy Lab, October 1948, with Charlie Magnum, Ivey Jacobs, and Spot Hunt.

Star Flash News. Left to Right: Carroll Blankenship, Alex Daley, and J. Roy.

In the radiology department.

J. Roy making hospital rounds with his nurse.

Bill signing Infant Mortality Awareness Day with Cong. Harris and Bilirakis, May 1990.

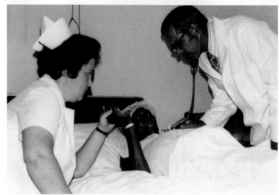

AIDS Commission with Sec. HHS Louis Sullivan, Sec. Veteran Affairs Ed Derwinski, and Surgeon General Jim Mason.

Deplaning CIA helicopter with Sonny
Montgomery, Jamales Valley, Honduras.

Visiting with Mike Bilirakis in his office.
"J. Roy – What an honor to be working with you!
Mike Bilirakis."

Mike Parker.

"To the best doctor a congressman could have.
Your friend, Mike Parker."

With President Bush in the Rabun Building.

Press Conference in Tegucigalpa, Honduras with Montgomery, Dana Roharbacher, and Chuch Douglas after visit with Contra.

Senators Johnny Isakson and Saxby Chambliss with Luella and J. Roy, 2006.

Signinig NIH Bill, 103rd Congress, with President Clinton, Sen. Edward Kennedy, and Cong. Fred Upton.

With Adolfo Calero (leader of the Contras) in Washington office.

With Bob Michel, Minority Leader.

*"Roy, we've had a good run together in the House.
All luck, my friend. Bob Michel."*

With Fred Grandy.

*"Roy, a pleasure doing business with you. Good
luck. Best, Fred Grandy."*

With Hillary Clinton in Normandy.

With Jim Cooper.

*"To my good friend Roy, it's been an honor to work
with a man of your ability and compassion. You
make Georgia and the nation proud. Jim Cooper."*

With Kennedy in Sparta, Georgia.

"To Roy, with my thanks for a wonderful day in Sparta. Ed Kennedy."

With Porter Goss, Bill Thomas, and Mike Bilirakis.

"Roy, you are a great leader of good works! With gratitude, Porter Goss."

"Roy, thanks! Bill Thomas."

"Roy, an honor, sir! Mike Bilirakis."

With Pres. Reagan, Vice Pres. Bush, Cong. Dyson, and Bonar meeting in Oval Office on MX Missile.

With Newt Gingrich, who was helpful with health care reform efforts. "To Roy, your friend, Newt Gingrich."

With President Clinton and Luella
at cookout on South Lawn of White House.

With President Reagan
meeting in Oval Office on Contra funding.

With Sen. Isakson, Distinguished Eagle Scout
Award Ceremony.

With Sonny Momtgomery and President Bush.

Captions on photo back:

"Roy, you and the President and my best buddies. Sonny Montgomery."

"To Roy Rowland, some threesome!! Warm regards, George Bush."

With Tip O'Neill.

"To Dr. Roy, with best wishes to a great man. Tip O'Neill, Speaker."

With Sonny Montgomery, Hillary Clinton, and Sen. Jay Rockefeller.

"To Rep. Rowland with thanks and best wishes. Hillary Rodham Clinton."

"Roy, proud of you. Sonny Montgomery."

"To my friend Roy. Jay Rockefeller."

With Denise Forbes, the CEO of The Community Mental Health Center of middle Georgia.

Three years later, in 1986, the Iran-Contra affair broke, greatly undermining the Reagan's Nicaraguan policy. The House had passed several amendments sponsored by Rep. Edward Boland of Maine restricting U.S. aid to the Contras. To circumvent the restrictions, Lt. Col. Oliver North, the top assistant to Admiral John M. Poindexter, the president's national security advisor, engineered the sale of U.S. arms to Iran and diverted the money to the Contras through a Swiss bank account. When exposed by investigative journalists, the affair touched off a national and international furor that led to the resignation of Poindexter and firing of North.

"I think it really hurts our credibility as a nation," I said when the media asked me about the secret deal. Although supportive of Contra aid, the Iran-Contra affair hurt rather than helped the Contra cause.

When the last Boland amendment expired, President Regan and his congressional allies proposed a $100 million Contra aid measure with $70 million designated for military supplies. With his support in Congress wavering, the president had to twist a lot of arms to have any chance of getting the proposal enacted. He invited House members to meet with him on the issue in small groups. I was one of four House members who met with him in the Oval Office on a Wednesday, March 12, 1986. He and his advisors told us the Soviet-Cuban influence in Latin America was as threatening as ever and supplying the Contras with the tools they needed would help prevent the spread of that influence.

We had heard the same argument many times and my doubts were growing. I listened politely, but was careful not to say anything that could be interpreted as supportive. The Contra revolution had cost many lives and, along with an embargo imposed by the Reagan administration, had severely disrupted the Nicaraguan economy, contributing to widespread poverty and suffering. The Sandinistas had also prevailed in a previous election that international observers considered honest. Moreover, some of my constituents were asking why the federal government was spending so much money in Nicaragua when many farmers, workers in the collapsing textile industry, and others in the U.S. had to go without help many desperately needed.

When I left the White House, I told waiting reporters I was leaning against the president's proposal. "There's a perception… we shouldn't be spending money out of the country when we're not doing enough to help people at home," I said. However, when the president agreed to withhold appropriated funds for the Contras if certain human rights conditions weren't met, I stuck with the administration and voted for a new Contra aid plan when it came before the House near the end of March. It failed by twelve votes. The president's chief speech writer, Pat Buchanan, didn't help the president's cause when he was quoted as saying a vote against more military aid for the Contras would indicate communist sympathy, a statement that hardened the opposition.

From what I was hearing, the Contras needed medicine and other non-military supplies. But they had stockpiled an ample supply of weapons and ammunition. In addition to the arms and other supplies provided by the U.S., the Reagan administration had persuaded several friendly foreign governments to provide arms to the Contras.

Then, in 1987 and early 1988, the dynamics of the Nicaraguan revolution changed. Costa Rican President Oscar Arias, leader of a regional peace process to promote stable democracies, negotiated a cease-fire agreement between the Sandinistas and the Contras designed to lead to another election under international oversight. The Contras agreed to cease terrorist activities and not accept military aid from anyone. The Sandinistas agreed to call an election, create an independent commission to oversee the campaign and voting, give political opponents access to the print and broadcast media, and allow political exiles to return without fear of punishment.

I'm sure both sides agreed to an election because both sides believed they would win. For the Contras, the armed uprising hadn't worked and an election appeared to be the only way they could remove the Sandinistas and gain power. For the Sandinistas, an election that would end the revolution and lift the embargo would give them a more secure hold on power. I publicly stated the U.S. should suspend military aid to the Contras while the peace process was moving forward. If the Sandinistas obeyed the rules and held a fair election, the U.S. should accept the results and end economic sanctions and Contra aid, I said. But I emphasized that if the Sandinistas cheated in the election, or refused to relinquish power if they lost, the U.S. should renew all-out support of the Contras.

As soon as the 1988 session convened, President Reagan presented Congress a $36.2 million Contra aid request including $3.6 million for military supplies. The purpose of the military aid, the president explained, was to put pressure on the Sandinistas to comply with the peace agreement. This made no sense to me. I knew the Contras didn't need more military supplies. In fact, they didn't want more U.S. military help at that moment. Adolpho Calero, a Contra leader who periodically met with members of Congress to solidify Contra support, told me at a meeting in our office that military aid wasn't needed. In a *Washington Times* interview, Contra spokesperson Marta Sacasa publicly affirmed what Calero told me privately. "Right now," she said, "lethal supplies are not needed. If the Sandinistas don't comply, then, yes, we will need them eventually."

With the Contras securely encamped in Honduras and ready to resume the revolution, plenty of pressure existed without more U.S. military aid. It was my guess President Reagan and his advisors didn't believe the Contras could win the popular vote and were seeking to intensify the revolution. But, based on my talks with Contra leaders, I thought the Contras had a good chance. While the Contras could have refused the new military aid if approved by Congress, the Sandinistas could have used congressional approval of the military funding as an excuse to cancel the peace agreement. I told reporters approval of the token $3.6 million in U.S. military aid would only enable Nicaraguan President Daniel Ortega to "get out of the corner he's backed himself into."

The White House apparently believed I could be persuaded to vote for its latest Contra military aid request. I had, after all, voted for previous Contra military aid measures. The President himself called to ask for my vote. White House Chief of Staff Howard Baker also called me for the same reason. I thanked them for calling, but declined to make a commitment.

The House defeated the Reagan proposal 219 to 211. I was one of 14 House members who consistently supported Contra military aid in the past who voted against the package, providing the swing votes that made the difference. Rep. John Lewis and I were the only members of the Georgia House delegation to vote against it. I immediately came under attack. Conservative editorial writers and commentators in Georgia and even nationally accused me of aiding and abetting the communist cause. A number of constituents wrote or called to heatedly accuse me of caving in to communist sympathizers. A political supporter told me there was so much negative talk about my vote at home that I could be in serious trouble in the next election.

My vote caught Democratic House leaders by surprise. Jim Wright, who succeeded Tip O'Neill as speaker following the Massachusetts lawmaker's retirement, asked me to serve on a ten-member task force chaired by Rep. David Bonior of Michigan to draft a new Contra aid package that provided only humanitarian help including medicine, food, and clothing. He wanted someone serving on the task force representing the party's moderate-to-conservative wing. When I suggested adding Republican representation, Jim Wright agreed. But Republican House leaders decided to put their own plan together and turned down the invitation to participate in a bipartisan effort.

Rarely is anything easy in Congress, and our effort to get a humanitarian package passed during this heated stage of the debate illustrated this fact. Most members of both parties agreed the Contras needed non-military help. Two partisan plans were produced to provide the needed assistance. They were almost identical. But the Republican proposal included parts for vehicles, making it a plan that could have been seen as having military value. Both proposals were defeated in the House and, for a while, it looked like gridlock would prevail. But we eventually crafted a bipartisan compromise that comfortably passed by a vote of 345 to 70.

Even this relatively modest Contra aid package was enough to seriously upset the Sandinistas. Citing the latest Contra aid, they would
soon refuse to let the first U.S. observers into the country, including me,
a decision that made it look like the Sandinistas were about to scuttle
the peace process.

As the Nicaraguan election approached in February 1990, President
George H. W. Bush, who had succeeded President Reagan, named his
close friend Sonny Montgomery to head a twenty-member bipartisan
congressional delegation to observe the campaign, a group called the
Presidential Monitoring Commission on Nicaragua. Sonny planned to
travel to Nicaragua in advance of the other commission members to get
an early insight into how the election process was developing. He invited
me and two Republican House members to accompany him, Reps. Dana
Rohrabacher of California and Chuck Douglas of New Hampshire. In
effect, we were to serve as deputy observers.

While flying to Central America in an Air Force plane, Sonny received
a call from the White House advising him the Sandinista government
had denied us permission to enter Nicaragua. In a note to the president,
Nicaraguan Foreign Minister Miquel d'Escoto reacted angrily to the
latest Contra aid. "In these circumstances," he said, "Nicaragua cannot
permit any U.S. presidential commission to come here and masquerade
as innocent and impartial election observers." If they were that bothered
by humanitarian aid, one can imagine how they would have reacted to
military aid. "It's a dumb move," I remember Sonny saying, one that made
it look like the Sandinistas had something to hide.

Instead of visiting Nicaragua, we flew to Honduras to visit the Contras who were encamped in a virtual city of some 12,000 guerillas and
families in the Jamales Valley. We landed at the Tegucigalpa airport in
pre-dawn darkness where we boarded an unmarked CIA helicopter. As
daylight appeared, we could see we were flying barely above the tree tops
over heavily-wooded, mountainous terrain. When I asked the pilot why
we were flying so low, he said if we flew any higher it would be easier to

spot us and shoot us down. This didn't give me a very good feeling. But we landed safely on the side of a mountain where we were met by friendly and excited Contra representatives.

At a large single-story wooden building where the Contra hospital was located, doctors confirmed they were in urgent need of medicine. But, for the most part, we found the Contras well-supplied and in good spirits. They assured us they were ready to resume raids on targets in Nicaragua at a moment's notice. The Contra representatives we met were doubtful the Sandinistas would allow a fair election to be held. After we were barred from Nicaragua, we were skeptical ourselves.

But the Sandinistas surprised us. They cooperated in the formation of a delegation by Jimmy Carter to make sure the election was carried out openly and honestly. Among the campaign monitors were representatives of the United Nations and the Organization of American States. Although a number of crises arose during the voting, they were all resolved to the satisfaction of all sides. The result was stunning. With eighty percent of the Nicaraguan electorate participating, the Sandinistas were defeated by a fourteen percent margin. The Sandinista regime fell without a shot being fired and a democratically-elected pro-Contra government took office. For the first time ever, a regime that came to power in an armed revolution relinquished control in a free election.

In my view, it wouldn't have happened without U.S. support for the Contras, or without the efforts of the international monitoring team, or if Congress hadn't rejected the untimely proposal to provide $3.6 million in new U.S. military aid. Although I felt vindicated by supporting the terms of the peace process, those who had attacked me in the media never admitted they were wrong. Once the Sandinistas were overturned, those in the media who had denounced opponents of the military aid simply didn't mention the issue.

When Sonny Montgomery decided to go to Nicaragua, President Bush asked him to include a visit to Panama to get a first-hand feeling for the critical situation that existed there. Sonny and those of us accompanying him had also planned to visit El Salvador where Cuban-influenced rebels were waging a new offensive. But that part of the trip was cancelled when we were told after landing it would be too dangerous. Panama was scary enough. The country was in turmoil.

Earlier in the year, Gen. Manuel Noriega, Panama's corrupt dictator, first tried to steal an election for his hand-picked candidates and then nullified the results when his candidates lost. An anti-Noriega coup attempt subsequently failed. Dangerous confrontations had occurred between Noriega's soldiers and U.S. personnel, including a recent incident in which a car carrying U.S. soldiers was stopped by troops loyal to Noriega and a young Marine was fatally shot in the melee that followed. Ample evidence had come to light that Noriega was running a vast drug empire and deep unrest existed among the Panamanian people as a result of Noriega's murderous human rights' abuses.

After landing in Panama City, we were driven to the U.S. embassy with an armed escort. The sense of tension and danger was palpable as we drove cautiously to the embassy. Our ambassador had been recalled. But we stayed at the ambassador's well-guarded residence. We were accompanied by armed guards everywhere we went for the next two days. We met with U.S. military leaders in the Panama Canal Zone and with Panamanian opposition leaders Arias Calderon and Guillermo Ford. We came away from those meetings concerned about the security of the Panama Canal and the safety of U.S. citizens and military personnel in Panama as well as for the Panamanian people.

When we returned to Washington, Sonny briefed President Bush about what we saw and heard in Panama. The three of us who accompanied Sonny on the trip issued statements urging U.S. intervention. Several weeks later, a U.S. military force stormed into Panama, overturned Noriega, and enabled Panama's opposition leaders to establish a democratic government.

This wasn't an easy decision for President Bush to make. The United Nations General Assembly and the Organization of American States condemned the invasion. Twenty-three American soldiers and hundreds of Panamanians were killed in the attack. But as long as Noriega remained in power, Americans stationed in Panama and many Panamanian citizens were in danger and the security of the canal was in jeopardy. The invasion brought down a brutal dictatorship and gave democracy a chance to take hold in Panama. I've always believed Sonny's report to the president, and the bipartisan congressional support for a U.S. invasion, helped convince the president that immediate intervention was the right decision.

The tobacco issue was a difficult one for me. No congressional district in Georgia and few in the country grew more tobacco than Georgia's Eighth District. Without the federal tobacco price support program, many families in the Eighth District would have experienced financial stress and some bankruptcy as many more small family farms went broke. Although I never hesitated to talk about the danger of consuming tobacco, I saw no contradiction in supporting a program that enabled tobacco farmers to compete on the world market. Even with a federal tobacco price support program in place, thirty-one percent of the tobacco in American-made cigarettes was coming from overseas, up from fourteen percent ten years before. Exports of flue-cured tobacco, the kind produced in Georgia, had plummeted by fifty percent in fifteen years.

Alcohol prohibition hadn't worked and few members of Congress advocated tobacco prohibition. I agreed government should do what it could to protect the public. I supported educational programs about the health risks of tobacco, warning labels on tobacco products, advertising restrictions, laws against selling tobacco to minors, and laws protecting people from exposure to second-hand smoke. Ralph Nader, the famous consumer advocate, attacked me and others supporting tobacco support programs as "death dealers." But I didn't think U.S. tobacco growers were causing people to consume tobacco. If U.S.-grown tobacco wasn't competitive, producers and consumers of tobacco products would have used foreign-grown tobacco. I just wanted to give U.S. growers a fair chance in the marketplace.

As both a physician and a consumer, I knew how addictive tobacco could be. Starting as a teenage soldier, I smoked Lucky Strikes for more than twenty years. I was 41, in mid-career as a doctor, when I gave up smoking at exactly 11:30 p.m. on November 30, 1967. I generally watched the 11 p.m. news on television and would light up a cigarette before going to bed. Although I hadn't planned to quit, on this evening I decided to forego my final cigarette of the day. Although I always smoked my first cigarette just after breakfast, the following morning I again decided not to smoke.

After I started abstaining, I refused to give in even when I began to suffer unpleasant withdrawal symptoms. I wasn't easy to live with for weeks to come. Although I don't think she was really serious, Luella threatened to go to the store and buy me cigarettes several times. But I never smoked again.

Congress had a responsibility to help the independent farm community survive at a time when net farm income had fallen from $32 billion to $20 billion and farm debt had increased from $182 billion to $218 billion during the two years before my election to the U.S. House. A decade before, farmers were receiving forty-four cents out of every dollar spent on food and now they were receiving thirty-five cents out of every dollar. The U.S. Agriculture Department estimated that twenty-five percent of Georgia's farmers were in severe financial trouble with many facing bankruptcy or foreclosure. According to Georgia Farm Bureau President Bob Nash, the actual percentage of Georgia farmers who were in big financial trouble was closer to fifty.

Representing an agricultural area, I regularly attended House Agriculture Committee hearings to learn more about farm issues. I formed my own advisory committee of farmers and agribusiness people from the Eighth District. We met periodically, especially when Congress considered the quadrennial omnibus farm bills.

My role was not only to support farm programs benefiting farmers in my own area, but also to support programs primarily benefiting other areas to help keep the agricultural bloc in Congress as unified as possible. Having other budget priorities, President Reagan wasn't particularly supportive of farm programs. His budget director, David Stockman, once called farm programs "handouts." But with the farm bloc standing together, we collectively kept family farming from declining at a more precipitous rate. For the public at-large, this helped keep consumer food prices from becoming more burdensome.

CHAPTER SIXTEEN

From the moment I was elected to the U.S. House, I planned to propose a nationwide prohibition on prescribing methaqualone, better known by its brand name, Quaalude. The widely-abused drug was killing thousands of people who took it for its euphoric quality. This would be first of many bills I would author or co-author during my years in Congress. Although more than half would pass, few would clear both houses of Congress and become law without a struggle. Unexpectedly, this would include the proposed national Quaalude ban.

On January 26, 1983, I released a statement to the media announcing I would introduce the bill to take Quaaludes off the market as a prescribed medication. I had already drafted the measure with the assistance of the legislative counsel's office. But I wanted to take a few days to sign up cosponsors before dropping it in the hopper. Among those signing on as principal cosponsors were Reps. Elliott Levitas, dean of Georgia's House delegation; Ed Jenkins, the Georgian who served on the Democratic Steering and Policy Committee; Newt Gingrich, the rising Republican from Georgia; and Mickey Leland, a prominent member of the Congressional Black Caucus from Texas.

While serving in the Georgia General Assembly, I had sponsored the bill that made Georgia the first state to impose such a prohibition. Florida had followed Georgia's lead. But the death toll from Quaalude overdoses had continued to rise nationally. So-called "stress clinics" that sold the dangerous drug to anyone who came in the door, including teenagers, were continuing to flourish in a number of cities. Prescribed as a sleeping aid, there were other less-dangerous medications that served the same purpose. If Quaaludes were placed in the same category as heroin and couldn't be legally prescribed, they would become unavailable to the few unethical medical professionals who sold the drug to anyone who could pay for it.

I introduced the bill on January 31 after taking five days to recruit cosponsors. Meanwhile, I was surprised when Rep. Larry Smith of Florida, a fellow freshman, introduced his own bill to ban Quaaludes on January 27, a day after news stories appeared about my intention to sponsor virtually the same bill. His version had no cosponsors. It looked like Larry had rushed to get a Quaalude bill drafted and introduced in order to preempt me as the point person on the issue. As a state legislator, Larry had worked for a state ban on Quaaludes in Florida just as I had in Georgia. His background qualified him for a frontline role in the Quaalude issue in Congress. But when he learned an organized effort to enact a national ban was already underway, he could have offered to work together. Instead, he took what appeared to be a competitive approach.

Larry and I would be named the principal cosponsors of the Quaalude bill reported out by the Energy and Commerce Committee. But our relationship was strained. Larry was an aggressive legislator who would later rise to positions of leadership in the House. But we didn't work closely together for passage of the Quaalude bill and many in the media regarded me as the leading voice on the issue.

In May, I was invited to appear on the Today show on NBC-TV. I flew to New York City and was picked up by a network limousine. At the Manhattan studio I was interviewed along with an American Medical Association representative, Dr. Joseph Skom, and Chicago television newsman Rich Samuels, whose documentary about Quaalude abuse in his city prompted the Today segment. The interviewer asked me why it was necessary to override the authority of the states to decide whether to legalize or ban a medication. The answer was obvious. Quaalude dealers who were shut down by a state could simply move to another state where they could operate legally. Rich Samuels backed me up, saying, "stress clinics" in Atlanta and Miami had moved to Chicago after Georgia and Florida prohibited the drug.

Although I detected little opposition among my colleagues, a few groups weren't supportive of a congressionally-imposed ban. The American Medical Association was concerned about banning a drug that some physicians considered useful and were still prescribing in spite of the drug's history of abuse. Because the AMA wouldn't endorse a ban on Quaalude prescriptions, the Food and Drug Administration and Justice Department were unwilling to reclassify the drug under the federal rule-making authority. President Reagan declined to support the bill because his administration didn't want Congress intruding on the authority of the executive branch. From the administration's point of view, it was the responsibility of the FDA and the Justice Department to reclassify a drug.

I publicly offered to withdraw the bill if the FDA and Justice Department would act. But the agencies wouldn't budge. If this wasn't exactly a Catch 22 situation, it was close to it.

The Justice Department refused to support methaqualone reclassification as long as the FDA listed it as a safe medication when used as prescribed. The FDA wouldn't label methaqualone as an unsafe drug as long as the AMA felt the drug had a useful medical purpose. The AMA was evidently sensitive to doctors who still considered it a safe medication for patients who needed it. Personally, I didn't think the drug was safe even when used as prescribed. As long as a small percentage of unethical doctors were freely dispensing Quaaludes, the record showed deaths from overdoses would continue to rise.

With the media showing considerable interest, Henry Waxman agreed to hold an Energy and Commerce Health and the Environment Subcommittee hearing on the issue. It was scheduled for October 3. I arranged for two Georgians to be among those giving testimony, former Georgia Secretary of State David Poythress, who started the Quaalude ban movement in Georgia, and a Macon psychiatrist, Dr. William Dudney, III. Together I thought we presented an irrefutable case. About the time the hearing was held, the White House quietly let me know the president wouldn't oppose or veto the bill even though he wasn't supporting it.

John Dingell and Henry Waxman had assured me they would move quickly, and they did. The subcommittee favorably reported the bill to the full committee within several weeks and the full committee reported it out for a vote on the House floor in early November. In mid-November, the bill passed in the House by a voice vote.

"I don't know of any opposition to it in the Senate," I told *The Telegraph and News* the day after House passage. I was overly confident. The bill was reported out of the Senate Judiciary Committee in April 1984, ready for final consideration on the Senate floor. The committee was chaired by Sen. Strom Thurmond of South Carolina who strongly supported the bill. Then, after Sen. Thurmond's committee favorably reported the bill, the Senate leadership left it in limbo without scheduling it for a vote on the floor.

Several issues delayed Senate action. Some critics argued the bill wasn't needed because the Lemmon Company of Sellersville, Pennsylvania, the U.S. manufacturer of Quaaludes, had voluntarily quit producing and distributing the drug, raising doubts about the bill's need among some senators. This was easily countered. If it remained legal to prescribe the drug, production and sales could be resumed at any time. Critics also questioned whether it was appropriate for Congress to approve or disapprove medications when it could be done under the FDA's regulatory authority. As a general rule, the answer is no. But methaqualone was an exception.

Most of all, consideration was delayed in the Senate by Sen. Dennis DeConcini, a Democrat from Arizona, who was determined to add a provision to the Quaalude bill to reclassify heroin so it could be used to treat pain for terminally-ill cancer patients. If such a provision was put into the Quaalude bill in the Senate, I would have opposed my own bill when it came to the House. Sen. Thurmond also opposed heroin legalization. As long as there was any chance the heroin amendment would be considered on the floor and possibly adopted, the South Carolina senator had decided not to ask Senate leaders to call up his committee's Quaalude bill for a floor vote.

I made several trips to Senate offices to see if I could get the bill moving. I tried to meet with Sen. Paula Hawkins of Florida, Senate sponsor of the Quaalude bill, to coordinate my Senate lobbying with any efforts she might be making. But when I showed up at her office for our appointment, she was tied up with reporters. I cooled my heels for a long time and finally left. Lobbying on my own, I met with Sen. DeConcini, pointing out how many lives could be saved by a Quaalude ban and urging him not to jeopardize the Quaalude bill by using it as a vehicle for the heroin proposal. I met with Sen. Ted Kennedy, who supported the heroin amendment. If the Massachusetts senator used his influence to separate the heroin proposal from the Quaalude bill, I knew there was a good chance it would happen.

Although Sens. DeConcini and Kennedy made no promises, I came away from these meetings thinking they might be having second thoughts about offering an amendment that might kill the Quaalude ban without helping legalize the prescribing of heroin. In early June, Sen. DeConcini dropped his heroin amendment. It would be better strategy, he explained, for the House to pass its pending heroin legalization bill and send it to the Senate. Once the heroin provision was withdrawn, it didn't take long for the Senate to pass the House-passed Quaalude bill. Several days later, while waiting for a flight in an Eastern Airlines lounge, an attendant told me the White House was calling. A presidential staffer had tracked me down to let me know the president had signed the Quaalude bill.

Although Henry Waxman and John Dingell had helped me with the Quaalude bill, I rose in opposition to the heroin bill they sponsored after it was approved by the Energy and Commerce Committee. I told colleagues I "reluctantly" opposed the bill. "I say 'reluctantly' because I know those who support this legislation do so from the heart. They do it because they are concerned about these people who are having severe pain with terminal cancer, and they want to do what they can to help relieve the situation." But, I continued, it would be wrong to "legitimize a drug that has caused so many problems."

In response to the argument that heroin was more effective in controlling extreme pain, and it made no sense to deny it to people with a terminal condition, I could cite the opinions of leading pain management experts such as Dr. Kathleen Foley, chief of pain service at Memorial Sloan-Kettering Cancer Center, who pointed out that other less dangerous pain killers were just as effective, if not more so, than heroin.

The heroin bill was overwhelmingly defeated by a vote of 355 to 55. An Associated Press story said, "The House followed the doctor's orders." This was a reference to what Associated Press called my "tenacious" opposition. Maybe the bill wouldn't have passed even if I hadn't taken a strong stand against it. But my views on health care issues did, in fact, influence a significant number of fellow House members. The landslide defeat made it difficult for proponents to bring up the proposal in the years ahead.

I hoped Dingell and Waxman would understand my opposition was as heartfelt as their support. But whether they understood or not, they weren't immediately forgiving and my outspoken position on heroin legalization was a major factor in their resistance to my joining the Energy and Commerce Committee.

If my relationship with Dingell and Waxman had been strained, I made new friendships in the Senate. Luella and I got to know Strom Thurmond, the legendary South Carolinian who had once led the fight to preserve segregation but later embraced racial justice. When we ran into Sen. Thurmond in a social setting, he regaled us with fascinating, often funny stories about politics and politicians, a real history lesson. I also developed a friendly association with Sen. Kennedy. Although we differed on a number of issues, I appreciated his accessibility and frankness in our discussions on the Quaalude bill, HIV-AIDS, and other issues.

I introduced a second major legislative initiative during my first term in Congress, the so-called "atomic vet" bill. An estimated 250,000 veterans had been exposed to ionizing radiation while stationed in Hiroshima and Nagasaki following World War II and during military exercises that were a part of atmospheric nuclear testing conducted by the U.S. between 1945 and 1962. The danger of nuclear radiation was not fully understood at the time and military personnel were subjected to a degree of exposure that would be unthinkable today.

Many "atomic" veterans suffered from cancers and other diseases that could have been attributable to radiation exposure. But, with rare exceptions, the Department of Veterans Affairs had rejected claims for military-connected assistance. At the time, only forty-four of more than 6,000 claims had been approved. According to the VA, the cause-and-effect relationship between radiation exposure and radiological disease wasn't conclusive.

It wasn't possible to conclusively prove a connection. But based on common sense, it was certain the exposure to radiation had caused many if not all the cancers and other diseases that had already taken the lives of thousands of these veterans and were threatening the lives of many more. As I saw it, it was fair and reasonable to give the benefit of the doubt to veterans whose lives were put in danger while serving their country. I considered it unjust and callous for the VA to oppose disability payments because these suffering veterans couldn't prove the unprovable.

With Republican Rep. John Paul Hammerschmidt of Arkansas as a co-sponsor, I introduced the Atomic Veterans Relief Act in September of 1983. The measure called for a temporary five-year benefit program for atomic vets while an in-depth study could be carried out to establish a scientific basis for presuming a link between radiation exposure and certain diseases. While it would still be difficult to qualify for benefits, we hoped a temporary program would help some veterans while we accumulated information supporting a more comprehensive benefit program.

The estimated cost of the program was fairly modest. But if the VA endorsed an atomic vet disability program, the agency would have had little choice but to accept a similar program for many thousands of Vietnam veterans who had been exposed to the defoliant Agent Orange. Many of the veterans who were suffering from diseases that could have been caused by Agent Orange were also denied disability claims. The Reagan administration apparently had other priorities it considered more important. The addition of costly new benefit programs for veterans exposed to nuclear radiation and Agent Orange would make it all the harder for the administration to get a budget through Congress with an acceptable deficit level. In the case of radiation and Agent Orange exposure, I thought just treatment of veterans should have the highest priority.

Rep. Hammerschmidt and I had the support of Sonny Montgomery, other members of the Veterans' Affairs Committee, and organizations representing the atomic and Agent Orange veterans. These organizations had lobbied for the benefits. But the Department of Veterans Affairs had lobbied just hard against such benefits. Backing up the agency's argument was a Defense Department-sponsored report. The department's Defense Nuclear Agency had commissioned a study by the private National Research Council that purportedly found the rate of bone cancer among veterans exposed to nuclear radiation during the U.S. occupancy of Hiroshima and Nagasaki to be no higher than that experienced by the general population. In the absence of countervailing information, many House members were reluctant to support atomic vet or Agent Orange benefits over the adamant objections of the VA agency.

At my request, the House VA Committee called on the Office of Technology Assistance, an arm of Congress, to evaluate the National Research Council's report. The evaluation found that the NRC study lacked an epidemiologist or statistician with sufficient expertise to accurately determine what constituted an abnormal rate of disease; it failed to consider many of the cancers and other diseases attributable to nuclear and Agent Orange exposure; and, although roughly half of bone cancer patients die within the first year of diagnosis, the study dealt only with living veterans and didn't take into account those who had already died. Shoddily done, the NRC study was simply a waste of the $19,000 the Defense Department spent for it.

Once we had the results of our evaluation in hand, the chances of getting an interim benefit program out of committee and through Congress improved. The atomic vet bill was merged with the Agent Orange bill and unanimously reported out of the VA Committee in November. In mid-December, it was passed by a voice vote in the House. It would take a few months to move through the Senate. In October 1984, the legislation to authorize the payment of benefits while in-depth studies were carried out over the next five years cleared the Senate and was sent to President Reagan who signed it into law.

If we thought the bill would suddenly open the door for the payments of legitimate claims, we were wrong. While the measure authorized benefits, it didn't mandate them and the VA simply continued its policy of dismissing most claims. Over the next few years I did everything I could to bring public attention to the issue, including pushing through a bill in the spring of 1985 to declare July 16 as Atomic Veterans Day to increase public awareness of the plight of atomic vets.

In 1987, armed with studies confirming the possible connection between exposure and certain diseases, I introduced a bill to require the VA to pay service-connected benefits to all veterans who were subjected to exposure, who acquired one of the illnesses covered by the legislation within thirty years of exposure, and who had suffered a significant disability. The bill established a presumption the disability in such cases was service connected. The VA Committee's Hospital and Health Care Subcommittee on which I served called a hearing on the bill in May. At the hearing, I engaged in a sharp exchange with VA General Counsel Donald L. Ivers.

According to Ivers, approving the atomic vet claims would be a "radical departure" from the VA's longstanding principle of paying benefits only if the illness or disability was directly traceable to military service. If the law called for a "presumption" of a military connection, it would dilute eligibility criteria, he said. If the VA provided benefits for non-military health problems, the agency feared it would erode public support for all benefit programs for veterans, he added.

Such a position was damaging the VA's credibility, I responded. Noting it was obvious the radiation exposure these veterans experienced had serious health consequences for many, I said the VA was undermining the compensation process by brushing this fact under the rug. Ivers insisted only one percent of the veterans covered by the bill received radiation exposure greater than the annual exposure federal rules then permitted for radiation workers. But, I pointed out, the tests for measuring radiation exposure were far from dependable and there wasn't any way the VA or anyone else could know the full extent of the exposure.

It would take another year to build support among House members. In early May 1988, the House finally approved the bill by a vote of 326 to two. The case we were able to make, and the respect in the House for Sonny Montgomery, had a lot to do with the one-sided margin. Who knows whether the bill would have prevailed in the Senate if it hadn't been for the overwhelming House vote? In light of the House vote, I'm sure a number of undecided senators realized they might appear to be unsympathetic to veterans if they voted against the "presumption" principle. The margin was much closer in the upper chamber, but it passed by a 48-30 vote.

Administration sources had said President Reagan would veto the bill. At $36 million annually, the projected cost estimates were rising, a big factor in the administration's opposition. Based on the close Senate vote, it was apparent a presidential veto couldn't be overturned. In fact, a veto is exactly what I was expecting. But in late May, the president surprised many people by signing the bill.

Many atomic veterans and their families would continue to face a difficult claim process in the years ahead. The records were often sketchy at best, and, in spite of the new law, the VA would reject claims where the information about the degree of exposure left sufficient room for doubt. But as a result of the atomic vet legislation, many claims that probably would have previously been rejected were approved. If we failed to achieve justice for all, at least we minimized the injustice.

Perhaps no issue in which I took a leading role was more critical than HIV-AIDS. The Centers for Disease Control (CDC) began reporting the mysterious cases of AIDS in the early 1980s. Within a decade, the U.S. death toll from AIDS would exceed 50,000 and federal funding to fight the disease would increase from $8 million to nearly $2 billion. Although HIV-AIDS was primarily associated with homosexual activity, it was spreading in the heterosexual population as well. After a few years, it was evident the country had never faced a disease so deadly, so rapidly spreading, with such complex moral, legal, and political ramifications.

Although I helped address HIV-AIDS within the veterans' population as a member and later chairman of the Veterans' Affairs Hospitals and Health Care Subcommittee, at first I wasn't directly involved in developing policies and programs relating to AIDS research, treatment, education, and protection of the general public. But this changed in 1985 when Congress considered the Higher Education Reauthorization Act. It occurred to me college students were a high-risk population. HIV can be transmitted in blood transfusions and by sharing unclean needles among drug abusers. But it's mainly a sexually-transmitted disease, and unprotected intimacy among college students needed to be prevented if possible. I introduced an amendment to the education bill calling on local health agencies and the CDC to carry out a study to establish a targeted AIDS educational program for college students. It was approved.

Meanwhile, I was growing more concerned over the fragmented, inefficient way the federal government was dealing with the AIDS crisis. What triggered the idea of creating a new AIDS commission in which both the president and Congress would have a stake was a call from a CNN reporter who asked for my reaction to a story about a dispute within the federal Centers for Disease Control near Atlanta over the role the

CDC was supposed to play in the AIDS effort. The question was soon settled and the CDC went on to do outstanding work. But the call made it all the more obvious to me no one was really in overall control of the many diverse federal AIDS initiatives.

In July 1987, President Reagan had created a thirteen-member presidential commission to make recommendations about what should be done about AIDS that wasn't already being done. The commission was given a lifespan of only one year. Included among the members were experts in health care and also several controversial political appointees, including those associated with the "moral majority." A few leaders associated with the "moral majority" movement had described AIDS as God's punishment for sinful behavior and were less than supportive of many AIDS initiatives. As a physician, I didn't believe God wanted us to turn our back on efforts to treat and prevent an illness causing widespread suffering and costing taxpayers untold billions of dollars in health care costs.

Although the make-up was criticized by AIDS activists, the president's commission made a number of beneficial recommendations in June 1988, including increased federal spending for AIDS' programs. I had met with the commission's chairman, retired Admiral James D. Watkins, and was impressed with the job he did. Yet, the commission's report didn't go far enough. It focused mainly on specific needs. What was needed was a comprehensive, coordinated strategy.

A 1986 Institutes of Health report had cited a "lack of cohesiveness and strategic planning throughout the national effort." AIDS programs of various kinds were managed by the departments of Defense, Education, Justice, State, Labor, Veterans' Affairs, Health and Human Services, and the Social Security Administration. In Health and Human Services alone, the CDC, National Institutes of Health, Public Health Service, Food and Drug Administration, and Health Resources and Services Administration were all dealing with different aspects of the AIDS fight. The result was interagency conflict, duplication, gaps in needs, and unclear policies for medical, ethical, and legal questions.

One example was a disagreement between two top leaders in President Reagan's administration, Surgeon General C. Everett Koop and Secretary of Education William Bennett. The surgeon general advocated a promotional campaign to promote condom use by people who weren't modifying their behavior and were potentially transmitting the disease to others. The education secretary opposed such a campaign because he believed it would lead to increased sexual activity. As a result, nothing was done about Dr. Koop's recommendation.

During the 1987 session, I proposed establishing a new bipartisan national AIDS commission with the broader mission of unifying the government's fight against AIDS. The bill I introduced called for the appointment of fifteen members by the Democratic and Republican leadership in the House and Senate and by the president. The measure required that a majority of the appointees have certain professional rather than just political qualifications.

When my bill came before the House in August 1987, a few Republicans like William Dannemeyer of California attacked it as "unnecessary duplication." But it was vigorously supported by Henry Waxman. With Henry's influence among Democrats to the left of center, and my friendships with Democrats and Republicans in the middle and to the right of center, the new AIDS commission was overwhelmingly approved by a vote of 355 to 68. Then it went to the Senate where it was referred to the Senate Labor and Human Resources Committee chaired by Sen. Ted Kennedy. Then, for quite a while, nothing happened. When our staff sought information at the staff level about why the bill had stalled, we couldn't get a clear answer.

For some reason Sen. Kennedy had pigeonholed the measure. As the 1988 session began, I met with the senator in his office. He was friendly. He was also frank. He didn't think much of ad hoc commissions in general and wasn't convinced a new AIDS commission was needed. But as we talked the issue through, he agreed to include the AIDS commission as part of an AIDS research and education bill he expected his committee to send to the Senate floor.

Sen. Jesse Helms of North Carolina was responsible for another obstacle facing the AIDS commission bill. The arch-conservative Senator, who was critical of just about any initiative to combat the disease, threatened to filibuster the measure by introducing an extensive list of time-consuming amendments. The Senate leadership delayed scheduling the AIDS commission bill for floor action rather than tie up Senate proceedings in what would amount to a form of filibustering. Eventually Senate supporters of the AIDS bill made a bargain with Helms. They agreed to drop a confidentiality provision Helms opposed and Helms agreed to withdraw his filibuster threat.

Before the year was out, the legislation establishing the National Commission on AIDS was enacted and signed into law. It would take the remainder of the year for all the members to be appointed. But by early 1990, the commission was finally in business. People with prominent credentials in health care, law, and ethics were appointed including two cabinet members, Health and Human Services Secretary Louis Sullivan and Veterans Administration Secretary Ed Derwinski. Magic Johnson, the Hall of Fame basketball player who was HIV-positive, joined. As the principal sponsor of the bill creating the commission, I was also appointed.

During the next few years, the commission held well-publicized hearings in communities throughout the country, including those I requested in Macon, Waycross, and Albany in Georgia's Eighth District, and issued a series of reports. The commission elevated public awareness about the disease and the president and Congress adopted a number of its recommendations. Some coordination was achieved within one key agency when Congress enacted the National Institutes of Health Revitalization Act in 1993 establishing an office to oversee the diverse NIH HIV-AIDS research programs. However, an overall coordinated federal strategy was never put in place.

Magic Johnson made national headlines when he resigned in protest to inaction on some key commission recommendations. I appreciated his effort to stir things up. But in the end, I agree with President Clinton who told me in a letter dated June 25, 1993, that the commission made an "enormous contribution." He pledged to "strive to carry out your (the commission's) recommendations with concern, commitment, and resolve." He did, in fact, strongly support many AIDS initiatives.

Although HIV-AIDS remains a serious public health issue, federal research helped develop the anti-viral drugs that have made it possible for many people infected with the disease to survive.

My sponsorship of the commission made me a well-known figure among AIDS activists and I was invited to speak on federal AIDS policy to a major gay activist conference in San Francisco. Also on the program was Dr. Louis Sullivan, the African-American from Georgia who had founded and headed the historically black Morehouse University medical college in Atlanta and who was then serving as Secretary of Health and Human Services. Although he did everything he could to control HIV-AIDS, the audience wrongly perceived him to be someone who wasn't sympathetic to the AIDS fight because he was part of a conservative Republican administration. When he spoke, he was greeted with boos and catcalls. When I arose to speak, I was cheered. I opened my remarks by admonishing the audience for treating Dr. Sullivan unjustly. Afterward, a couple of the conference's leaders apologized for the rudeness toward Dr. Sullivan, an extraordinary person.

At home, a minister attacked me for appearing before a gay rights' organization. It was important to have a dialogue with all constituencies, including the gay community, about what they could do to help deal with the crisis. But I didn't think I could influence this particular critic and I ignored the criticism. All too often, the political discourse over the HIV-AIDS crisis seemed uninformed and misguided.

The environment was another area where I took a leading role. As a member of the Public Works and Transportation Committee, I helped write six provisions in the reauthorization of the Clean Water Act and was the principal author of the storm water runoff provision. Congress had been unable to pass a stronger Clean Water Act for several years, and disagreements over controversial requirements to control runoff into waterways from all kinds of sources including industries, farmland, and streets had been a perennial snagging point. Some analysts believed such runoff was responsible for up to half of the country's water contamination.

After hearing from all sides, my staff aide Karen Mogen and I authored a compromise that included civil and criminal penalties for water standard violations as well as limited waivers on water quality standards and extensions on compliance deadlines to ease burdensome requirements. This wasn't exactly what environmentalists or commercial interests wanted. But by balancing the conflicting interests, the proposed compromise was eventually approved by both houses of Congress without a dissenting vote.

When I was named to the Energy and Commerce Committee, and came off of the Public Works and Transportation Committee, circumstances made me an intermediary between John Dingell and Henry Waxman over the federal standard for vehicle tailpipe emissions in the Clean Air Act. A bitter disagreement between Dingell, who was allied with the auto industry, and Waxman, a champion of environmentalism, had kept the committee from reporting out an updated Clean Air Act for the previous twelve years. When the committee took up the issue again in 1989, representatives of both sides talked to me and other committee members about what would be acceptable to them. Although Dingell and Waxman had long been at loggerheads, it seemed to me a compromise was possible.

I arranged to talk one-on-one with both of the powerful chairmen. Over a period of some days, I bounced back and forth between their two offices. After laying out a number of proposals and counter-proposals, I sensed they were both ready to reach an agreement. The deal they finally struck was given a thumbs up by most environmentalists and grudgingly accepted by industry representatives, although some made it clear they weren't too happy with the tougher requirements. John Dingell deserves credit for reaching an agreement that apparently didn't sit too well with his constituents in the auto industry.

Congressional Quarterly's Politics in America publication noted that "Rowland worked behind the scenes to help fashion a compromise on that key provision (tailpipe emission standards), enabling the overall bill to move ahead." I was appointed to the conference committees that worked out the final versions of the clean air and water bills.

The purchase of Bond Swamp in middle Georgia was another environmental success story. This made it possible to establish the Ocmulgee National Wildlife Refuge, a diverse ecosystem along the Ocmulgee River in middle Georgia. Georgia's U.S. Sen. Wyche Fowler and I worked together to persuade the Interior Department to make the Bond Swamp acquisition a priority and to include funding for that purpose in the 1990 Interior Department Appropriations Act. Although President Bush and his Office of Planning and Budget shifted their natural resources' emphasis from conservation to recreation, posing a threat to our efforts, we eventually won the administration's support. Since Mercer University owned part of Bond Swamp, a total of $2.4 million of the funds for land acquisition went to Mercer's School of Medicine.

While still a member of the Public Works and Transportation Committee, I authored two innovative bills aimed at stimulating growth in rural areas. Neither passed, but they received considerable media coverage. Both ideas would be worth considering today.

One bill proposed to build a rural-based system of auxiliary airports, called "wayports," to divert much of the traffic at big city airports including freight-carrying airliners and private aircraft. The proposal originated with James E. Sheppard, manager of the Federal Aviation Administration's district office in Orlando, FL. He presented the concept to the committee and I was taken with it. We worked on and off together for several years to promote the plan and draft it into legislative form. By establishing a revolving loan fund from a $5 billion surplus in the federal Airport and Airway Trust Fund, four to six wayports could have been built in rural areas without increasing the deficit, facilities we believed would have been self-sustaining.

Another bill called for shifting some interstate highway funding to build a network of interstate connectors to rural communities, something that would attract business and industrial development in less populous areas. Georgia Transportation Commissioner Tom Moreland designed the plan and I drafted it into a bill, the Federal Aid Highway Reform Act. The measure would have consolidated twenty-five separate federal highway programs into five and authorized $15.5 billion a year for the connectors, money that would have come from federal motor fuel taxes.

Ed Bodenhamer, executive director of the Southeast Georgia Area Planning and Development Commission, testified at a Public Works and Transportation Committee hearing in 1984 about the glaring disparity in the distribution of federal highway funds. He pointed out rural citizens were paying a much bigger share of motor fuel taxes than they were receiving in federal road development. This means "rural areas are paying for their own economic demise," he said. Although the 1984 Surface Transportation Act included a provision I sponsored calling for a U.S. Transportation Department study to determine how badly communities of less than 50,000 people were being shortchanged, nothing ever came of it and rural areas continued to pay for their economic demise.

Many of my legislative goals were achieved as a member of ad hoc caucuses or commissions. One was a total flop. I was appointed to a twelve-member House and Senate biomedical ethics advisory committee created by Congress in 1988 to recommend government policy relating to stem cell research, cloning, and other biomedical issues. The committee disbanded when some of the appointees became so entangled over abortion nothing could be accomplished. But I helped achieve a number of goals as chairman of the Physician's Task Force of the Rural Health Care Coalition, a caucus of House members representing rural areas; chairman of the Infant Mortality Committee of the Sunbelt Caucus of Southern House members; member of the House-created Select Committee on Children, Youth and Families; and vice chairman of the National Commission to Prevent Infant Mortality, a commission created in 1986 under a bill sponsored by Sen. Lawton Chiles of Florida who served as chairman.

Thanks to great leadership and teamwork by Sen. Chiles, U.S. Education Secretary Dick Riley of South Carolina, Lynda Johnson Robb, and others serving on the commission, major progress was made in fighting the country's shamefully high rate of infant mortality. The commission developed and pushed through the Healthy Birth Act, a measure that established a program to identify at-risk pregnant women and send nurses, social workers, and trained volunteers to their homes to help assure healthy pregnancies and births; sponsored a national campaign to provide at-risk women information about how to access prenatal care; and raised awareness by holding public hearings around the country.

Although the U.S. had made gradual advances in combating infant mortality over the previous few decades, a 1987 study by the Children's Defense Fund, a children's advocacy organization, reported the country still stood last among the twenty most industrialized nations in the percentage of children who died before their first birthday, an average of eleven deaths out of every 1,000 births. In Georgia, the number was even worse, 12.6 per 1,000 births. This was not only a tragedy for the affected families, studies at the time found that every low birthweight birth that was averted saved the country's health care system between $14,000 and $30,000. When the federal government funded family planning and other services for pregnant woman after World War II, the infant mortality rate declined. The rate increased when funding for such services was cut, demonstrating that the programs made a difference.

During my second term, Speaker O'Neill named me to the nearly-created twenty-five member Select Committee on Children, Youth and Families chaired by Democratic Rep. George Miller of California. I served on the select committee for all ten years of its existence, helping address issues dealing with foster care, child abuse, youth suicide, mental health, battered spouses, prenatal care, and the impact of the tax code on families.

The Physician's Task Force of the Rural Health Care Coalition, which I chaired, led the way in eliminating the Medicare reimbursement differential between rural and urban hospitals. Congress had decided urban hospital costs were higher than rural hospital costs and a lower rural reimbursement rate should therefore be set. But rural hospitals were closing at an alarming rate and the inequitable Medicare reimbursements were a contributing factor. Although we had to do some compromising, the rural coalition successfully sponsored legislation to gradually equalize the rate over a five-year period to stem a disparity that was increasing by $1 billion a year.

Membership of the bipartisan coalition expanded rapidly. Founded in 1987 by Rep. Charles Stenholm, a leader of conservative Democrats in the House from Texas, and Republican Rep. Pat Roberts of Kansas, a community newspaper publisher, the coalition grew from a starting membership of forty-six to some 170 from forty-seven states. With power in numbers, the coalition also succeeded in establishing the Rural Health Care Policy office within the Department of Health and Human Services; creating the Rural Health Transition Grant program to help hospitals meet changing needs in rural areas; funding the Essential Access Community and Rural Primary Care Hospital programs to help form rural health care networks; revitalizing the National Health Service Corps; and helping establish state offices of rural health.

In 1990, I introduced a so-called "anti-hassle" bill to eliminate unnecessary and wasteful red tape imposed on health professionals, one of my top priorities when I came to Congress. It had taken some years to build support for at least some health care deregulation. Many colleagues advocated more government regulation, not less, as the answer to the country's health care problems. Rep. Waxman, chairman of my health subcommittee, supported some of my deregulation proposals, although not all. But another influential liberal voice in health care issues, the Ways and Means Committee's Pete Stark of California, vehemently opposed every regulatory reform we proposed.

As my co-sponsors and I negotiated and fought over a number of anti-hassle provisions, the bill remained stuck in committee for most of the year. But with support for Medicare reform growing, agreement was reached late in the session to include most of the provisions in the Budget Reconciliation Act, which passed. The first anti-hassle bill mandated studies in six carrier areas to determine the effect of releasing prepayment medical review screens and parameters; permitted reciprocal agreements; authorized a study in at least four carrier areas on the effect of permitting certain changes in the aggregation rule with respect to claims under appeal; and established a Practicing Physicians' Advisory Council to review proposed regulations and carrier manual instructions relating to physician services.

During the 1991-92 term, I worked hard to get a second anti-hassle bill passed. But history repeated itself. Again it got bogged down in committee and couldn't pass as a free-standing bill. But late in the term, my cosponsors and I managed to get some of the provisions included in an urban aid bill. Frankly, I didn't much like the bill that served as a vehicle for the anti-hassle provisions. It passed but was vetoed by President Bush and Congress didn't override the veto. The second anti-hassle bill would have repealed the pre-certification requirement for certain surgical procedures; amended existing Medicare Secondary Pay authority to prohibit the Health Care Financing Administration from denying physician payments for medically-necessary services if patients failed to complete questionnaires; prohibited HCFA from charging for filing paper claims, errors or rejected claims, unsuccessful appeals, and applications for unique provider identification numbers and medical review requirements; and allowed physicians to bill for services of locum tenens physicians through the ordinary billing practices established for regulation patients.

We planned to try again during the 1993-94 term. But with the election of President Clinton, and the coming of his effort to transform the whole health care system, whatever we tried to do about regulatory reform would have to be done in a broader context. I was about to take on the greatest challenge I would ever face in health care policy.

CHAPTER SEVENTEEN

Countless words have been written and spoken about President Clinton's 1993-94 health care reform initiative, one of the country's great lost causes. Health care experts, journalists, academics, and political figures who were involved in the process have analyzed what happened and why in books, articles, blogs, and on television and radio talk shows. But no one has told the whole story as I experienced it as a leader in efforts to enact a bipartisan compromise.

None of the post-mortem analyses have focused on the market-oriented House plan produced by five Democrats and five Republicans late in the debate that would have made dramatic progress toward achieving universal care. It was rejected by President Clinton and his key congressional allies without sufficient consideration like every bipartisan compromise introduced in the House. And none have pointed out that a far-reaching bipartisan compromise might have passed in spite of all the conflict and confusion if it hadn't been for the partisan inflexibility of one person during a critical point in the debate, House Democratic Majority Leader Dick Gephardt of Missouri.

With final adjournment of the two-year Congressional term approaching, I stopped by Dick Gephardt's office to ask him when he planned to give the full House a chance to act on health care reform. Although House Speaker Tom Foley of Washington State was ultimately in charge, he had placed the majority leader in command of the debate in the House. I was shocked when Dick Gephardt brusquely told me no plan would be considered because the public wasn't interested in health care reform any more. He had assured me a few weeks earlier he would bring three plans to the floor-- a Clinton-like plan, a single-payer plan, and a bipartisan plan—and let the membership make the choice. A lack of public interest wasn't the real reason he changed his mind. The majority leader was a presidential hopeful from an urban St. Louis district with a labor constituency. From my perspective, it looked like he terminated the debate in the House because he couldn't get the votes to pass the Clinton plan or another government-driven plan acceptable to labor.

Analysts have commonly pointed to three major factors contributing to the debacle:

▶ **COMPLEXITY AND CONFUSION.** The complexity of health care reform in general, and the Clinton plan in particular, left people confused, making it difficult for Congress to reach a constituent-friendly agreement. Although this was a factor, public opinion polls and my own contact with constituents led me to believe most Americans understood the broad outline of reform, even if they didn't grasp the specific details, and were ready to accept a plan that wouldn't create bigger federal deficits and didn't impose too much government control.

▶ **SPECIAL INTERESTS.** A wide range of special interests campaigned against the more government-oriented Clinton plan and against more market-oriented bipartisan alternative plans, spending many millions of dollars in attack ads. Although such ads sowed uncertainty and fear about health care reform, the fact that most members of Congress supported a number of the same major reforms indicated a substantial reform plan could have passed with public approval.

▶ **PARTISANSHIP.** The two-year debate took a series of partisan twists and turns. Although President Clinton originally advocated a bipartisan approach to health care reform, he abandoned bipartisanship by introducing a plan few could support other than Democratic factions well to the left of center. The president and his Democratic majority allies in Congress believed they had the power to push through a costly, highly-bureaucratized plan that would quickly provide all of the new and expanded benefits they proposed. They kept pushing until it was too late. As the end neared, the president and a number of his allies in Congress changed course and finally sought a bipartisan compromise. But these efforts were stonewalled when the Democratic majority leader ended the debate in the House rather than consider a bipartisan compromise and a Republican faction effectively shut down the debate in the Senate soon thereafter by mobilizing for a filibuster.

J. Bradford DeLong, an economist who served as undersecretary of the Treasury Department during the Clinton years and an advisor in drafting the Clinton plan, blamed the "crash" on what he described as moral, intellectual, and political bankruptcy. He described Republicans who promoted gridlock for political gain as morally bankrupt; President Clinton and his team as intellectually bankrupt for failing to construct and promote the kind of plan to improve the health care system that had a chance of passing; and the Democratic majorities in the House and Senate as politically bankrupt for failing to use their overwhelming strength to reach an acceptable compromise.

In a memoir, former President Clinton insisted his plan wasn't a "big government" scheme. He believes opponents' misrepresentation of his plan caused its downfall. In fact, his plan would have created a new government bureaucracy that looked to me as if it would have been very big. But this argument aside, the former president failed to explain why he didn't more forcefully get behind bipartisan efforts to achieve as much reform as possible after it became clear to almost everyone his own plan wouldn't pass and bipartisanship was the only way anything could be accomplished. If he did anything to encourage Gephardt to focus on a meaningful alternative, it wasn't apparent to those of us involved in bipartisan efforts. To us, the president's handling of the health care reform process appeared indecisive and weak.

The president designated the first lady, Hillary Clinton, to take charge of the administration's health care reform initiative. Her failure to produce and reach agreement over a politically-viable plan in the 1993-94 debate came back to haunt her in her presidential campaigns. This was early in her career on the national stage. If she could have called on the wealth of national political experience she later gained, perhaps she would have led the administration toward an acceptable bipartisan compromise before it was too late.

Senate Democratic Majority Leader George Mitchell of Maine eventually called on the administration to move in a more realistic direction. But when Sen. Mitchell and other key Senate supporters of the Clinton plan tried to come up with a worthwhile compromise in the debate's final stages, they were tripped up by the Republican filibuster threat. In the House, Dick Gephardt and Energy and Commerce Chairman John Dingell of Michigan didn't ever move in a bipartisan direction. From the outset they demonized bipartisan alternatives, making it difficult for them to reverse course even if they had wanted to.

I don't doubt they believed their all-or-nothing position was best for the country as well as for their own political interests. Most of my constituents opposed the Clinton plan. So I, too, was doing what was in my political interest as well as what I thought was best for the country. As for labor's position, I had labor support in my own campaigns and I recognized the right of labor representatives to take whatever stand they believed was right. But I couldn't understand, and still can't, why President Clinton and Democratic leaders in Congress made such a feeble effort to reach a worthwhile compromise when the Clinton plan was obviously dead, leaving themselves open to the oncoming disaster.

A substantial health care reform compromise would have passed if the wishes of most members of Congress had prevailed. This assumption is based on the number of Democrats and Republicans who co-sponsored or verbally committed to bipartisan proposals during the debate, including the consensus plan co-authored by Mike Bilirakis of Florida and myself. When a health care reform bill based on the consensus model came before the next term of Congress following a voter backlash in the 1994 mid-term elections, the Kassebaum-Kennedy bill, it passed in the House and Senate with only two dissenting votes. President Clinton and many of the same lawmakers who opposed a consensus plan two years before were now wholeheartedly in favor of it. The Kassebaum-Kennedy bill lacked a number of the major provisions included in the Rowland-Bilirakis bill. If the president and his Democratic congressional allies had turned to a consensus plan in 1993-94 when popular momentum for health care reform was at a peak, a much more far-reaching plan would likely have passed.

Several lessons can be learned from the 1993-94 debate. One, rigid partisanship existed within both parties, and still does. Two, when Democratic and Republican leaders take an unyielding stand, whether for political advantage or an unwillingness to balance one's strongly-held opinions with the opinions of others, it can overwhelm a goal supported by a majority. And three, when uncompromising partisanship leads to a stalemate over important goals, it violates a fundamental principle of good governance: Don't sacrifice progress on the altar of perfection.

President Clinton deserves credit for taking on the overwhelmingly-difficult task of reforming the health care system even if his execution failed. Presidents Woodrow Wilson, Franklin D. Roosevelt, and Harry Truman were among those who had previously sought to comprehensively change the health care system without success. But times had changed.

Even before the 1992 presidential race, Pennsylvania Democrat Harris Wofford had demonstrated how explosive health care reform could be as a political issue. Running for election after he was appointed to fill the term of Sen. John Heinz who had perished in a plane crash, Wofford appeared to be too far behind to have a chance in his race against a former Republican governor, Richard Thornburgh. Then Wofford saturated television with ads aligning himself with sweeping health care reform. Suddenly he surged in the polls and won with fifty-five percent of the vote. When Sen. Tom Daschle of South Dakota, who headed the Democratic Senate Policy Committee, asked his fellow Democratic senators to identify the issues they believed should be emphasized by Democratic candidates in 1992, every one placed health care reform at or near the top.

While many people were satisfied with their coverage and care, the system's imperfections were causing hardship for millions of patients and the professionals who provided the care. Millions of people couldn't afford health care coverage and many of them weren't receiving adequate care. Self-employed and unemployed citizens faced obscenely high costs for individual coverage. People couldn't change jobs because they would lose their coverage and many couldn't get coverage because they were already sick. Low-income citizens often couldn't take minimum wage jobs because it would make them ineligible for Medicaid. Government red tape often interfered with the care physicians felt was best for patients.

Although the U.S. was spending a bigger portion of its gross national product for health care than most nations, the country stood thirty-first in life expectancy and twenty-eighth in the rate of infant mortality. While many factors affect life expectancy, the system's defects were a significant contributing factor. Federal and state health care outlays were absorbing ever larger portions of government budgets, exceeding twelve percent at the federal level and much higher percentages in most states. Fraud, waste and excessive malpractice litigation were driving health care costs higher.

Within days of taking office, First Lady Hillary Clinton took charge of the health care reform initiative. To serve as their plan's chief architect, she recruited a Clinton presidential campaign advisor, Ira Magaziner, a forty-five-year-old business consultant from Rhode Island who was known for the complex business reorganization schemes he designed.

Like many observers, I presumed President Clinton and his team would come up with a health care reform plan driven substantially by free market principles, an approach he and his advisors endorsed early in his administration. Addressing the National Governors' Conference in Tulsa, Oklahoma, President Clinton stated health care reform could only succeed on a bipartisan basis. Speaking to the American Medical Association in Chicago, Hillary Clinton said the Clinton plan would include safeguards to prevent government bureaucrats from second guessing medical decisions. "This kind of micromanagement and regulation has not improved quality and has wasted billions of dollars," she said. According to *Washington Post* reporters David Broder and Haynes Johnson in *The System*, a definitive book on the debate, Ira Magaziner privately warned they couldn't win with a liberal Democratic coalition alone and would need more than token support from Republicans.

As the process was getting underway, President Clinton hosted a series of get-togethers with small groups of House members and senators to hear their views on health care reform. When invited, I was escorted into a White House drawing room and seated in a semi-circle around the president with seven or eight House colleagues. During a free-wheeling discussion covering many aspects of health care reform, I urged the president to include physicians and other health care professionals in designing the plan. When he nodded without saying a word, I took it as an affirmative nod.

I've read the administration used the Jackson Hole Plan as the administration's beginning model. This managed competition concept was developed by Stanford University economist Alain C. Enthoven and a group of academic thinkers and business leaders who met regularly in Jackson Hole, WY, a concept emphasizing competitive forces and limited government oversight. A *New York Times* editorial endorsed the Jackson Hole Plan in 1991, saying unfettered competition would leave Americans at the mercy of insurers and health care entities but a hybrid system based on managed competition principles would provide the best solution ever devised for controlling costs, assuring quality, and guaranteeing access. A plan based substantially on market forces appealed to moderates in both parties.

But if the administration really planned to embrace bipartisanship, limited government control, and professional expertise in developing its plan, such guidelines got lost in the tortured drafting process.

Hillary Clinton and Ira Magaziner established an Interagency Task Force to help work out the details. Asked to participate in the process were representatives of federal agencies, staff members from congressional committees, aides of select Democratic House members and senators, health care experts and academic figures who served as consultants. From January until the task force was disbanded in late May, more than 600 people met in separate working groups behind closed doors every weekday at the Old Executive Office Building adjacent to the White House. Although the proceedings were kept secret, and I didn't exactly know who was participating, it was my impression medical professionals were woefully underrepresented.

Early in February I sent a letter to Hillary Clinton volunteering to work with the task force. I certainly didn't expect the administration to agree with me on everything. But as a physician, one deeply involved in health care issues, I believed I could make some useful suggestions. In a letter dated February 19, the first lady said, "As both a policymaker and family physician, you are well aware of the enormous challenges we face. I am grateful for your offer of assistance and hope that you will share with us your views on how we may achieve our goal of providing affordable health care to every American. I look forward to working with you." But as the weeks and months passed, my staff and I weren't invited to participate in the planning process.

In mid-May, Sonny Montgomery, Sen. Jay Rockefeller of West Virginia, and I met with the first lady in Sen. Rockefeller's Senate Hart Building office to brief her on veterans' health issues. At that get-together, I understood her to say my staff and I would finally be included in the task force process then still underway. Subsequently I sent more information in writing I thought would be helpful. But we still weren't invited to the task force meetings, which soon ended. Although I didn't really realize it at the time, the door apparently wasn't open to any voices perceived as potentially incompatible with the emerging vision held by the first lady and Magaziner.

This was the first indication the president's health care reform plan might not conform to the president's commitment to market principles. Based on information filtering out to members of Congress, I was beginning to think the Clinton plan would over-emphasize government control and have to be substantially modified when it came to Congress in order to attract a consensus needed for passage. According to many reports, top administration figures like Health and Human Services Secretary Donna Shalala, Treasury Secretary Lloyd Bentsen, Budget Director Leon Panetta, and Deputy Budget Director Alice Rivlin were privately raising concerns about the complex bureaucracy, unfunded costs, and political uncertainty of the plan devised by the first lady and Magaziner.

Evidently Hillary Clinton dismissed most if not all of these concerns and the president mostly sided with the first lady.

The president had promised during his campaign to send a health care reform plan to Congress within one hundred days. But he was well past that deadline on November 20, 1993, when he finally sent a first draft of his 1,342-page Health Security Act to Capitol Hill. The plan's scope was breathtaking. Mandating insurance coverage for every uninsured American within a financially-viable context would have been a huge undertaking on its own. But the plan also included expensive new programs to provide assistance for long-term care, catastrophic care, mental health care, and prescription drugs. It proposed the creation of a new bureaucracy to control government and consumer health care costs involving scores of new oversight and regulatory commissions, councils, boards, and alliances. It called for a presidential-appointed national board to establish a national health care budget setting caps on state and federal health care spending.

It required employers to not just to provide employee coverage, but also to pay most of the cost. Although it called for tripling tobacco taxes, it would have increased budget deficits by billions of dollars.

The Clinton plan was a "monster in Jackson Hole clothing," in the words of Alain Enthoven. Instead of a system based on managed competition, President Clinton was proposing a top-down command-and-control system governing just about every aspect of the delivery and financing of the country's health care services. Although the plan's goals were all laudatory, I believed the Clinton plan would ration care; interfere with medical decisions; impose more burdensome paperwork on professionals, some of whom were already spending twenty percent of their office work time dealing with bureaucratic rules; increase health care costs; and lower the quality of care for many.

While polling showed most Americans wanted more secure health care coverage for themselves and their family, and for a system assuring access to care for everyone, events would prove they didn't support reform if it came with bigger deficits and more government control over the delivery of health care. The Clinton plan would have required most insured Americans to give up their past coverage and receive new coverage controlled by federally-regulated regional alliances that would serve as purchasing co-ops. According to some estimates, forty percent of the insured population would have paid more for their premiums. This was a hard sell and it's no wonder much of the public turned against it. Much of the business community passionately opposed the Clinton plan from the outset.

Perhaps the most controversial feature of the Clinton plan was its mandated employer-paid employee health insurance coverage. Employer-based health insurance is one of President Franklin D. Roosevelt's unintended legacies. Faced with a wage and price freeze during World War II, many companies helped provide employee health care coverage in lieu of pay raises. This fringe benefit has always been something employers provided voluntarily.

Hillary Clinton knew a mandate requiring employers to provide group insurance coverage and pay a big share of the coverage would create a political problem that wouldn't be easy to overcome. But as she explained in meetings with members of Congress, it would take a massive tax increase or the kind of employer mandate she was proposing to finance universal coverage and all of the new benefits provided in the Clinton plan. The employer mandate, she noted, was less politically troublesome than a massive general tax hike. What was not apparent to the first lady until too late was that both a big tax increase and mandated employer payments were deal breakers in Congress.

The employer contribution would have been eighty percent of a standardized plan with contributions capped at nearly eight percent of company payrolls for businesses with fifty or more employees or three and a half to six and a half percent for businesses with fewer than fifty employees. Although much of the share paid by employers would have actually been borne by employees in reduced wages, the U.S. Labor Department estimated it would cost businesses $30 billion annually and would eliminate more than a million jobs the first year. Many small businesses feared the insurance costs would force them to close.

By putting the same burden on low income as high income workers, it was a regressive proposal. According to the independent consulting firm, Lewin-VHI, Inc., "Most economists agree that workers will bear nearly all of the cost of employer-provided health care insurance in the form of reduced wages." Employees would have fared better under any one of a number of bipartisan alternatives offered in the House and Senate, none of which would have driven employers to offset higher costs with lower wages. When the Clinton plan bogged down, the White House tried to soften the administration's mandate by proposing to exempt companies with fewer than ten employees and to lower the employer share to fifty percent. But these compromises didn't generate much new support.

Standing resolutely with the president's plan throughout the debate was the single-payer bloc of congressional Democrats supporting a government-run health care system. Since a single-payer plan didn't stand a chance in Congress, the Clinton plan was viewed as the best possible option for single-payer advocates, including organized labor. A total of eighty-nine House members co-sponsored the single-payer health care reform bill introduced in the House. That was a sizable number, but it was an isolated group that couldn't grow. Leading the single payers in the House was Rep. Jim McDermott of Washington State, the only other physician serving in Congress. I held Jim in high regard personally and professionally. But we held diametrically opposing views over the kind of health care system the country needs. He believed a government-run system could assure the care everyone needs and the problems I envisioned would pale compared to the humanitarian benefits.

Fair enough. But I wish Jim could have accepted significant improvement over none at all. At the outset, the president vowed to veto any plan providing less than he proposed. This fired up labor and single- payer supporters to fight for all or nothing. After pushing through the North Atlantic Free Trade Agreement (NAFTA) early in his administration, a treaty opposed by labor but considered essential to U.S. trade leadership by the administration, it became more difficult for the president to back off of his all-or-nothing pledge on health care reform without alienating labor and other core supporters of the Clinton plan. It was the president's vow, I suspect, that locked in labor-allied House Democratic leaders like Gephardt and Dingell to an all-or-nothing stand until the end.

A few weeks before President Clinton formally introduced his plan, entitled the Health Security Act, I attended a joint session of Congress where the president called the existing health care system "too uncertain and too expensive, too bureaucratic and too wasteful." When the president's plan was introduced soon thereafter, many of us who were listening to him in the House chamber that day remembered his words and thought they described his own extraordinarily-convoluted proposal.

CHAPTER EIGHTEEN

Waving a pen in the air, President Clinton issued this unequivocal warning to me and other members of the House and Senate who gathered to hear his State of the Union address on January 25, 1994: you better not send me a health care reform bill that doesn't guarantee private coverage for every single American or "you will force me to take this pen, veto the legislation, and we'll come right back here and start all over again."

What a bind this put the administration in. Neither the president, nor congressional supporters of the Clinton plan, nor anyone else could ever figure out how to ensure ninety-five to one hundred percent health care coverage, the administration's range for defining universal coverage, without expanding the bureaucracy, raising taxes, and mandating employer-paid coverage. None of these measures for controlling costs and financing new benefits were politically tenable.

If many observers, including me, thought his aim wasn't realistic, the president and his allies on health care reform were obviously convinced they had the power to force their partisan plan through Congress. They would keep pushing until nearly the bitter end. The first step was to get the Clinton plan favorably reported out of Senate and House committees.

In the House, health care reform proposals were referred to three committees with jurisdiction over general health care issues, the Energy and Commerce, Ways and Means, and Education and Labor committees. All three were expected to report the Clinton plan or a variation of the Clinton plan out of committee. But the Energy and Commerce Committee's version was generally expected to be the one considered on the House floor. The Energy and Commerce Committee had broad jurisdiction over much of the legislation considered in the House. Its balanced membership reflected the diversity of the whole House. Under its powerful chairman, John D. Dingell, Jr. of Michigan, it had a high success rate in getting the bills it reported to the floor enacted.

The sixty-seven-year-old Dingell had succeeded his late father in representing an industrialized congressional district in Dearborn, MI dominated by auto makers and auto unions. Ranked sixth in seniority among the 435 House members, he was called "Big John" in recognition of the power he wielded with political finesse and a strong personality. Passing legislation to nationalize the health care system had been his abiding goal from the day he entered Congress in 1955. His father had unsuccessfully led efforts to enact a national health care plan during FDR's final years in the White House and the younger Dingell had introduced a national health care insurance bill every term he had served in Congress.

Knowing passage of a single-payer plan to establish a government-run system wasn't possible, the chairman backed the Clinton plan because it came close enough to fulfilling his and his father's dream of nationalizing the system.

Following proper procedure, the chairman assigned the Clinton plan to the Energy and Commerce Committee's Health and the Environment Subcommittee chaired by Rep. Henry Waxman, a liberal from California who was among the powerful supporters of the Clinton plan. I was a member of the subcommittee and I know how hard Henry worked to favorably report the Clinton plan to the full committee. But too many of the Democrats on the subcommittee were unwilling to vote for the

Clinton plan and Henry wasn't open to a big enough compromise. In spite of Henry's arm-twisting, the bill remained stalled in the subcommittee for many weeks.

When Congress returned from an Easter recess in April 1994, John Dingell took decisive action to get the process moving by pulling the bill out of the subcommittee and placing it with the full committee. Although the delay wasn't helping the Clinton cause, Henry was far from pleased when his subcommittee's authority was usurped. This was an early indication the Clinton plan was in trouble and the Clinton forces were in disarray.

Under the rules, Dingell needed twenty-three votes to report the Clinton plan out of committee. There were twenty-seven Democrats and seventeen Republicans on his committee. None of the Republicans would vote to send the Clinton plan to the House floor. Needing the votes of twenty-three of the twenty-seven Democratic committee members, the chairman went into overdrive, buttonholing uncommitted members on the House floor, in the Capitol hallways, in their offices, and anywhere he spotted them to urge them to cast the decisive twenty-third vote.

He secured the support of twenty-two of the Democratic members, one tantalizing vote short. The committee's five Democratic holdouts, including me, wouldn't budge.

One of the holdouts was Rep. Jim Cooper, the son of three-time Tennessee Gov. Prentice Cooper. Jim's resume included a Rhodes scholarship and a degree from Harvard Law School. He was the principal author of the bipartisan "Clinton lite" plan, which many people thought would be the plan Congress would eventually enact. Jim was running against Republican Fred Thompson for the Senate. For not supporting the Clinton plan, labor organizations in Tennessee were campaigning against Cooper. If Cooper had voted to report the Clinton plan out of the committee, he could have potentially turned labor in his favor. Dingell reportedly offered him a deal. If Cooper would vote to report the Clinton plan out of committee for a vote on the floor, the chairman would make sure Cooper's "Clinton lite" plan would also be reported out. But there was no guarantee

"Clinton lite" would be scheduled for a floor vote even if reported out of committee. Cooper held firm.

Dingell twisted the arms of Reps. Billy Tauzin of Louisiana, Ralph Hall of Texas, and Jim Slattery of Kansas, who was running for governor. None of them could be convinced a vote for the Clinton plan would be good for themselves politically or for the country. As quoted in *The System*, the chairman reportedly commented in a private conversation there were "SOB's" in the Democratic ranks who "deserve to be punished," an indication of how his frustration boiled over.

It was late in June 1994 when the chairman stopped me on the House floor and said he wanted to talk. I followed him off the House floor, through the speaker's lobby, and through a door onto a narrow balcony overlooking the Washington mall called the "Speaker's Balcony." We sat in a couple of straight-backed chairs that were probably used to watch concerts and fireworks displays held on the Capitol's west lawn. I've always wondered why he chose this picturesque location to make his pitch. Possibly he hoped the inspiring view would reinforce an appeal based, in part, on my sense of duty.

While I don't remember his exact words, I haven't forgotten the gist of our conversation. He explained the committee's responsibility to perfect legislation as much as possible and to report it out so every House member would have a chance to consider it. I knew it wouldn't be good for the chairman's prestige and the committee's prestige to fail to report out any health care reform proposal. But more than that, he suggested, I could defend a vote to send health care reform to the floor as a vote of fairness to give the whole House an opportunity to consider one of the most important bills in history.

Then he got to the clincher. If I would vote to bring the Clinton plan to the floor, he would accompany me to the White House to meet with President Clinton who was ready to grant me any political favor I wanted. It wasn't easy to turn down a powerful committee chairman who potentially controlled the fate of my legislative goals. But I couldn't vote for a plan I believed would be harmful to patients, health care professionals, and the country's economic well-being, and I couldn't sell out my colleagues who were working with me on a bipartisan alternative. I had to tell him thanks but I was already committed.

There went my chance to become U.S. surgeon general. Later in the year, when the U.S. surgeon general's position opened up, more than one hundred colleagues urged President Clinton to name me to the prestigious post. While I realized I had virtually no chance because of my stand on health care reform, I was honored. I also had no regrets. I had made the only choice I could make. The president never acted on my recommendation for surgeon general and, as far as I know, never commented on it.

On June 28, Dingell sent a letter of surrender to the House speaker. He said it would be "counterproductive" to continue seeking approval of the Clinton plan by the committee he chaired. Ironically, he blamed Republican partisanship for the committee gridlock. While some Republicans opposed any health care reform, at this point many Republicans in Congress, perhaps most, supported a bipartisan alternative offering extensive reform. Dingell never made any real effort to work for a bipartisan agreement. I've read that the chairman broached the idea of working with Republicans in a conversation with Rep. Carlos Moorhead of California, the senior Republican on the Energy and Commerce Committee. But that conversation went nowhere, and if the chairman made any further attempt to seek common ground with the other party it wasn't revealed.

In his letter, Dingell denounced the two main bipartisan bills in the House, the consensus bill introduced by Mike Bilirakis and myself and the "Clinton lite" bill introduced by Jim Cooper and Fred Grandy of Iowa, saying they would "perpetuate or worsen" the health care system's existing problems. Although the Rowland-Bilirakis proposal wasn't nearly as far-reaching as the Clinton plan, while avoiding the unfunded costs and much of the bureaucracy of the Clinton plan, most of the provisions in the Rowland-Bilirakis bill were included in the Clinton plan. Dingell didn't explain how dealing with some of the problems addressed in the Clinton plan could be worse than failing to deal with any of the system's problems.

If John Dingell had opened the door to bipartisanship, a plan could have been developed within the Energy and Commerce Committee by pulling together features from the president's plan and the two principal bipartisan plans in a more market-oriented context. This would eventually be done with the development of a breakthrough comprehensive bipartisan plan developed by the so-called "Gang of Ten" in the House, which would have increased guaranteed coverage to ninety-two percent of the population, just short of the ninety-five percent that served as the president's final threshold for defining universal coverage. If the Energy and Commerce Committee had reported a market-driven plan such as this to the House floor, it might well have had enough clout behind it to pass whether the House majority leader liked it or not.

When Dingell threw in the towel, the spotlight in the House turned on Dick Gephardt, 53, an attorney and veteran congressman who had been designated by the speaker to lead the House effort to enact a health care reform plan, preferably the president's plan. Although I hadn't had many direct dealings with him, we had always been friendly. I had said encouraging things when he once talked to me about supporting him in a future presidential race.

With the Energy and Commerce Committee deadlocked, he turned to two other committees with jurisdiction over health care for a plan he and other supporters of the Clinton plan could accept. The Education and Labor Committee chaired by Rep. Billy Ford of Michigan, a liberal bastion, reported out both a variation of the Clinton plan and a single-payer plan. The House Ways and Means Committee chaired by Rep. Dan Rostenkowski of Illinois and, when he stepped aside to deal with personal legal problems, Rep. Sam Gibbons of Florida, reported out a plan that differed from the Clinton plan but still relied on strong government control.

In the Senate, the Clinton plan was referred to the Labor and Human Resources Committee chaired by Sen. Kennedy and the Finance Committee chaired by Sen. Pat Moynihan of New York. Following long and difficult negotiations, both committees approved offshoots of the Clinton plan. But neither bill came close to attracting enough support to pass. Sen. John Chafee of Rhode Island, chairman of the Republican task force on health care reform in the Senate, and Democratic Sen. John Breaux of Louisiana, the "Clinton lite" sponsor in the Senate, led a sizable faction of moderate senators, dubbed the mainstream coalition, in working on a bipartisan option. Although the Senate bipartisan plans attracted substantial support, for most of the debate the Democratic leadership under Democratic Majority Leader George Mitchell resisted consideration of an alternative to the Clinton plan.

By July 1, 1994, President Clinton and congressional allies finally agreed to a seismic shift in strategy. Based on the events that followed, it was evident that President Clinton, Hillary Clinton, Tom Foley, Dick Gephardt, and George Mitchell had communicated with one another and agreed to modify universal coverage and some of the other provisions they were insisting upon in the Clinton plan. They began working for a compromise that would hopefully appeal to centrists without upsetting their core supporters too much.

In a speech to the National Governors' Conference in Boston, President Clinton announced he was ready to work for a more centrist compromise, one that was "in the ballpark" of the ninety-five percent threshold for universal coverage and might be funded by some mechanism other than the mandated employer contribution. This was a big story. For the first time, he had publicly backed off of his threat to veto anything failing to guarantee universal coverage and all of his plan's other benefits.

His remarks touched off a firestorm of protest by his supporters on the left. Rep. McDermott said the president was about to lose the support of the single-payer bloc. Labor leaders hotly criticized such a compromise. The reaction obviously alarmed the White House. For the next few days, Hillary Clinton, Vice President Al Gore, and others representing the administration appeared on talk shows to say nothing had really changed. The president was still fighting to enact the kind of plan he had introduced, they said. But when Sen. Mitchell soon joined with the mainstream coalition in trying to work out a bipartisan agreement, the president didn't object.

Toward the end of July, Gephardt and Mitchell held a joint news conference to make it clear they would move away from the Clinton plan and work for a budget-friendly plan that could attract broader support. Mitchell would do exactly what he told the country he would do. Gephardt would go in a different direction. Selecting the Ways and Means Committee bill as his vehicle, he consulted a wide range of experts and colleagues about how to re-write the committee's measure so it would offer enough reform to appease many on the left and somehow attract the support of a sufficient number of moderates. But the bill he cobbled together would dismay many Democrats in Congress looking for a centrist solution, including a number of other key supporters of the Clinton plan.

Instead of moving toward the center, the majority leader's revised plan would appeal only to the same relatively small base supporting the Clinton plan. The stalemate would continue. Congress could either enact health care reform on a bipartisan basis or nothing at all.

CHAPTER NINETEEN

Mike Bilirakis and I introduced a bill in 1993 aimed at making publicly-supported community health centers available to every community in the country, a step that would lead us more deeply into the stormy health care reform debate the following year. These centers provide primary care to everyone whether or not a patient has money or insurance to pay for care.

Our proposal was inspired by the development of a community health center in my birthplace. Dr. Jean Sumner, a Mercer University School of Medicine honor graduate, now dean of the medical school, had opened a practice in Wrightsville in 1990, becoming the only physician then serving an area with a twenty percent poverty rate compared to six percent statewide. Reading about the federally-funded centers in a newspaper, she realized such a facility could save lives and improve the health of this severely underserved part of the state.

With Dr. Sumner spearheading the project, a core team was put together, community support organized, a federal application prepared, and a partnership worked out with the Medical College of Georgia. The U.S. Department of Health and Human Services (HHS) awarded funds for one community health center in the Southeast that year, the Johnson

County Center for Community Health. Free or affordable care was soon available to every citizen, whether insured or not, from Johnson County and many neighboring counties including Laurens, Wilkinson, Washington, Jones, Jefferson, Twiggs, Baldwin, and Hancock.

I marginally assisted by providing information and support from Washington. I also stepped in when a real threat arose. A state legislator from nearby Swainsboro, Butch Parrish, decided his community would compete for the federal funds. He was looking after the area he represented as he should have done. But I didn't think HHS would fund two centers in communities that close together in the same year, and if politicians like me and my colleague in the U.S. House representing Swainsboro were competing for the limited HHS funding it could eliminate both projects from consideration. Although a tough call to make, I contacted Butch Parrish and asked him to wait until another day. I'm sure he didn't appreciate my interference. But, to his credit, he agreed to withdraw rather than potentially put the Wrightsville application at risk.

Community health centers were founded in 1965 as part of President Lyndon Johnson's "War on Poverty." Although some of the anti-poverty programs didn't live up to expectations, the health centers turned out to be a resounding success. They're sustained by a mix of federal, state, local, and even private funding. Located in neighborhoods accessible to low-income families, they provide care for anyone for a fee, or no fee at all, based on a patient's ability to pay. They are governed by boards with patient representation. According to studies at the time, the average cost of treatment at the centers was forty-one percent lower than the cost by other sources. Studies also showed the quality of care at the centers was generally excellent. In fact, studies indicated fewer babies died, emergency room lines were shorter, and overall health was improved in areas where community health centers were located.

After recruiting Mike as a principal co-sponsor, we introduced the Community Health Improvement Act on November 19, 1993, the day after the Clinton plan was formally introduced. The legislation proposed to accelerate the development of community health centers by using Medicaid funds in a more cost-effective way. It would have authorized states to require Medicaid patients to receive state and federally-funded care at their local community health center, greatly reducing Medicaid costs and facilitating the establishment of more centers. Approximately 1,000 community centers already existed. But we wanted to develop an expanded nationwide network of centers to make primary care accessible to everyone.

Although twenty of the bill's twenty-one co-sponsors were Democrats, Mike's involvement made it a bipartisan measure. Our idea wasn't controversial. Just about everyone on all sides of the health care reform debate understood that community health centers were providing quality care in communities where they existed. Even if a system guaranteeing universal coverage was eventually created, former South Dakota Sen. Tom Daschle pointed out in a book he co-authored on health care that community health centers would still be needed as a safety-net for low income patients who could still fall through the cracks.

Some medical doctors expressed concern that shifting Medicaid patients from private practices to publicly-supported centers could financially undermine some private practices, leaving fewer doctors in physician-deprived areas. But I doubted many practices would be hurt by the loss of relatively low-paying Medicaid reimbursements. The benefit of a national network of community health centers would greatly out-weigh any problems. In any case, our bill called for our proposed program to first be tested in demonstration projects to make sure it would work as anticipated.

Although the Community Health Improvement Act got brushed aside in the debate over comprehensive reform, Mike and I included the community health center expansion plan in two broader bipartisan health care reform plans we would author and introduce. The two of us made good partners. Although Mike, at 63, was four years younger than me, we belonged to the same generation. We came to Congress the same year, became Justice Court neighbors, and served together on the Energy and Commerce health subcommittee. Although we belonged to different parties, we both preferred bipartisan solutions over partisan bickering.

President Clinton inadvertently nudged Mike and me to take our next step in the health care reform debate. When flying on Air Force One, the president sometimes invited one or more members of Congress from a state or district where he was stopping to join him on the flight. The president asked Mike to accompany him on a return flight to Washington, D.C., after visiting Florida on a health care reform barnstorming tour. The Clinton plan was still at the beginning of the drafting stage. The president obviously thought the moderate, easy-going Republican from Florida who served on the key House committee would be someone whose support would be worth wooing.

As Mike recalled, he told President Clinton during the flight he looked forward to working with him on a financially-sound health care reform plan with bipartisan support and thought they could reach agreement on one that could achieve much of what the president wanted. According to Mike, the president responded with enthusiasm, saying bipartisan cooperation was the way to go. Based on their chat, Mike and I prepared a letter to send to the president suggesting a gradual phase-in of the many benefits he was proposing in order to make the package deficit free. We asked him to consider including our community health center proposal as part of his plan. When we asked House colleagues to co-sign the letter, a time-consuming task, we collected 103 signatures.

At the time, we thought he would send us a reply reiterating his eagerness to shape a fiscally-sound, market-based plan that could potentially attract centrist bipartisan support. We were ready to join him as allies on health care reform and hoped he would agree to our community health expansion plan. But his reply politely stated his intention to provide universal coverage, period. It said nothing about bipartisanship, market principles, fiscal soundness, or community health centers. I always found Bill Clinton to be personally likeable. But critics have described him as a master of faking sincerity. As we would learn, the president sometimes said things people in his company wanted to hear whether he meant it or not.

I sent two letters to President Clinton offering to help him reach a bipartisan agreement. In both I suggested full health care reform might have to be achieved incrementally in order to adhere to market principles and fiscal responsibility. In mid-October 1993, he responded with a note saying, "I appreciate your offer to work together in a bipartisan effort. However, I disagree that we should start this debate by taking the package apart. I believe this issue should be tackled in whole and I look forward to working with you." In early November, he replied to my follow-up letter with another note saying, "I respectfully acknowledge your candor and frankness. Although we disagree on how health care reform should be addressed by Congress, I look forward to continued dialogue and debate on this issue of such great importance to the American people."

If President Clinton and his team were departing from a managed competition concept, Mike and I thought somebody better do something if we were going to get the kind of reform we thought was best for the country and that had a chance of passing in Congress.

I'm not sure who first suggested focusing on health care reforms included in every one of the plans introduced by the president and several Democratic and Republican members of Congress. But it was an idea Mike and I began to discuss and study after our exchange of correspondence with President Clinton. When Mike and I looked at the Clinton plan after it was introduced, and a wide variety of alternative plans, we were surprised to learn how many of the same major reforms were included in all of them.

If the Clinton plan couldn't pass, a consensus plan would be something virtually everyone could accept, we figured. While the Rowland-Bilirakis consensus bill didn't offer universal coverage all at once, it would have moved the country considerably closer to universal access to care and would have addressed some of the most perplexing problems in the system. We thought the consensus concept would be a non-controversial fallback plan for the White House and members of both parties in Congress.

A major bipartisan alternative to the Clinton plan was already pending in the House, the Cooper-Grandy bill, cosponsored by Democrat Jim Cooper and Republican Fred Grandy, a bright up-and-coming lawmaker who had played a comic character in the long-running television series, *Love Boat*. Both were running for statewide office, Cooper for the U.S. Senate in Tennessee and Grandy for governor of Iowa. Their measure was an updated version of a health care reform bill introduced by Cooper without much fanfare during the previous term. "Clinton lite" was an impressive proposal modeled on the Jackson Hole plan that would have guaranteed ninety percent coverage without a big new bureaucracy or price controls. It didn't include price controls, a bigger bureaucracy, or a mandate requiring employers to pay for employee coverage.

For a few months, the widely-publicized Cooper-Grandy bill was seen by many as the most likely health care reform bill to pass if the Clinton plan stalled. The bill quickly attracted forty-four co-sponsors, twenty-six Democrats and eighteen Republicans. It received the endorsement of the Business Roundtable, a highly influential organization in the business world made up of more than 200 of the country's top CEOs. From what I was hearing, the White House energetically courted Cooper in hopes he would give up on his own plan and support the administration. It didn't work. For a long time, Jim and Fred remained convinced their plan would ultimately prevail.

But following the early burst of support for "Clinton lite," the number of co-signers dwindled to a trickle and then stopped altogether when its reliance on a tax increase and deficit spending sunk in. It called for taxing high-end "Cadillac" insurance plans, a proposal opposed by members on the left and right, including those opposing any tax increase and labor organizations which had negotiated generous coverage. The plan also depended on projected savings and revenue-raising provisions to cover its estimated costs. But, according to a Congressional Budget Office (CBO) analysis, the savings and revenue would have fallen short. With federal budget deficits soaring in recent years, any plan that would put the country deeper in the red was anathema to many members of Congress in both parties, including Mike and me. We didn't sign on as co-sponsors.

The Cooper-Grandy bill was competing with the Clinton plan. The Rowland-Bilirakis bill really wasn't. The two main bipartisan health care reform bills in the House proposed two distinctly different plans designed for distinctly different purposes. Both the Clinton plan and the Cooper-Grandy "Clinton lite" plan were seeking to extensively revise the system, one based more on government control and the other more on the free market. The Rowland-Bilirakis bill simply proposed to fix as many problems as possible, a plan designed to pass if nothing more far-reaching could. Our consensus plan would have accomplished a lot, however.

It would have restricted insurers from denying coverage for preexisting conditions; protected employees who were covered in the workplace from losing coverage when changing jobs; fully deducted the cost of individual health care coverage on tax returns; minimized paperwork costs and hassles by streamlining the administration of government health care programs; strengthened anti-fraud rules; enacted anti-trust reform to allow more consolidation of medical technology to avoid costly duplication; and set limits on pain and suffering awards in medical malpractice suits to reduce the cost of defensive medicine.

The Clinton plan and the major alternative plans included a limit on malpractice awards. These tort reform proposals were more modest than many medical professionals would have liked. But any step in the right direction would have been welcome.

The Rowland-Bilirakis bill would have been financed without a tax increase, deficit spending, bureaucratic expansion, price controls, or a mandate requiring employers to pay for employee coverage.

On March 3, 1994, we introduced the Rowland-Bilirakis bill, officially entitled the Health Reform Consensus Act. Several weeks later, *The Washington Times*, ran an op-ed column written by Mike and me. "We need to face facts," we said. "Unless altered considerably, none of the high-profile plans are likely to pass." We said it was misleading to describe the Rowland-Bilirakis bill as a half-measure, pointing out it would "embody the most far-reaching changes in our nation's health care system since the creation of the Medicare and Medicaid programs" and "provide real relief" for millions of Americans.

CHAPTER TWENTY

Early in the summer of 1994, the syndicated newspaper columnist and well-known TV commentator Morton Kondracke wrote a column identifying the Rowland-Bilirakis bill as the only health care reform plan with a chance. He pronounced the Clinton plan and all pending health care reform plans other than the Rowland-Bilirakis bill dead if not yet buried. The national media had previously paid only passing attention to our "minimalist" bill. Following Kondracke's column, media coverage of the consensus plan dramatically increased. ABC network television newsman John Cochran, arranging an interview with me in front of Wrightsville's community health center, echoed Kondracke's assessment of the Rowland-Bilirakis bill as the last chance for health care reform.

Forty-nine Democrats and forty-nine Republicans signed the Rowland-Bilirakis bill as co-sponsors. To give the bill a strictly bipartisan appearance, Mike and I decided to keep the number of Democratic and Republican co-sponsors the same. But many other Republican members assured us they would cosponsor the bill anytime we were ready. Although the Republican House Whip Newt Gingrich has never denied he conspired to kill health care reform in an effort to overturn Democratic control of Congress, he supported the Rowland-Bilirakis bill. Newt even offered to join as a cosponsor. But he was a partisan lightening rod and we turned him down. Rep. Dennis Hastert, the moderate Republican from Illinois who was appointed coordinator of a House Republican task force on health care reform by House Minority Leader Bob Michel of Illinois, backed the Rowland-Bilirakis bill.

Considering the hostility of House Majority Leader Dick Gephardt and Energy and Commerce Committee Chairman John Dingell, it was remarkable as many as forty-nine Democrats signed the measure. Many House Democrats frankly told us they didn't want to put their names on the bill and risk offending their party's leadership if it wasn't going to be considered on the House floor. But many told us we could count on their votes if the bill ever reached the floor. We were confident the consensus bill could pass if the House Democratic leadership would ever let it out of committee.

Although we hoped key leaders like Gephardt and Dingell would eventually agree to consider the measure rather than settle for nothing, it didn't look encouraging based on what they were saying. In a *New York Times* article, the House majority leader called the Rowland-Bilirakis bill the "Rowland-Republican bill," derisively suggesting I was consorting with Republicans to defeat legitimate reform. When Dingell commented publicly on our bill, he illogically insisted it would perpetuate the system's problems and even make them worse.

Why were they hostile? The reforms in the consensus bill were reforms they supported. I understand they didn't like our bill because it didn't do as much as they wanted. But, while I would like to have addressed the problems more extensively myself, I thought it just made good sense to accomplish as much as possible. If Democratic leaders like Dick Gephardt and John Dingell thought our "minimal" bill was luring Democratic support from the more expansive Clinton plan, they were mistaken if not delusional. The real reasons more Democrats weren't supporting the Clinton plan were its costs, bureaucracy, and political unpopularity. Bipartisanship wasn't standing in the way of the great humanitarian cause of health care reform. But their resistance to a bipartisan agreement was.

I can only guess that Gephardt and Dingell needed a scapegoat for the gridlock they created by refusing to consider a true compromise. I also believe the increasingly-polarized environment in Congress made it easier for them to reject bipartisanship and adhere to their all-or-nothing position.

It was late in the debate when Dick Gephardt told me he would bring a Clinton-type plan, a single-payer plan, and the bipartisan consensus plan to the House floor following the August 1994 recess. At that point, the debate was still alive in the Senate. If the House majority leader had promptly done what he said he would do when Congress returned to work after the recess, a window of opportunity appeared to exist for passing a plan and sending it to the Senate before Senate Republicans had mobilized for a filibuster. Instead, Dick Gephardt pulled the plug in the House. George Mitchell pulled the plug in the Senate when it was clear the number of Republicans supporting a filibuster had grown to the point where a cloture motion to stop a filibuster couldn't pass.

If the House Energy and Commerce Committee had reported out the Rowland-Bilirakis bill with John Dingell's blessing, the majority leader and speaker might well have let it come to a vote in the whole House. But I had learned a couple of months earlier John Dingell didn't intend to let the committee he chaired consider the consensus plan.

I was part of the congressional delegation that flew to France in early June to participate in the fiftieth anniversary observance of the D Day invasion of Normandy while Congress was in recess. As I stood in a line with others in our delegation to enter a building where a D Day ceremony was to be held, the chairman approached me from behind and draped his arm around my shoulder. "Roy," he said, "your bill will never see the light of day." He was referring to the Rowland-Bilirakis bill. Taken by surprise, I said "I know that, Mr. Chairman." But I hadn't really known for sure until then. While Dingell couldn't get enough votes within the committee to report out the Clinton plan, he had the power to keep our consensus bill in deep freeze.

After this encounter, Mike and I talked about forming an independent House group to expand our consensus bill so it would come closer to achieving the goals of the Clinton plan while avoiding the Clinton plan's policy and political problems. As improbable as it seemed, we still thought it was possible to somehow figure out a plan that would come close enough to providing universal care to force Dick Gephardt and other House Democratic leaders to consider it. We knew such a plan had so far eluded everyone seeking a bipartisan solution. But if we could consolidate the bipartisan forces in the House behind one plan, we thought it was worth a try.

Jim Cooper wasn't interested when we approached him earlier about merging our efforts. Even if the Cooper-Grandy bill was locked-up in the Energy and Commerce Committee like the Rowland-Bilirakis bill, he was convinced his plan would eventually prevail in the Senate where the majority leaders were more receptive to a bipartisan option. When we approached him again, he still wasn't interested. But Mike and I decided to organize a new bipartisan task force whether or not Cooper and Grandy participated.

Considering how confused and volatile the debate had become, it was surprising we were able to talk six of the strongest personalities in the House into taking part in a longshot attempt to save health care reform. Joining us were Democratic Reps. Charles Stenholm of Texas, Dave McCurdy of Oklahoma, and Mike Parker of Mississippi and Republican Reps. Hastert, Bill Thomas of California, and Porter Goss of Florida. The media dubbed us the "Gang of Eight."

Rep. Stenholm, a farmer and vocational education teacher who held a Master's Degree from Texas Tech, had co-founded and led the caucus of conservative House Democrats called the Conservative Democratic Forum, later called the Blue Dog Coalition. Rep. McCurdy, an Oklahoma University law school graduate, was a fast-rising figure in the Democratic Party who served as chairman of the House Intelligence Committee. He had been a major campaigner in Bill Clinton's presidential race and, while still in his forties, was seen as a future presidential candidate himself.

Rep. Parker, a businessman who graduated from William Carey College in Mississippi, represented the most conservative wing of the Democratic Party, the only Democrat to vote against his party's candidate for speaker in the next term, Dick Gephardt.

Rep. Hastert, a former high school teacher and coach who graduated from Wheaton College in Illinois, was a moderate Republican leader who later served as House speaker longer than any Republican in history. I was shocked when he was accused long after his retirement from Congress of moral transgressions when he was a coach and teacher years before. In the 1990s, he was respected on both sides of the aisle. Rep. Thomas, who held a master's degree from San Francisco State University, later served as chairman of the House Ways and Means Committee, a moderate described by *Washingtonian Magazine* as one of the smartest and hardest working members of Congress. Rep. Goss, a Yale graduate, was a former CIA operative. He later served as chairman of the House Intelligence Committee and CIA director, a moderate who was especially productive on environmental as well as security issues.

Not long after we went to work, Fred Grandy decided bipartisan unity over health care reform was a good idea. Fred had gotten in trouble with some Republican leaders for generically criticizing those in his party who didn't work as hard to pass a health care reform bill they could support as they did in opposing the Clinton plan. Now he privately urged Jim Cooper to join with our new bipartisan initiative and the Tennessean finally agreed. The "Gang of Eight" became the "Gang of Ten."

We worked at a feverish pitch through July and into August, attending lengthy, exhausting work sessions just about every day we were in session, often staying late into the night. The group designated me as chairman and we met regularly in my office. We secured the help of a number of outside health care experts who joined us as advisors, augmenting the advice we received from our own staffers who specialized in health care. We studied tons of information and explored countless ideas, adopting some, revising others, and discarding many.

Time was running out and we were under extreme pressure to get the job done. We constantly fought fatigue and frustration and more than once came close to giving up, only to return the next day and make a breakthrough that kept us going. Although we knew getting the House Democratic leadership to consider any proposal would be a tough challenge, we felt a sense of extraordinary accomplishment on the day we signed off on the new plan entitled the Bipartisan Health Care Reform Act. Although it would take a while to draft a formal bill, we produced an extensive outline on August 11 for consideration by President Clinton, Congress, the media, and the public.

No measure of this magnitude could be perfect from everyone's point of view. But our group had found a way to address the health care system's deficiencies more comprehensively than any other market-oriented plan conceived during the long and contentious debate. An impartial CBO analysis calculated it would have extended coverage from eighty-five percent to ninety-two percent of the population. Although we couldn't come up with a cost-effective way to reach President Clinton's ninety-five percent threshold, our plan would have provided coverage for more than twenty-one million Americans who had none.

The CBO said the plan would slightly elevate national health care costs. But the CBO also found it would bring Medicaid spending under better control and reduce the federal budget deficit by $65 billion over ten years. It didn't provide the prescription drug, mental health, catastrophic, and long-term care programs offered in the Clinton plan. But it also didn't include the political deal-breakers in the Clinton plan such as a bigger government bureaucracy, price controls, or a mandate requiring employers to pay for employee coverage.

However, the Bipartisan Health Care Reform Act would have been a better deal for employees by not including the Clinton plan's employer mandate. It also would have subsidized coverage for low income citizens; provided financial incentives for individuals to purchase coverage; made health insurance premiums fully deductible for the self-employed and partly-deductible for employees whose employers didn't contribute to their coverage; provided all of the reforms in the consensus plan including assured coverage for people with preexisting conditions and portability of coverage from job to job; and included our community health center expansion plan, starting with demonstration projects.

"We sought to develop a new plan that truly fixes what is broken and keeps what works," I told *The New York Times*. The *Times* quoted Jim Cooper as saying, "The principles that united people from both parties were that health care reform should be voluntary, it should be market-driven, and it should offer maximum consumer choice." That's what this new plan would do while reaching a higher level of guaranteed coverage, he noted.

At this point, it was doubtful Newt would support this or any new proposal. We may have lost the support of his wing of the Republican Party. But the ten of us wouldn't have produced such a plan if we weren't sure it would be acceptable to many moderate members on both sides of the aisle.

Knowing labor would oppose any plan without a mandated employer contribution, the White House quickly issued a statement denouncing our plan. According to a White House spokesperson quoted in *The New York Times*, the new bipartisan plan wouldn't help middle class people, older Americans, or small businesses. But, in fact, it would have made coverage affordable and available for millions of middle income, elderly, and business people. The *Times* quoted an unnamed White House official as saying our plan wouldn't came close to the president's goal of guaranteed health insurance for all Americans. Although ninety-two percent was less than ninety-five percent, it was a lot closer to the president's goal than staying at eighty-five percent.

Rep. Vic Fazio of California, chairman of the Democratic Congressional Campaign Committee, stated that Republicans had "an inordinate amount of influence" in designing the plan. That wasn't accurate. Democrats had as much input as Republicans, including Dave McCurdy who had campaigned for Clinton in thirty-seven states and seconded Clinton's nomination at the Democratic National Convention. But Rep. Fazio's comment provided an insight into the thinking of some Democratic leaders, especially in the House, who weren't eager to share credit with Republicans on health care reform and were quick to reject any bipartisan proposal.

This was one of President Clinton's lowest moments. Even if he wasn't thrilled with the plan, he could have opened negotiations to see if it could have been altered to his liking. After all, our plan included a number of the same provisions as his plan. As I saw it, his instant rejection of this last chance for health care reform was prompted by short-sighted political considerations.

Dick Gephardt finally spoke out a couple of weeks later. With the media hounding him with questions about the latest bipartisan proposal, he called a news conference at the Capitol. Scores of reporters filled the room. Gephardt attacked the new bipartisan plan in the most inflammatory language possible, saying it would "steal from our seniors." Although it didn't include all the benefits promised in the Clinton plan, no one had accused sponsors of health care bills in the past that didn't include these same benefits of stealing from seniors. A representative of an organization supporting the Clinton plan, the Consumer Union, who appeared at the Gephardt news conference, declared it "didn't come close to providing universal care." Some critics could never accept the fact that ninety-two percent was better than eighty-five percent.

After the House majority leader tried to modify the health care reform vehicle reported out of the Ways and Means Committee in an apparent attempt to make it acceptable to more moderates without offending labor and other-single payer advocates, he must have realized he had created a dud. It would have been politically embarrassing if the plan he helped write was overwhelmingly defeated and a plan he had attacked was passed.

When I returned to Washington from Georgia following the Labor Day recess, Kathy Hennemuth, my legislative health care aide, informed me she heard a rumor that Gephardt no longer intended to bring any plan to the floor. After calling to make sure he was in, I went to the majority leader's office to find out what was going on. This time his manner was terse and hardly friendly. That's right, he said, no health care reform plan would be considered by the full House. I asked why. That's when he told me people were no longer interested in health care reform. I didn't prolong the conversation. He was telling me the debate was over and I knew nothing I said would change his mind.

By quietly siding with Gephardt, Speaker Tom Foley let the debate end without giving the full House an opportunity to vote on any plan. Other backers of the Clinton plan in the House disagreed with this decision. Key Democratic leaders like John Dingell, Billy Ford, Sam Gibbons, and Dan Rostenkowski let it be known behind the scenes that they would have preferred a showdown on the floor. But with the speaker's apparent backing, Gephardt was the first to shut down the debate in Congress.

Meanwhile, the debate was also faltering in the Senate. But it wasn't quite over in the upper chamber. Sen. Mitchell and the bipartisan mainstream coalition had frantically hammered out a new compromise during the Labor Day recess. They still believed a compromise could pass. But suddenly they were confronted by two huge obstacles.

Some Senate Republicans were mobilizing for a filibuster and Newt Gingrich had openly warned the White House that a continuation of the debate would jeopardize Republican support for the General Agreement on Tariffs and Trade (GATT), another treaty the administration considered essential to U.S. influence in international economics. With labor opposing GATT, Republican support was needed for ratification of the trade pact.

Had the emerging filibuster and the threat to GATT already effectively killed health care reform on both sides of the Capitol by the time members returned from the recess? Some members thought so. Democratic Sen. Frank Lautenberg of New Jersey was one of those who was certain no compromise could attract the 51 votes needed for passage by then, let alone the 60 votes needed to invoke cloture. "Republicans played gridlock politics... and their behavior was disgraceful," he declared.

To be sure, some Republicans were playing gridlock politics. But so was the Democratic majority leader in the House. If Dick Gephardt had allowed a bipartisan compromise to reach the House floor immediately following the recess as he first said he would, I'm confident it would have passed with broad bipartisan support. And if the House had promptly sent the Senate such a compromise, I don't see how Republicans could have mounted a filibuster against it without the blame for the downfall of health care reform shifting to their party. Moreover, I question whether the Republicans would have retaliated against GATT, a separate issue with different dynamics.

Just before the recess, a moderate Republican freshman from New Jersey, Jim Saxton, stated on the House floor, "There is tremendous bipartisan desire by Republicans and Democrats alike to pass a bill. We should take an approach that we can all agree on rather than try to push through a bill regardless of the views of the American people." He was absolutely right. At the time of the recess, and immediately thereafter, a substantial compromise could have passed.

On September 26, Sen. Mitchell announced at a news conference the debate was over. "Under the rules of the Senate, a minority can obstruct the majority," he said, adding, "This is what happened to health care reform." While he was correct, he didn't mention his House Democratic counterpart had already ended the debate on his side of the Capitol.

The failure of a Democratic president and the Democratic majorities in the House and Senate to deliver on the health care reform promise was a major factor in the upheaval that occurred in the 1994 mid-term elections on November 6, 1994. Democrats lost control of the House and Senate. Tom Foley became the first speaker since 1862 to lose a race for reelection. Jim Cooper and Jim Slattery, the two Democrats John Dingell tried to recruit to get the Clinton plan out of the Energy and Commerce Committee, lost to GOP candidates in their races for the Senate and governor. Democrat Harris Wofford, who had pulled an upset in his Senate race against a better-known Republican candidate by emphasizing health care reform, lost to Republican Rick Santorum. Health care reform didn't help Republican Fred Grandy, either. He lost his race for governor in the Republican primary.

Dick Gephardt and John Dingell were reelected. But, of course, they lost their majority positions. Gephardt became House minority leader instead of majority leader and Dingell became the ranking member of the Energy and Commerce Committee instead of chairman.

The Health Insurance Portability and Accountability Act, more commonly known as the Kassebaum-Kennedy bill, wasn't as far-reaching as the Rowland-Bilirakis bill. But it was based on the same concept. The big difference, wrote *The Macon Telegraph and News* Washington correspondent Nolan Walters, was that President Clinton and Democratic congressional leaders "wanted it this time (and) last time they didn't." No longer was a consensus bill worse than nothing. In the words of President Clinton, it was now a "long step toward the kind of health care our nation needs." When Americans spoke out at the ballot box, political leaders in Washington finally listened.

David Broder wrote these words when he signed a copy of *The System* for me: "To Doc Rowland, who tried so hard to give this story a better ending." So did many others. But those of us who worked to enact the best plan possible didn't control the process.

The miracle hasn't yet occurred. Following the 2016 elections, virtually everyone agreed the Affordable Care Act should be extensively changed if not repealed in its entirety. I still believe passage of a managed competition system guaranteeing affordable, quality care for everyone is possible. But I doubt it will happen until the country's vital center is empowered more than it was during the tragicomic 1993-94 debate over health care reform.

CHAPTER TWENTY-ONE

As the 1984 election approached, I viewed my first race for reelection with some apprehension. Two years had passed since I carried Georgia's Eighth Congressional District soundly in 1982 and I had no assurance my base of support had remained secure. I had worked hard to stay in touch with the people I represented. But I didn't know what kind of political backlash to expect from some of the controversial issues we dealt with during my first two years on Capitol Hill, most notably the Martin Luther King, Jr. holiday bill.

I was fortunate. Although Billy Evans had said he might run against me again in two years, the qualifying deadline passed with no one challenging me in either the Democratic or Republican primaries.

I had maintained a close relationship with Democratic activists, local government officials, and state legislators throughout the Eighth District. During the General Assembly session, I had hosted the state legislators from my area at a luncheon in Atlanta, something I would do every term I served in Congress. I had passed the Quaalude bill, one of the few first-termers to get a major bill enacted. I had made many appearances at town meetings and other events in the district. We had maintained an effective constituent services program and had answered constituent calls and letters promptly. I had received extensive coverage from our dailies, weeklies, radio stations and WMAZ-TV in Macon, our principal television station. If my vote for the King holiday left some constituents angry, it also solidified support within the black community and among some Democratic movers and shakers like Macon's Gus Kaufman who generally sided with the party's national agenda.

All of these factors put me in reasonably good political standing in my district. The Republican Party was growing stronger in most areas of the state, including the Eighth District. But it would be a few more years before the GOP would become Georgia's dominant party.

Even without opposition, I conducted an active reelection campaign in 1984, running newspaper, television and radio ads, doing media interviews, and making personal campaign-related appearances. Reporters asked me why I bothered. As I saw it, campaigns give elected officeholders an opportunity to tell their side of the story. I had held fund raisers in anticipation of a competitive race and had the means to finance a media campaign. I could have saved the contributions for use in a later race. But running campaign ads in 1984 was an effective way of emphasizing what I was doing to live up to my promise to be a congressman people could be proud of. By not doing more campaigning when unopposed, my predecessor had contributed to the impression he had lost touch with constituents.

Two years later, my luck continued. Once again I had no Democratic opposition. This time I was opposed in the Republican primary, but it was token opposition. A resident of Waycross, Eddie McDowell, an African American who identified himself as an entertainer and a manager of musical groups, entered as the only Republican candidate. He qualified as a pauper, enabling him to get his name on the ballot without paying a qualifying fee. Although I heard he had once run as a self-styled candidate for president, few people involved in politics and few among the public at-large knew him. To my knowledge, he never attacked me during the campaign. If he campaigned at all, I never crossed paths with him when traveling around the district.

Once again, I sponsored an ad campaign emphasizing my record. I received eighty-six percent of the vote. Although I won by an overwhelming margin, it was striking for an unknown candidate who barely participated in the campaign to receive as much as fourteen percent of the vote. Apparently he attracted a significant number of votes just by running as a Republican. This was a sign an historic change was taking place after more than a century of Democratic dominance.

From this point on, my campaigns for reelection would get more difficult. Fortunately, as an incumbent, it was easier to raise funds and I was able to organize better-financed, more professional campaigns. I retained political consultants of national stature like Deloss Walker of Memphis, Hank Sheinkopf of New York, and Saul Shorr of Philadelphia to advise us on the advertising and strategizing. I never stopped holding occasional fund-raisers in the district and in Washington, D.C.

In the 1988 race, I escaped a Republican challenge. But a former Democratic state legislator from Hazlehurst, Bayne Stone, entered the Democratic primary. Unlike Eddie McDowell, Bayne was politically experienced, had some organized support, and modest campaign financing. He campaigned energetically, attacking me for ineffectiveness, failing to develop "rapport" among my House colleagues and the House leadership, and for supporting big business and the "elite" over working men and women of the Eighth District. In response, I cited examples in my record contradicting his criticisms. The media endorsed me across the board.

An editorial in *The Macon Telegraph* said that "in his quiet way" I had gained the respect of my colleagues, adding I had "often acted as a bridge between liberals and conservatives and played a pivotal role on issues such as anti-drug laws, clean water, and help for veterans suffering from atomic radiation." The editorial also noted I had introduced the legislation that established a National Commission on AIDS and had kept in close contact with the home folks.

This time I received eighty-eight percent of the vote. Bayne told the media he could hardly believe the lopsided outcome. "I thought I had a better message than that," he said. While I thought his message missed the mark, I was surprised by the margin myself. Bayne received only twelve percent of the vote, two percent less than Eddie McDowell. Apparently I had solidified my political support. But the results also reflected the fact that Bayne wasn't running as a Republican at a time when more Georgians were voting a straight Republican ticket.

If I hoped all my races would be as easy as the first three, it was wishful thinking. Over the next four years I would twice be challenged by a Republican candidate who would run strong campaigns with an experienced campaign staff and the backing of his party's establishment on the local, state and even national levels. These races would get as mean as politics can get and my margins of victory would narrow. With the Republican party rising in Georgia and the South, the advantage of incumbency for a Democratic officeholder like me was fading.

Robert F. "Bob" Cunningham, who owned and operated a Macon insurance agency, was the Republican nominee in the 1990 and 1992 Eighth District congressional races. An Atlanta native who moved to Macon in 1959, he had served as chairman of the Bibb County Republican Party. A strongly-conservative ex-Marine, he viewed a moderate conservative like me as a big-spending liberal. Except for Evans, Cunningham was the strongest candidate I had faced. His political strength came from the same affluent Republicans in Macon and other areas of the district who had backed Billy in his last race.

While he had to engage in negative campaigning to have a chance, he would hurt himself by resorting to accusations that stretched credibility.

He accused me of "unbridled and extravagant" spending, a message he promoted in television, radio and newspaper ads, in interviews, and in campaign appearances. I had cosponsored a constitutional amendment to require balanced federal budgets and had consistently voted against budgets proposed by the Democratic and Republican leadership because they failed to cut deficit spending enough while supporting alternative deficit-reducing measures. But my Republican opponent could back up his big-spending accusation by citing surveys on congressional spending by two conservative organizations, the National Taxpayers Union and the American Conservative Union. These organizations issued congressional voting surveys on spending issues that I believed relied on "cherry-picking." Because they selected spending measures the organizations considered fiscally responsible while excluding competing measures I believed were just as fiscally responsible, if not more so, I thought their surveys produced biased results.

Jim Wooten, *The Atlanta Journal's* conservative editor of the editorial page, wrote a column prior to the 1990 general election supporting Cunningham's accusation. Wooten stated my votes on spending issues matched that of Rep. John Lewis of Atlanta, one of the more liberal members of Congress. This was ludicrous. My voting record was strikingly different than John's. Although Jim Wooten's basis for such a comparison wasn't entirely clear, his assessment was apparently based on voting surveys I considered misleading.

The Conservative Democratic Forum, the moderate-to-conservative House caucus in which I participated, periodically compiled composite ratings of all the major congressional voting surveys including the National Taxpayers Union, the American Conservative Union, the U.S. Chamber of Commerce, and others. Using a liberal-to-conservative scale of zero to 1,000, the Conservative Democratic Forum survey placed members of Congress into five categories—liberal, moderate liberal, moderate, moderate conservative, and conservative. In the latest compilation before Jim Wooten's column, I scored 580 and John Lewis scored 104, making me a moderate conservative and John a liberal. My career-long composite score was the same as it was for that year, 580.

Criticizing me for not voting to cut the country's social safety-net as much as Jim Wooten would have liked was certainly fair. But trying to portray me as a flaming liberal on spending issues was inaccurate and unbelievable. It didn't wash with the rest of the media or with most constituents. Among the newspaper endorsements I received in the 1990 campaign was one by *The Waycross Journal-Herald* which said, "We believe the record categorically reveals Rep. Rowland to be on the conservative-to-moderate side of the fiscal ledger and we heartily support him for reelection to Congress."

I won with sixty-eight percent of the vote. The rising tide of Republicanism was a factor in Cunningham's thirty-two percent vote total. He finished twenty percent stronger than Bayne Stone did as a Democrat. The black electorate was a big factor in my sixty-eight percent margin. In 1990, thirty-seven percent of the population in the Eighth District was black. At the time, about ninety-five percent of the black vote was dependably cast for Democratic candidates in races against Republicans. A substantial decrease in the district's black population in 1992 would enhance the chances of a Republican challenger even more.

Under the U.S. Constitution, states must realign congressional districts every ten years to adjust for population trends over the previous decade. The Georgia General Assembly was called upon to adopt a congressional redistricting plan in time for the 1992 election. The plan had to be acceptable to the U.S. Justice Department under the Voting Rights Act. Prior to 1992, Georgia had one black-majority district. But with the state's black population at twenty-seven percent, the Justice Department wouldn't accept any congressional redistricting plan that didn't include three black majority districts out of the state's eleven congressional districts. This goal couldn't be achieved without making alterations in every congressional district. The creation of two new black-majority districts inevitably had a domino effect on the configuration of the remaining districts.

Most of Georgia's incumbent members of the U.S. House, including myself, repeatedly visited the Georgia Capitol while the redistricting process was underway to lobby for keeping our current districts as intact as possible. Every member from a white-majority district, including myself, was certain to lose black citizens who mostly voted for Democratic candidates and gain more citizens who voted for Republican candidates. I lobbied for a redistricting plan that would minimize this shift as much as possible in the Eighth District. My colleague representing the neighboring Third District, Richard Ray, was doing the same thing for his area. As the General Assembly got deeply into the process, it came down to an unspoken tug-of-war between Richard and myself.

Richard's brother, Robert Ray, was a member of the House Reapportionment Committee. Robert did everything within his power to protect Richard's interests as he should have done. If Richard had ended up with a district with a minimal Democratic-to-Republican shift, it would have left me with a more extensively altered district. But I, too, had help. While Tom Murphy didn't have anything against Richard, I was closer to the Georgia House speaker than he was. And Tom Murphy would have a significant influence on the final outcome.

I also had an ally in Jim Comerford and the Medical Association of Georgia (MAG). Jim had gone to work for the MAG following law school. He had convinced the organization to purchase a sophisticated computer program in order to design redistricting proposals that would meet the Justice Department guidelines while creating congressional districts favorable to candidates the MAG particularly supported, including me. The nuts-and-bolts work on redistricting was primarily done by the General Assembly's outstanding reapportionment staff. But the MAG shared its proposals with key legislators and I believe these proposals influenced the final plan enacted by the General Assembly.

Late in the process, I was contacted by key legislators working on reapportionment and told Richard Ray and I could work out the details of our own districts from among the counties that would potentially be placed in the Eighth and Third districts. I went to Richard and suggested we agree on a plan that would balance the problems for both of us. He turned me down. With the help of his brother, he was confident the legislature would give him an advantageous district. If this left me with a politically-disadvantageous district, that wasn't his problem. He misread the political dynamics.

One of Tom Murphy's main objectives in congressional reapportionment was doing as much damage to Newt Gingrich as possible. The speaker didn't care for Newt. Tom also looked after me as much as possible. When the final plan emerged from a House and Senate reapportionment conference committee, much of the Republican-dominated urbanized southern portion of Newt Gingrich's Sixth District was shifted into Richard Ray's Third District. This put Richard in an almost-hopeless situation. It didn't help that his vote against the King bill made it difficult to energize the black vote remaining in the district. Newt moved into a more favorable district and was reelected in spite of the speaker's efforts. But Richard lost by nearly ten percentage points to his Republican opponent, Mac Collins of Henry County.

Although I fared much better in reapportionment than Richard, I was still left with a different district. The black population dropped from thirty-seven percent in the old Eighth District to eighteen percent in the new Eighth, boosting Cunningham's chances. The district now extended into new areas of southwest Georgia including a portion of Albany.

An Albany high school teacher, Bill Lightle, challenged me in the 1992 Democratic primary. He was a beginner as a political candidate. But he was keenly interested in politics, taking a moderately-liberal position on many issues. In spite of his lack of campaign experience, he put together a fairly strong campaign organization and attracted a substantial following, especially in the district's new areas. As a bright new figure on the Democratic political scene, he appealed to many Democratic Party workers in the Eighth District who gave him campaign advice even while most continued to support me. Since I viewed him as a long-shot in the primary, I decided to save campaign money for the more difficult general election race against Bob Cunningham and wage a minimal primary campaign. This was a factor in the outcome. So was the growing public discontent with politics in general, which Bill Lightle capitalized on.

When my Democratic opponent received thirty-two percent of the vote, I was surprised. Although we were aware from our polling he was doing fairly well, we weren't expecting him to receive nearly a third of the vote. His impressive showing undoubtedly buoyed the hopes of Bob Cunningham and encouraged state and national Republican strategists to target the Eighth District. Former Vice President Dan Quayle came to Georgia's Eighth District to campaign for Cunningham, an indication of the high-powered national Republican help Cunningham received. Republican challengers were defeating Democrats in increasing numbers throughout the South and the latest congressional reapportionment plan would accelerate this trend.

This time, Cunningham turned the heat up even higher than he had two years before. Fortunately for me, he got off on a bad foot and never fully recovered.

In TV campaign commercials, he accused me of missing more than a hundred votes as a result of junkets he said I had taken to thirteen foreign countries at taxpayers' expense. Professional political operatives say candidates in competitive races should run hard-hitting campaigns. But they also say candidates should be careful not to make factual mistakes in attacking opponents. Erroneous attacks usually come back to bite the attacker. Cunningham and his campaign advisers got their facts wrong.

I called a news conference and produced documented proof that I had made four congressional-sponsored foreign trips, not thirteen. Each of them was for a legitimate congressional purpose. I also showed I had compiled a ninety-eight percent voting record, among the highest in Congress, missing 116 of 4,789 votes during my ten years in office. But none of the missed votes was due to congressional travel, which I did during congressional recesses. A number of the 116 votes were missed as a result of my mother's death and my son's serious illness. At the news conference, I called on Cunningham to apologize for spreading misinformation.

When confronted by reporters, he said he had no intention of retracting or apologizing for anything. "I don't have time to fool with whether the trips were thirteen, sixteen, eighteen or whatever," he said. This was not his best response. By saying he didn't have time to fool with the facts, *The Telegraph* said in an editorial, "We are left to conclude he only wanted to fool the voters." The editorial also said, "Taking off the gloves and punching hard is within the rules. But hitting below the belt is not. Spouting obvious untruths is not. Cunningham loses points on both."

Cunningham remained on the attack, at one point joking he wished I had skipped more votes such as my vote for a congressional pay raise. When politicians give themselves a pay raise, it can be a major political problem. But in this case he wasn't telling the whole truth. The bill I voted for did include a pay raise, but one that wouldn't take effect until the next term. I had voted against increases in congressional pay during current terms and even sponsored legislation to prohibit current pay raises. In this case, the bill was really more of a pay reform than a pay increase bill. It offset the future raise by imposing tight restrictions on outside income received by members.

The long-overdue 1989 bill was entitled the Ethics Reform Act. It banned honoraria, money received for speeches, articles written for organizational publications, and personal appearances. When special interests paid big sums to lawmakers for making speeches, writing articles, or attending various functions, it could amount to influence peddling. The bill prohibited members from receiving directors' fees, legal fees, and other income for professional services. It banned gifts of more than $200 from anyone outside the family. It limited all outside income to no more than fifteen percent of the members' official salary. The pay increase and the reform bill actually reduced the overall income of many members. If I had voted against it, Cunningham could have attacked me for voting against pay reform. When the media interpreted the purpose of the bill as more about ethics than a pay raise, it neutralized the criticism.

Cunningham portrayed me as a supporter of the national homosexual agenda, a pronouncement featured in a flurry of TV ads. He was referring to my work on HIV-AIDS. The policies and programs I supported to combat a disease that was spreading at a devastating rate were those supported by leading authorities in the health care community including the

American Medical Association. He linked my positions on AIDS to the gay rights' agenda because gay rights' organizations generally supported the same policies and programs endorsed by the leading health care authorities.

Specifically, Cunningham attacked me for not supporting a U.S. ban on HIV-infected foreign travelers. In fact, I opposed the immigration of HIV-infected foreigners. Our health care system was already over-burdened by the disease. But banning HIV-infected travelers would have had harmful consequences without providing any real protection. A person infected with the virus posed no danger to anyone when simply traveling from one place to another. There were foreign scientists and health care experts who were working with their U.S. counterparts to bring the disease under control. If our borders had been closed to HIV-infected foreign travelers while foreign borders remained open to U.S.-infected travelers, these vitally-important cooperative efforts would have been disrupted. Scientists abroad were saying they wouldn't participate in AIDS initiatives in the U.S. if a travel ban was imposed. A proposed travel ban was a political issue that would have needlessly compromised international efforts to combat AIDS. The National Commission on AIDS, on which I served and was responsible for creating, recommended against an HIV-related travel prohibition.

It was my impression his attacks on this issue offended more people than they influenced.

Late in the campaign, my opponent ran ads calling me a big spender for voting against a Republican-backed bill aimed at reducing the budget deficit. My problem with the measure was its severe cuts in Medicare and several other important social programs. I supported an alternative deficit-reduction bill with more balanced spending cuts between defense and domestic programs. If Cunningham and his campaign advisers had carefully read the bill that I voted against, they would have found it proposed a whopping $27.2 billion cut in Medicare. As events would soon reveal, they didn't pay close enough attention to the specific provisions in the legislation. All they apparently focused on was the fact that it was a deficit-reduction bill and I had voted against it.

We produced an ad stating Bob Cunningham supported legislation that would slash Medicare by $27.2 billion. We taped the ad one day and had it running it on TV stations throughout the district the following day. This was a major threat to his campaign. Most senior citizens depend on Medicare coverage. Many react furiously when they think Medicare is seriously threatened. Seniors could make a big difference in the outcome of our race.

Cunningham called another news conference and denounced me for saying he would cut Medicare funding. He said he had never supported such a proposal and accused me of outright lying. As soon as the news conference ended, reporters called to ask me for an explanation. We were ready. We faxed every reporter a copy of the page of the lengthy bill Cunningham had publicly supported with the $27.2 billion cut in Medicare underlined. The stories that followed confirmed that our ads about the Medicare cut were accurate and Cunningham didn't seem to know what was in the legislation he supported. A newsman who covered the Cunningham campaign told us later that one of Cunningham's campaign staff members said they believed they would win until this incident occurred. Our polling indicated we would probably have won anyway. But it would have been a much closer vote.

We ran ads accusing my opponent of lies and distortions. If Cunningham had accepted responsibility for making inaccurate accusations, I couldn't have used such strong language in responding. But he steadfastly refused, and our strongly-worded counterattacks took a toll on his campaign. When the votes were counted, I won the hard-fought race with fifty-six percent of the vote. According to Charles Bullock, a University of Georgia political science professor, the Eighth was the only Georgia congressional district where the bulk of the white vote went Democratic. The reason, he said, was an "attachment to Rowland."

However, the fact that Cunningham had gained twelve percentage points over the previous two years in spite of running an error-filled campaign was a sign the political landscape was changing. In another *Atlanta*

Journal editorial Jim Wooten observed, "Democrats who attract moderate and conservative white voters, like J. Roy Rowland of Dublin, are a species headed for extinction." This time I knew he was probably right.

After his second defeat, Cunningham publicly announced he wouldn't run again. The Eighth District Republican candidate in 1994 was a prominent Moultrie attorney, Saxby Chambliss, who had started laying the groundwork to run not long after Cunningham's final loss. Chambliss had lost to Cunningham in the 1992 Republican primary. But now he had the solid backing of his party. By early 1994, he had already accumulated substantial campaign funds and developed a strong district-wide campaign organization. Although I didn't know him very well at the time, I thought Saxby Chambliss would probably be the most formidable challenger I had faced. He would confirm this impression by eventually winning congressional races multiple times, serving a long and distinguished career in the U.S. House and U.S. Senate.

Meanwhile, the 1993-94 term of Congress was perhaps the most exhilarating and disappointing two years I spent in Congress. I emerged as a leader among the moderate voices in the House and had co-produced the only House health care reform plan that could have passed if some Democratic House leaders hadn't refused to let it come to a vote. I held positions of leadership as the ranking Democrat in the Georgia House delegation, chairman of the House Veterans' Affairs health subcommittee, and, along with John Lewis, one of two Georgians on the House Democratic Steering and Policy Committee. But, like everyone else, I ended up emptyhanded in the health care reform debate and became somewhat isolated within the House Democratic Caucus.

Liberal Democrats particularly criticized me for voting against a job stimulus bill sponsored by President Clinton and the House Democratic leadership in 1993. Considering the bill too costly, I was the only Democrat in the Georgia House delegation and one of only twenty-two Democrats in Congress opposing it. I thought the bill would do more economic harm than good. In past years, I suspect little notice would have been taken within the

Democratic House Caucus over such a vote. But leaders within both parties were becoming less tolerant of those who took independent positions.

Sometime in late winter or early spring of 1994, I began thinking about retiring from Congress. The upcoming campaign certainly wasn't going to be a sure thing. While I was fairly confident I could continue to receive most of the black vote, I was also aware it would be difficult to retain enough of the white vote to survive. Even if I was reelected, I would not only face the party polarization in Congress, but also the deepening ideological polarization within the Democratic party.

A number of Democratic elected officeholders in Georgia and the South were switching to the Republican party. One of my colleagues in the Georgia House delegation, Nathan Deal, who was elected as a Democrat in his north Georgia district, switched parties and was eventually elected governor of Georgia as a Republican. Some friends suggested I should switch. But I had long stated I would rather fight than switch. Moreover, switching would have been a poor choice from a political standpoint. Saxby Chambliss had already cornered the support of most Republicans in the Eighth District. I started my political career as a Democrat and I would end it as a Democrat.

For several days I struggled with the question of whether or not to run. I discussed it with Luella, who would only say it was my decision. Then one morning as we were sitting at the breakfast table, I said, "I don't think I'll run again." "I'm glad," she responded.

That was it. After notifying my staff, and calling close supporters, we issued a news release early in April announcing my decision. It was big political news in the Georgia media. It was enough of a national story to appear on the inside pages of newspapers throughout the country.

The Associated Press said my efforts to enact a compromise health care reform plan were in keeping with the "reputation he built over the years as a conservative Democrat who could help bridge differences between the party's conservative and liberal wings." Washington correspondent Mario Christaldi, who represented a group of newspapers including

The Valdosta Daily Times in the Eighth District, also noted Democratic leaders viewed me as an "important link between conservative Southerners and more liberal Democrats."

Jeanne Cummings of *The Atlanta Journal-Constitution* Washington Bureau wrote that my retirement was a "blow to the already diminished influence of the Georgia congressional delegation." The Georgia House delegation had lost six veteran incumbents to retirement and election defeats in the previous election. Democratic Georgia Sen. Sam Nunn told her my retirement would be "a great loss to our state" and Republican Georgia Sen. Paul Coverdell called me a "legislator of unequalled vigor and character." The University of Georgia's Charles Bulloch was quoted as saying my departure would reduce the clout of the Georgia delegation and potentially hurt the whole Congress. "They've got all kinds of attorneys but they don't have someone like him who has that kind of expertise on health care," he said. My retirement left one physician among the 535 members of the House and Senate, Jim McDermott. *The Albany Herald* said it was "unfortunate" someone with my knowledge in health care had chosen not to run and recommended the voters replace me with someone who held the same political philosophy.

I appreciated a column by Bill Boyd in *The Macon Telegraph* that concluded with these words, "Let the record show we had a gentleman in Washington for the past twelve years."

Early in October, as the congressional term neared final adjournment, a number of House colleagues rose on the floor to express best wishes to me upon my retirement from the House. It's traditional for members to say nice things about someone who retires. But I was surprised and gratified by the remarks made about me that day. Among those who wished me well were Democrats and Republicans, liberals and conservatives. Here is a sampling of the remarks:

Sonny Callahan (R-AL): "He is a free spirit... who didn't take a position for party or political reasons and... often bucked conventional wisdom on how he might be expected to vote." Tillie Fowler (R-FL): "His kindness and good nature are legendary; his word is his bond, and he always gives a hundred and one percent to the task at hand." Charles Stenholm (D-TX): "In an era when politics has become increasingly contentious and heated, Dr. Rowland has always managed to maintain the soft voice and courteous manner." Jake Pickle (D-TX): "In my thirty-one years in Congress I have seldom met a member who was more caring, more compassionate, or more dedicated to the service of his district and country." Tom Bevill (D-AL): "He is one of the finest, most highly-respected members to ever serve in Congress." Buddy Darden (D-GA): "He made the hard vote when the political consequences could have been disastrous." Bill Hughes (D-N.J.): He is "one of the hardest working and most effective members of Congress... and a man of honesty and integrity who represents the very best in public service." Bill Thomas (R-CA): "He has demonstrated a strong sense of service to his fellow man.... Through his leadership (in health care reform) he showed that Republicans and Democrats can cooperate to achieve an end." Richard Lehman (D-CA): "Having practiced medicine, his ideas on specific medical issues and comprehensive health care reform always attracted the interest and consideration of his colleagues." Carlos Moorhead (R-CA): "As a member of the (Energy and Commerce) committee, he has made outstanding contributions to the committee's unparalleled record of achievement." Sanford Bishop (D-GA): "With Roy's hard work and medical knowledge, millions of Americans have been spared the addictive horrors of Quaalude use." Porter Goss (R-FL): "He is known as a true Southern gentleman... and a strong and independent voice for his constituents." Jim Cooper (D-TN): "It's been an honor to work with you.... You made Georgia and this nation proud." Jack Kingston (R-GA): "All of us in the Georgia delegation and those that have been fortunate to work with him through the years will miss Roy's counsel, his loyalty and his friendship." Cass Ballenger (R-NC): "Thanks for your years of dedicated service. You will be missed."

Also taking the floor to bid me farewell from the House was Rep. John Lewis, the Atlanta congressman who made history as a courageous young civil rights leader, a liberal with whom I was often in disagreement over the issues and a friend I greatly respect. He said: "I have known this man for several years. He is a good and decent man. He is a leader in the truest sense of the word." At the other end of the spectrum, Rep. Newt Gingrich said, "Congress and the American people have been enriched by the dedicated public service of Dr. Rowland." According to my longtime partner in health care reform, Mike Bilirakis, "Congress is losing one of its finest and most respected members."

I received a written note from Lee Hamilton, a Democratic from Indiana, whose scholarly expertise in foreign affairs made him one of the most highly-respected House members of our times, someone who was long considered a prime candidate for a place on the Democratic presidential-vice presidential ticket. "Throughout my years in Congress," he said, "only a few members stand out in my mind for their exceptional dedication to their tasks, and you are easily among them. It has been a high privilege to work with you."

Not everyone agreed. Dick Gephardt let his ill feelings toward me be known. After announcing my retirement, I asked a number of colleagues with whom I worked to have a photo taken with me as a remembrance, including those who generally sided with me on the issues and some who didn't. Although I wasn't happy about the way Dick Gephardt handled health care reform, I recognized his right to deal with issues according to his conscience. I certainly wasn't holding a personal grudge. When I asked him if he would take a moment to have a photo taken together, he told me to call his office and arrange it. When we called to make an appointment, we were advised by someone on his staff they would call back. We never heard from Gephardt.

The next year, after I had left Congress, I ran into Leon Panetta at a fund raiser for Rep. Ike Skelton of Missouri, a veteran Democratic House member who served as chairman of the House Armed Services Committee. Ike was a friend who had endorsed me for U.S. surgeon general. Leon's manner toward me was plainly unfriendly. When he was President

Clinton's budget director, he had appeared at a meeting of the House Conservative Democratic Forum to give a briefing on an administration budget proposal. I was among those asking some tough questions. Leon became testy and left. Although this incident might have been a factor, I suspect my opposition to the Clinton health care reform, one he also had qualms about, primarily prompted his unfriendliness.

These were just two incidents. But they were examples of how the environment was changing in Congress.

In December, after Joycelyn Elders left as surgeon general, one hundred House members signed a petition urging President Clinton to name me as the country's new "first doctor," a position that can exert national influence over health care. Democratic Rep. Gene Taylor of Mississippi, a close friend, initiated the petition. He said it took less than twenty-four hours to obtain the signatures. In the petition sent to the president, the signers said I was a person of "unwavering honesty and undeniable intelligence. Most importantly, he has the ability to communicate with all citizens in a manner that every American can understand." It concluded, "As former colleagues who know first-hand the dignity he would bring to that position, we respectfully request that you consider Dr. Rowland for the post of U.S. surgeon general."

Although I knew my role in the health care reform debate made it unlikely President Clinton would choose me for the post, I was honored by the trust many House members had in me.

When I left Congress at the age of sixty-eight, I had kept my medical license current and thought I would find a job connected to medicine. But I received a telephone call from Chuck Merrin, a lobbyist with a small Washington, D.C. "legislative strategies" (lobbying) firm, Gold and Liebengood. Chuck represented clients who opposed the Clinton health care reform plan and supported a bipartisan plan such as the one I co-sponsored with Mike Bilirakis. As allies working for the same cause, I had become well-acquainted with Chuck over the past couple of years. Through Chuck, I was offered a job as a lobbyist making more money than I had ever made before. Although I wasn't sure that's what I wanted to do, I took it. As I saw it, my job was to provide factual information in support of the clients we represented much like an attorney advocating the position of a client.

My career as a lobbyist lasted a couple of years. I couldn't shake the feeling I was asking for a favor when I talked to former colleagues in Congress about supporting issues I was paid to promote. I wasn't as aggressive as the firm would have liked. One day our boss, John Scruggs, called me into his office and offered to buy out my contract. In effect, he was firing me. It was embarrassing to get the boot for the first and only time in my life. But it was also a relief.

Back in Georgia, the Medical Association of Georgia asked me to temporarily serve as a consultant during the upcoming session of the Georgia General Assembly. In this capacity, I met Marge Smith, commissioner of the Georgia Department of Medical Assistance, the state's Medicaid agency. Marge offered me a position as the department's medical director on a three-days-a-week schedule so Luella and I wouldn't have to move to Atlanta fulltime. During my two years working with Marge, we made progress in improving the medical services for Georgia's lower-income population. When a new governor took office, Marge stepped down and so did I.

Meanwhile, the Laurens County Commission appointed me to a regional mental health oversight board. At a board meeting in June 1999, Patsy Thomas, the CEO for mental health services in the Dublin area, offered me a position on her staff, serving as general consultant with Patsy and later, when she passed away, with her successor, Denise Forbes. The work I do three days a week utilizes my medical training. Once again, I'm working hard to keep up with new medical developments.

In 2007, Gov. Sonny Perdue appointed me to the Medical College of Georgia Health System board of directors (the board's name has undergone several changes) and I was reappointed by Gov. Deal, eventually serving on the board for nine years. I've also contributed to medical education by endowing scholarships and sponsoring lectureships at The Mercer University School of Medicine and the Medical College of Georgia and helping pay the costs of the coats at the white coat ceremony for students at the Medical College of Georgia.

I've received the Medical College of Georgia Alumni Association's Distinguished Alumnus Award; the American Medical Association's Nathan Davis Award for governmental service to medicine and the Dr. Benjamin Rush Bicentennial Award for community service; the Shining Knight Award for work on infant mortality; and the Dublin and Laurens County Suicide Prevention Coalition Lifetime Achievement Award. The Mercer University School of Medicine has placed a plaque in the school's atrium recognizing my contributions to the school. I've also received the Distinguished Eagle Scout Award for lifetime achievement in public service by Eagle Scouts, an award presented by U.S. Rep. Sanford Bishop, a former recipient, with principal remarks given by U.S. Sen. Johnny Isakson, at an event in Dublin attended by family, friends, former congressional staffers, Boy Scout leaders, and an array of other dignitaries.

Under an act of Congress, the federal courthouse in Dublin was named in my honor. U.S. Rep. Charlie Norwood of Augusta sponsored the bill after U.S. District Judge Dudley Bowen, Jr. of the Southern District signed off on the idea. I was present when the House passed the bill by a voice vote. At the dedication ceremony, a professor from the Medical College of Georgia, Dr. Pepper Martin, Judge Bowen's father-in-law who had taught me when I was a student at the medical college, displayed a record of the class standings showing I had the second highest marks in the class. Several judges attended. Two former U.S. House members with whom I served were there, Buddy Darden and Lindsay Thomas. Three current members of Congress attended, Saxby Chambliss, John Linder, and Charlie Norwood. Several members of my congressional staff attended, which I greatly appreciated. My portrait now hangs in the foyer of the courthouse that bears my name.

CHAPTER TWENTY-TWO

When looking back on the turbulent times and personal ups and downs I've lived through for most of the 20th century and nearly two decades of the 21st, I'm hopeful about the future. I've confronted the challenges in my life as energetically and sensibly as I know how and have usually emerged all the stronger. With few exceptions, so has the country.

But I'm also concerned. Can we effectively deal with global terrorism, nuclear threats, the health care crisis, and other contemporary challenges if partisan conflict keeps the governmental process in disarray? Can we remain a shining model of self-government if solidarity over political interests replaces our solidarity over constitutional principles? Are we headed for a future of greater or diminished strength and security?

Some observers believe nothing has changed. No one can disagree that conflicts between Americans from separate parties and with different viewpoints have always existed. Slavery led to a devastating sectional war. The civil rights movement and the war in Vietnam deeply divided Americans. But without one overarching issue dividing the country, cultural and philosophical differences have polarized the federal process over the past several decades as they rarely have before. If the two major parties rule as hostile enemies rather than patriotic rivals, I believe our international security and domestic well-being will be dangerously compromised.

Some observers point out our system of governmental checks and balances has withstood attacks from the nation's beginning. No one can deny our history is full of examples of how the courts created rather than interpreted law and how the executive branch abused its rule-making authority. Unfortunately, such violations remain a threat. To possibly an unprecedented degree, the executive branch has adopted rules in recent years that amount to legislation. And to a degree that's uncomfortable to me, members of Congress have tended to support the positions of their party's presidents in the interest of partisan unity rather than serve as an independent voice. Violating the system of checks and balances can lead to an unhealthy concentration of power today just as much as it could have done in our founders' day.

Statistics document how the moderate center has lost ground and polarization around ideological extremes has increased. According to the Pew Research Center, thirty-seven percent of the American people label themselves strong liberals or strong conservatives. This leaves sixty-three percent somewhere in the middle. But the Pew Research Center findings show that fifty-seven percent of the people who are engaged in political activism come from the thirty-seven percent who identify as strong conservatives and liberals. To a degree, a more moderate majority has yielded political power to a minority more willing to accept stagnation rather than compromise over critical issues.

Several factors can be cited. Redistricting is one. Congressional reapportionment has trended toward more solidly Democratic and solidly Republican districts and fewer diverse districts, leaving fewer members of the U.S. House with an interest in seeking balanced solutions. Money is another. Wealthy contributors can skew the political process by helping elect representatives from one end of the spectrum or the other. Party realignment is still another.

Many white people who historically voted Democratic switched to the Republican party and many African Americans who historical-ly voted Republican switched to the Democratic party when President Johnson signed the Civil Rights and Voting Rights acts into law in the mid-1960s. When Republican Sen. Barry Goldwater of Arizona ran for president against Johnson in 1964, conservative Goldwater supporters, many of whom were newcomers to active Republican ranks, took control of GOP party offices from the precinct level up. Although Sen. Goldwa-ter favored equal rights, he believed voting reform and other civil rights initiatives should be a state rather than a federal responsibility. Wheth-er or not party realignment was his intent, the two parties became more ideologically uniform and divided.

Dynamics such as these are a natural part of our always-evolving representative form of government. If the U.S. Justice Department and the states adopt a policy of greater diversification in future reappor-tionment cycles, and the public at-large increases its percentage of the financing for campaigns, the process in Washington will likely to move toward the center. But only the electorate can make a quick difference. If voters demand that their elected representatives put the country ahead of their party and seek common cause to address the country's vital in-terests, it will happen.

While serving in Congress during the 1980s and 1990s, I witnessed a turning point in Washington's slide toward deeper partisanship.

Saving Social Security was the top issue on the day I first took the oath as a U.S. House member in January 1983. Some experts predicted the system would be bankrupt by the end of the year if President Reagan and Congress didn't take drastic action. Whether or not Social Security was headed for terminal insolvency within twelve months, doing nothing could have led to delays in payments, creating hardship for millions of recipients. Presidents and Congress had attempted to deal with the ap-proaching crisis by enacting four Social Security rescue bills during the previous seven years. None of these measures were substantial enough to stabilize Social Security for long.

The year before my arrival, a conservative president, Ronald Reagan, and a liberal speaker of the House, Tip O'Neill, had worked together to create the fifteen-member National Commission on Social Security Reform to produce a compromise plan for making the system financially sound for the foreseeable future. The president and many conservatives wanted to make the Social Security voluntary, insisting it could be done without destroying the system. The speaker wanted to put the burden for covering the Social Security deficit on higher income Americans while essentially preserving the existing system. If they had taken rigid partisan stands, there wouldn't have been enough votes on either side to get anything passed.

All of the compromise plan's provisions were politically unpopular—higher Social Security rates for workers, an income tax applied on half of the Social Security earnings for middle to higher income recipients with the revenue dedicated to the system, an increase in the age of eligibility, a six-month delay in the Social Security cost-of-living adjustment, new ceilings on Medicare payments to medical professionals, and the merger of Social Security and the Civil Service Retirement System. I particularly didn't like the Medicare payment-fixing provision because it would raise the cost of medical services for non-Medicare patients, or the consolidation of a healthy civil service system with the ailing Social Security System. Amendments to the compromise plan were disallowed under the rule adopted by the House Rules Committee. Members had to vote for or against the whole package.

I voted for it. Although I strongly believe in the "first-do-no-harm" principle, I decided this was a choice that avoided a greater harm.

A financial crisis again looms over Social Security and Medicare. According to the system's trustees, insolvency could overtake the Social Security Disability Insurance Trust Fund by 2023, the Medicare Hospital Insurance Trust Fund by 2028, and the Social Security Old Age and Survivor's Trust Fund by 2035. The private Committee for a Responsible Federal Budget calculates benefits would be immediately reduced by 21 percent for all Social Security recipients if nothing was done. Various solutions have been proposed, including the creation of a new bipartisan Social Security reform commission. But can agreement be reached in today's political climate?

President Reagan and Speaker O'Neill differed in their beliefs just as much as today's rival political leaders. Reagan once said the portly O'Neill was like Pac-Man, "a round thing that gobbles up money." O'Neill once compared President Reagan to Ebenezer Scrooge, calling him a voice of "greed." In spite of their sharp differences, they found ways to cooperate when the country's interests were at stake. So did the old-school political figure then serving as Republican minority leader, Bob Michel of Illinois, who also knew how to get things done without sacrificing bedrock principles.

The process sometimes bogged down during those years just as it has always done at times. But unlike today, cooperation across party lines was accepted as an integral part of the culture. As a number of studies have confirmed, congressional polarization began to intensify in the 1980s and peaked by the second decade of the twenty-first century when the federal government shut down for two and a half weeks in a dispute over health care funding in 2013 and came within a hair of defaulting on the national debt by refusing to raise the debt ceiling in 2011, almost triggering an economic calamity. Measures to address many of the country's major problems, like immigration reform, have been stalled for years.

Sometime in 1982, Newt Gingrich called together a few like-minded Republican friends in the House including Reps. Vin Weber of Minnesota and Robert Walker of Pennsylvania and organized the Conservative Opportunity Society (COS). The group met regularly at the Washington office of the strongly-conservative Free Congress Foundation. At the time, Newt was a Republican back bencher who was gaining a name for his biting, well-articulated attacks on Democrats. He believed Republicans in Congress could overturn the Democratic control of the House by pursuing an aggressive partisan strategy, one that seized on wedge issues like the balanced budget amendment and voluntary prayer in schools, branding

Democrats who opposed measures like these as radical socialists. Newt and his COS allies would lead the charge for a Republican takeover.

No one could have imagined how successful the so-called Republican "firebrands" would be. Their challenge to the more conciliatory leadership of Bob Michel increasingly appealed to Republican members of Congress and Newt's following rapidly grew. He was elected Republican House whip starting in the 1990 term and speaker of the House starting in the 1995-96 term. When Democratic leaders inadvertently helped Republicans politically by failing to deliver on the Democratic promise of health care reform in 1993-94, the GOP gained control of the House in the 1994 election. Knowing he couldn't defeat Newt, Bob Michel retired at the end of the 1993-94 term after serving fourteen of his thirty-eight years in Congress as Republican leader in the House. Newt resigned from Congress four years after his election as speaker when Republicans suffered a political setback as a result of a government shut down over a budget dispute. By then, severe party polarization was well entrenched.

Early in 1984, Gingrich, Weber, and Walker turned to C-SPAN as a useful medium for attacking Democrats. Launched in 1979, the private, non-profit television network provided gavel-to-gavel coverage of congressional proceedings. C-SPAN also covered special orders when members reserved time in the House chamber to speak on an issue following each day's business. The network drew an audience of half a million. The Republican "bomb throwers," as some in the media referred to them, regularly held special orders to present their conservative agenda and denounce Democrats, sometimes by name, in the strongest possible language. It's an understatement to say many Democrats were fuming over the inflammatory attacks.

A climatic moment came in May 1984, when Gingrich, Weber, and Walker sent a letter to prominent House Democrats inviting them to join them in the House chamber for two days of special orders to discuss foreign policy. I doubt if the three seriously expected any Democrats to attend. With occasional exceptions, Republicans who weren't participating didn't attend either. On the first day of the discussion, Democratic leaders were described as radicals with a pessimistic, defeatist view of the country's role in the world. Gingrich, Weber, Walker, and allies singled out some "radical" Democrats by name.

A furious House Democratic speaker, Tip O'Neill, thought the Republicans had questioned the patriotism of the Democrats they mentioned. At times calling them the "three Stooges," the speaker criticized the Republican insurgents for attacking people who weren't present to defend themselves. During a regular House session, Newt took the floor to explain why he and his allies believed it was important to engage in in-depth discussions of critical issues. The speaker interrupted, and the two engaged in a heated exchange. Tip took control and declared, "You challenged their (Democrats) Americanism and it is the lowest thing I have ever seen in thirty-two years in Congress."

This comment caused an uproar among Republicans. I was sitting in the House chamber a few feet away from Bob Walker when the Pennsylvania Republican jumped to his feet and demanded the House parliamentarian "take down his words." Bob was calling on the parliamentarian to rule O'Neill out of order. Under House rules, members are prohibited from engaging in personal attacks. When Bob's motion was upheld, members of his party gave Newt a standing ovation, although some, like Bob Michel, reportedly didn't join in the cheering.

No one could remember when a speaker had been officially rebuked like this. It was an embarrassing moment for the whole institution. Although the speaker could have expressed his concerns without using personal language, I also thought Bob Walker was out of line for demonstrating disrespect for the speaker and his office, especially before a national C-SPAN television audience.

On the second day of the special order on foreign policy, Tip O'Neill ordered the C-SPAN cameras to pan the nearly-empty House chamber. Previously, the cameras had remained fixed on the member speaking from the well. The speaker's purpose was to indicate to the TV audience that the special order was all for show. Republicans protested that the speaker didn't have the authority to direct the cameras, saying he was acting in a dictatorial fashion. But O'Neill pointed out he was authorized to adjust the camera "angles."

It was truly an angry atmosphere. It would get even angrier.

The next major eruption occurred in 1985 following a disputed congressional election in Indiana. Democratic Rep. Frank McCloskey of Indiana, who came to Congress in the same freshman class as I did, first appeared to be the winner by seventy-two votes in his 1984 race for reelection. But after a recount, Indiana's Republican secretary of state declared his Republican challenger the winner by thirty-four votes.

The Democratic-controlled House refused to seat the Republican challenger and named a three-member task force to conduct its own recount, two Democrats and one Republican. After nearly four months, the Democratic-majority task force named McCloskey the winner by four votes. The Democratic House majority then voted to seat the Democratic incumbent by a vote of 230-195.

Who knows who really won? But the way it was handled in the House was sure to leave Republicans believing it was blatantly a political decision. The affair touched off bitter partisan attacks and counter-attacks for months, intensifying the growing polarization. Frank, incidentally, was one of the House Democrats who would lose following the 1993-94 health care reform disaster.

Perhaps the most spectacular partisan tactic attributed to Republican "firebrands" involved the so-called House banking scandal, sometimes called "Rubbergate" in reference to bounced checks. Although an innocent bystander, I would briefly get caught up in the "scandal."

The bank in question was really a pool of money deposited by House members in an account managed by the House office of the sergeant of arms, a convenience for members who needed a quick source of cash in the days before ATMs. The rules were lenient, statements weren't consistently sent out, and deposits weren't always immediately recorded. Members had overdraft protection as long as they didn't exceed their next pay check, and overdrafts had become commonplace.

Arriving in my office early one morning in 1992, an alarmed staffer informed me *The New York Times* had listed me as a check bouncer in a story reporting that scores of House members had bounced checks on a House-run bank. In my case, I knew a mistake had been made. I had always deposited more than I had withdrawn and had the records of deposits and withdrawals to prove it. Cancelling everything, I rushed to our townhouse, gathered up the records, and hurried to the sergeant of arms office where someone confirmed I had never overdrawn my account and assured me this fact would be conveyed to inquiring reporters.

We called Howell Raines, then chief of *The Times* Washington Bureau, who ran a follow-up story with an accurate list. This time I wasn't named. But a Connecticut congressman named John Rowland was. The similarity in names evidently caused the error. In the next campaign, we ran an ad listing one of my accomplishments as not bouncing any checks.

It's been reported Newt's faction leaked the story. Republican candidates effectively used Rubbergate as an issue in the next election, attacking Democratic House members who had overdrawn their accounts as privileged people who were getting away with something the average citizen would get in trouble for doing. Although some Republicans as well as Democrats had overdrawn their accounts, more Democrats were on the check-bouncing list. The affair touched off a national furor that led to the defeat or retirement of seventy-seven House members, mostly Democrats. This reduced the Democratic advantage in the make-up of the next House, making it more difficult for President Clinton and Democratic leaders in Congress to pass their version of health care reform.

There are two or more sides to every story, of course.

Newt Gingrich and his followers believed the end they were seeking justified the means. As a close observer of Newt's rise, I realized he was pursuing his super-aggressive strategy as the most realistic way to achieve a Republican majority in Congress. From his viewpoint, he was pragmatically building a stronger and freer country. While Newt may have created gridlock at times, he also helped overcome gridlock on some big issues. He helped pass the King holiday bill, for instance. He also did his best to help get the bipartisan Rowland-Bilirakis health care reform plan passed.

No one should doubt the motives of President Clinton, Hillary Clinton, Dick Gephardt, John Dingell, and everyone who took a rigid position for the Clinton health care reform plan, either. They, too, were sincerely doing what they thought was best for the country. If they accepted anything other than the government-driven plan they proposed, I suspect they believed they would be giving in to forces who wanted to protect special interests rather than help people in need. If so, it was an unfair and self-destructive point of view.

Feuds often have a logical origin. People who engage in hostilities usually believe they are in the right. But our country's conflict between political parties and conservatives and liberals has reached illogical extremes and the long-term consequences are proving to be harmful to the governmental process. As I view it, all sides share the blame for governmental dysfunction and all sides have a responsibility to do something about it.

This is certainly true when it comes to health care reform. Americans on the left and right have passionately fought for nearly a century over what kind of health care system the country should have. On the left, many believe health care is a fundamental right and only a government-run system can guarantee affordable, quality health care for all. On the right, many believe a government-run system violates the right of free enterprise and only a system governed by free market forces can provide efficient, affordable, and innovative health care.

We've ended up with a hybrid system including government programs like Medicare, Medicaid, and the veterans' health care system and a vast private insurance market. The Affordable Care Act expanded the government health care safety net. But problems persisted. In spite of subsidies, millions still lacked coverage. Many who logged into the ACA's exchanges were hit by higher deductibles, less choice, and, for some, double-digit premium increases. ACA critics and supporters alike agreed the system still needed major surgery.

Will our political representatives get it right as the "repeal and replace" process moves forward? If they insist on a utopian solution as each side sees it, it's unlikely the result will be any different than it has been in the past. Perfection is unachievable because Americans define perfection differently. But if our political representatives follow the resourceful, old-fashioned example of Ronald Reagan and Tip O'Neill in finding ways to overcame partisan gridlock with bipartisan cooperation, it's likely they will finally get it as right as possible.

"The challenge of our times," President Clinton called health care reform, assuring the country, "Miracles can happen." I believed him. I've tried to help make it happen for much of my life. I'm now in my nineties and I may not have as much energy as I once had. But I'm just as stubborn and I'll stubbornly keep trying by voting, writing my representatives, and speaking out when anyone will listen. I'm still confidant the challenge will someday be met.

I still believe in miracles.

APPENDIX

Legislation Sponsored or Cosponsored by J. Roy Rowland

AMENDMENT

1. H.Amdt.503 to H.Amdt.502 — 101st Congress (1989-1990)

    Description: Amendment, as originally offered, sought to require States, as a condition of receiving grants under the bill, to require the confidential reporting of all HIV test results to State public health officials including information on sexual and intravenous needle-sharing partners of the individual tested. State health officials would have been required to establish a program for partner notification regarding cases of infection. \ As amended by the Rowland of Georgia substitute amendment (A005), language was added which gave each State flexibility in determining and establishing reporting requirements.

    Amends Bill: H.R.4785

    Sponsor: Rep. Rowland, J. Roy [D-GA-8] (Offered 06/13/1990)

    Latest Action: 06/13/90 On agreeing to the Rowland (GA) amendment (A005) Agreed to by recorded vote: 312 - 113 (Roll no. 166).

AMENDMENT

2. H.Amdt.492 — 100th Congress (1987-1988)

Description: An amendment to provide that tests for acquired immune deficiency syndrome be routinely offered to women of childbearing age when they apply for services available through migrant health centers.

Amends Bill: H.R.1326

Sponsor: Rep. Rowland, J. Roy [D-GA-8] (Offered 11/09/1987)

Latest Action: 11/09/87 Amendment Passed in Committee of the Whole by Voice Vote.

AMENDMENT

3. H.Amdt.1065 — 99th Congress (1985-1986)

Description: An amendment to require the Secretary of Transportation to make available for second and third priority projects, funds designated for first priority projects, if such funds have not been made available the the first priority project after 365 days.

Amends Bill: H.R.3129

Sponsor: Rep. Rowland, J. Roy [D-GA-8] (Offered 08/06/1986)

Latest Action: 08/06/86 Amendment Passed in Committee of the Whole by Voice Vote.

AMENDMENT

4. H.Amdt.677 — 99th Congress (1985-1986)

Description: An amendment to specify that the Administrator of the Agency for Toxic Substances and Disease Registry is to arrange for instead of "provide" medical testing and care to exposed individuals in cases of public health emergencies.

Amends Bill: H.R.2817

Sponsor: Rep. Rowland, J. Roy [D-GA-8] (Offered 12/06/1985)

Latest Action: 12/06/85 Amendment Passed in Committee of the Whole by Voice Vote.

AMENDMENT

5. H.Amdt.666 — 99th Congress (1985-1986)

Description: An amendment to require the Secretary of HHS through the Centers for Disease Control to conduct a study of sexually transmitted diseases (including AIDS) on college campuses. Consultation with local and State public health authorities, institutions of higher education, and Department of Education is required. Distribution to institutions of higher education is required of any information found in the studies that may help prevent the spread of sexually transmitted diseases.

Amends Bill: H.R.3700

Sponsor: Rep. Rowland, J. Roy [D-GA-8] (Offered 12/04/1985)

Latest Action: 12/04/85 Amendment Passed in Committee of the Whole by Voice Vote.

AMENDMENT

6. H.Amdt.1069 — 98th Congress (1983-1984)

Description: An amendment dealing with emergency relief and health surveillance. The amendment provides that any individual or group may submit a petition to EPA providing evidence which 1) demonstrates that they are being exposed to any hazardous substance and 2) provides an empirical analysis of the level of exposure. The Administrator must take action if he determines that there is a "reasonable likelihood" that the substance is from a facility is or was treated, stored, recycled, or disposed of on a regular basis or at which removal action is being taken. The amendment specifies what type of action must be taken by the EPA. The amendment also requires the Administrator to establish action levels for hazardous substances based upon toxicological and epidemiological evaluations, among other factors.

Amends Bill: H.R.5640

Sponsor: Rep. Rowland, J. Roy [D-GA-8] (Offered 08/09/1984)

Latest Action: 08/09/84 Amendment Passed in Committee of the Whole by Voice Vote.

AMENDMENT

7. H.Amdt.200 — 98th Congress (1983-1984)

Description: Amendment to the Shelby amendment in the nature of a substitute to add a new section "in fiscal year 1985 and 1986 the Consumer Product Safety Commission shall use funds appropriated under the amendment made by section 2 for the Flammable Fabrics Act to include within the definition of articles of wearing apparel surgical drapes which are used to completely or partially cover patients undergoing surgery".

Amends Bill: H.R.2668

Sponsor: Rep. Rowland, J. Roy [D-GA-8] (Offered 06/29/1983)

Latest Action: 06/29/83 Amendment Passed in Committee of the Whole by Voice Vote.

BILL

8. H.R.5228 — 103rd Congress (1993-1994) Bipartisan Health Care Reform Act of 1994

Sponsor: Rep. Rowland, J. Roy [D-GA-8] (Introduced 10/06/1994)

Cosponsors: (21)

Committees: House - Education and Labor, Energy and Commerce, Judiciary, Veterans' Affairs, Ways and Means

Latest Action: 11/14/1994 Referred to the Subcommittee on Labor-Management Relations.

LAW

9. H.R.3313 — 103rd Congress (1993-1994) Veterans Health Programs Extension Act of 1994

   Sponsor: Rep. Rowland, J. Roy [D-GA-8] (Introduced 10/19/1993)

   Cosponsors: (23)

   Committees: House - Veterans' Affairs

   Latest Action: 11/02/1994 Became Public Law No: 103-452.

BILL

10. H.R.3955 — 103rd Congress (1993-1994) Health Reform Consensus Act of 1994

    Sponsor: Rep. Rowland, J. Roy [D-GA-8] (Introduced 03/03/1994)

    Cosponsors: (98)

    Committees: House - Education and Labor, Energy and Commerce, Judiciary, Ways and Means

    Latest Action: 08/02/1994 See H.R.3600.

BILL

11. H.R.4013 — 103rd Congress (1993-1994) VA State Health Care Reform Pilot Program Act

    Sponsor: Rep. Rowland, J. Roy [D-GA-8] (Introduced 03/11/1994)

    Cosponsors: (19)

    Committees: House - Veterans' Affairs

    Latest Action: 06/09/1994 Message on Senate action sent to the House.

BILL

12. H.R.4425 — 103rd Congress (1993-1994) To authorize major medical facility construction projects for the Department of Veterans Affairs for fiscal year 1995, to revise and improve veterans' health programs, and for other purposes.

    Sponsor: Rep. Rowland, J. Roy [D-GA-8] (Introduced 05/16/1994)

    Cosponsors: (8)

    Committees: House - Veterans' Affairs | Senate - Veterans' Affairs

    Latest Action: 05/25/1994 Received in the Senate and read twice and referred to the Committee on Veterans.

BILL

13. H.R.1910 — 103rd Congress (1993-1994) Fairness in Product Liability Act of 1993

    Sponsor: Rep. Rowland, J. Roy [D-GA-8] (Introduced 04/28/1993)

    Cosponsors: (152)

    Committees: House - Energy and Commerce, Judiciary

    Latest Action: 05/03/1994 Subcommittee Hearings Held.

BILL

14. H.R.3573 — 103rd Congress (1993-1994) Community Health Improvement Act of 1993

    Sponsor: Rep. Rowland, J. Roy [D-GA-8] (Introduced 11/19/1993)

    Cosponsors: (22)

    Committees: House - Energy and Commerce

    Latest Action: 01/03/1994 Referred to the Subcommittee on Health and the Environment.

LAW

---

15. H.R.2535 — 103rd Congress (1993-1994) To amend title 38, United States Code, to provide additional authority for the Secretary of Veterans Affairs to provide health care for veterans of the Persian Gulf War.

    Sponsor: Rep. Rowland, J. Roy [D-GA-8] (Introduced 06/28/1993)

    Cosponsors: (33)

    Committees: House - Veterans' Affairs | Senate - Veterans' Affairs

    Latest Action: 12/20/1993 Became Public Law No: 103-210.

BILL

---

16. H.R.3082 — 103rd Congress (1993-1994) Women Veterans Health Improvements Act of 1993

    Sponsor: Rep. Rowland, J. Roy [D-GA-8] (Introduced 09/15/1993)

    Cosponsors: (1)

    Committees: House - Veterans' Affairs

    Latest Action: 10/06/1993 Subcommittee Consideration and Mark-up Session Held.

BILL

---

17. H.R.3081 — 103rd Congress (1993-1994) To amend title 38, United States Code, to extend and expand authority for the Secretary of Veterans Affairs to provide priority health care to veterans who were exposed to ionizing radiation or to Agent Orange.

    Sponsor: Rep. Rowland, J. Roy [D-GA-8] (Introduced 09/15/1993)

    Cosponsors: (1)

    Committees: House - Veterans' Affairs

    Latest Action: 10/06/1993 Subcommittee Consideration and Mark-up Session Held.

LAW

18. H.R.2034 — 103rd Congress (1993-1994) An Act to authorize major medical facility projects and leases for the Department of Veterans' Affairs, to revise and extend the authority of the Secretary of Veterans' Affairs to enter into enhanced-use leases, to revise certain authorities relating to Pershing Hall, France, and for other purposes.

Sponsor: Rep. Rowland, J. Roy [D-GA-8] (Introduced 05/06/1993)

Cosponsors: (3)

Committees: House - Veterans' Affairs | Senate - Veterans' Affairs

Latest Action: 08/13/1993 Became Public Law No: 103-79.

BILL

19. H.R.2714 — 103rd Congress (1993-1994) To amend title 38, United States Code, to extend to recipients of the Medal of Honor eligibility for medical and dental care furnished by the Department of Veterans Affairs.

Sponsor: Rep. Rowland, J. Roy [D-GA-8] (Introduced 07/22/1993) (by request)

Cosponsors: (1)

Committees: House - Veterans' Affairs

Latest Action: 07/23/1993 Referred to the Subcommittee on Hospitals and Health Care.

BILL

20. H.R.2713 — 103rd Congress (1993-1994) To amend title 38, United States Code, to provide that former prisoners of war are eligible for reimbursement for emergency medical expenses on the same basis as veterans with total permanent service-connected disabilities.

Sponsor: Rep. Rowland, J. Roy [D-GA-8] (Introduced 07/22/1993) (by request)

Cosponsors: (1)

Committees: House - Veterans' Affairs

Latest Action: 07/23/1993 Referred to the Subcommittee on Hospitals and Health Care.

BILL

---

21. H.R.1770 — 103rd Congress (1993-1994) Rural Physicians' Incentives Act of 1993

Sponsor: Rep. Rowland, J. Roy [D-GA-8] (Introduced 04/21/1993)

Cosponsors: (25)

Committees: House - Education and Labor, Energy and Commerce, Ways and Means

Latest Action: 05/12/1993 Referred to the Subcommittee on Health and the Environment.

BILL

---

22. H.R.1771 — 103rd Congress (1993-1994) Rural Access to Obstetrical Care Act of 1993

Sponsor: Rep. Rowland, J. Roy [D-GA-8] (Introduced 04/21/1993)

Cosponsors: (22)

Committees: House - Energy and Commerce

Latest Action: 05/12/1993 Referred to the Subcommittee on Health and the Environment.

BILL

---

23. H.R.862 — 103rd Congress (1993-1994) Long-Term Care Insurance for the Elderly Act of 1993

Sponsor: Rep. Rowland, J. Roy [D-GA-8] (Introduced 02/04/1993)

Cosponsors: (0)

Committees: House - Energy and Commerce, Ways and Means

Latest Action: 02/24/1993 Referred to the Subcommittee on Commerce, Consumer Protection and Competitiveness.

BILL

24. H.R.2824 — 102nd Congress (1991-1992) To provide for demonstration projects to test the feasibility of broader use of arrangements between the Department of Veterans Affairs and other Federal health-care providers for the sharing of health-care resources, and for other purposes.

Sponsor: Rep. Rowland, J. Roy [D-GA-8] (Introduced 06/27/1991)

Cosponsors: (18)

Committees: House - Armed Services, Energy and Commerce, Veterans' Affairs, Ways and Means

Latest Action: 10/08/1992 For Further Action See H.R.776.

BILL

25. H.R.1205 — 102nd Congress (1991-1992) Long-Term Care Insurance for the Elderly Act of 1991

Sponsor: Rep. Rowland, J. Roy [D-GA-8] (Introduced 02/28/1991)

Cosponsors: (24)

Committees: House - Energy and Commerce, Ways and Means

Latest Action: 07/23/1992 Subcommittee Hearings Held.

BILL

26. H.R.3524 — 102nd Congress (1991-1992) Controlled Substances and Forfeited Property Amendments of 1991

Sponsor: Rep. Rowland, J. Roy [D-GA-8] (Introduced 10/08/1991)

Cosponsors: (1)

Committees: House - Energy and Commerce, Judiciary

Latest Action: 10/25/1991 Referred to the Subcommittee on Health and the Environment.

BILL

27. H.R.3030 — 102nd Congress (1991-1992) Fairness in Product Liability Act of 1991

Sponsor: Rep. Rowland, J. Roy [D-GA-8] (Introduced 07/25/1991)

Cosponsors: (159)

Committees: House - Energy and Commerce, Judiciary

Latest Action: 10/09/1991 Executive Comment Received from Justice.

BILL

28. H.R.2695 — 102nd Congress (1991-1992) Medicare Physician Regulatory Relief Amendments of 1991

Sponsor: Rep. Rowland, J. Roy [D-GA-8] (Introduced 06/19/1991)

Cosponsors: (169)

Committees: House - Energy and Commerce, Ways and Means

Latest Action: 07/09/1991 Referred to the Subcommittee on Health and the Environment.

LAW

---

29. H.R.749 — 102nd Congress (1991-1992) To authorize the Secretary of the Interior to accept a donation of land for addition to the Ocmulgee National Monument in the State of Georgia.

Sponsor: Rep. Rowland, J. Roy [D-GA-8] (Introduced 01/30/1991)

Cosponsors: (0)

Committees: House - Interior and Insular Affairs | Senate - Energy and Natural Resources

Latest Action: 07/09/1991 Became Public Law No: 102-67.

BILL

---

30. H.R.2230 — 102nd Congress (1991-1992) Rural Physicians' Incentives Act of 1991

Sponsor: Rep. Rowland, J. Roy [D-GA-8] (Introduced 05/07/1991)

Cosponsors: (62)

Committees: House - Education and Labor, Energy and Commerce, Ways and Means

Latest Action: 06/17/1991 Referred to the Subcommittee on Postsecondary Education.

BILL

---

31. H.R.2229 — 102nd Congress (1991-1992) Rural Access to Obstetrical Care Act of 1991

Sponsor: Rep. Rowland, J. Roy [D-GA-8] (Introduced 05/07/1991)

Cosponsors: (54)

Committees: House - Energy and Commerce

Latest Action: 05/20/1991 Referred to the Subcommittee on Health and the Environment.

BILL

32. H.R.1581 — 102nd Congress (1991-1992) Wayport Development Act of 1991

Sponsor: Rep. Rowland, J. Roy [D-GA-8] (Introduced 03/21/1991)

Cosponsors: (0)

Committees: House - Public Works and Transportation, Rules

Latest Action: 04/16/1991 Referred to the Subcommittee on the Legislative Process.

BILL

33. H.R.926 — 102nd Congress (1991-1992) To amend the Internal Revenue Code of 1986 to exempt distributions to members of the reserves while on active duty from the additional tax on early distributions from qualified retirement plans.

Sponsor: Rep. Rowland, J. Roy [D-GA-8] (Introduced 02/06/1991)

Cosponsors: (0)

Committees: House - Ways and Means

Latest Action: 02/06/1991 Referred to the House Committee on Ways and Means.

BILL

34. H.R.4506 — 101st Congress (1989-1990) To require the Secretary of Health and Human Services to review and revise the list of dangerous contagious diseases used in the exclusion of aliens from the United States.

Sponsor: Rep. Rowland, J. Roy [D-GA-8] (Introduced 04/04/1990)

Cosponsors: (22)

Committees: House - Energy and Commerce, Judiciary

Latest Action: 11/29/1990 See S.358.

BILL

35. H.R.5619 — 101st Congress (1989-1990) To authorize the Secretary of the Interior to accept a donation of land for addition to the Ocmulgee National Monument in the State of Georgia.

   Sponsor: Rep. Rowland, J. Roy [D-GA-8] (Introduced 09/13/1990)

   Cosponsors: (0)

   Committees: House - Interior and Insular Affairs

   Latest Action: 09/20/1990 Referred to the Subcommittee on National Parks and Public Lands.

BILL

36. H.R.4941 — 101st Congress (1989-1990) To amend title 38, United States Code, to change from 30 years to 40 years the period during which the disease of leukemia occuring in a veteran after exposure (while serving on active duty) to nuclear radiation as a result of participation in certain radiation-risk activities shall be presumed to be service connected for purposes of compensation paid by the Department of Veterans Affairs.

   Sponsor: Rep. Rowland, J. Roy [D-GA-8] (Introduced 05/24/1990)

   Cosponsors: (30)

   Committees: House - Veterans' Affairs

   Latest Action: 07/26/1990 See H.R.5326.

BILL

37. H.R.4475 — 101st Congress (1989-1990) Medicare Physician Regulation Relief Amendments of 1990

   Sponsor: Rep. Rowland, J. Roy [D-GA-8] (Introduced 04/04/1990)

   Cosponsors: (266)

   Committees: House - Ways and Means, Energy and Commerce

Latest Action: 04/23/1990 Referred to the Subcommittee on Health and the Environment.

RESOLUTION

38. H.Con.Res.246 — 101st Congress (1989-1990) Congressional Commitment to Long-Term Care Concurrent Resolution

Sponsor: Rep. Rowland, J. Roy [D-GA-8] (Introduced 01/24/1990)

Cosponsors: (112)

Committees: House - Ways and Means, Energy and Commerce

Latest Action: 02/12/1990 Referred to the Subcommittee on Health and the Environment.

BILL

39. H.R.1638 — 101st Congress (1989-1990) Wayport Development Act of 1989

Sponsor: Rep. Rowland, J. Roy [D-GA-8] (Introduced 03/23/1989)

Cosponsors: (13)

Committees: House - Public Works and Transportation, Rules

Latest Action: 02/08/1990 Subcommittee Hearings Held.

BILL

40. H.R.3491 — 101st Congress (1989-1990) Long-Term Care Insurance for the Elderly Act of 1989

Sponsor: Rep. Rowland, J. Roy [D-GA-8] (Introduced 10/18/1989)

Cosponsors: (11)

Committees: House - Ways and Means, Energy and Commerce

Latest Action: 10/27/1989 Referred to the Subcommittee on Commerce, Consumer Protection and Competitiveness.

RESOLUTION

41. H.J.Res.405 — 101st Congress (1989-1990) To provide for the designation of the month of October 1989 as "National HIV and AIDS Awareness Month".

    Sponsor: Rep. Rowland, J. Roy [D-GA-8] (Introduced 09/14/1989)

    Cosponsors: (82)

    Committees: House - Post Office and Civil Service

    Latest Action: 09/21/1989 Referred to the Subcommittee on Census and Population.

BILL

42. H.R.1710 — 101st Congress (1989-1990) Healthy Birth Act of 1989

    Sponsor: Rep. Rowland, J. Roy [D-GA-8] (Introduced 04/05/1989)

    Cosponsors: (89)

    Committees: House - Energy and Commerce

    Latest Action: 04/24/1989 Referred to the Subcommittee on Health and the Environment.

BILL

43. H.R.2881 — 100th Congress (1987-1988) National Commission on Acquired Immune Deficiency Syndrome Act

    Sponsor: Rep. Rowland, J. Roy [D-GA-8] (Introduced 07/01/1987)

    Cosponsors: (85)

    Committees: House - Energy and Commerce, Veterans' Affairs | Senate - Labor and Human Resources

    Committee Reports: S.Rept 100-400

    Latest Action: 06/24/1988 Placed on Senate Legislative Calendar under General Orders. Calendar No. 761.

BILL

44. H.R.4812 — 100th Congress (1987-1988) A bill to amend the Internal Revenue Code of 1986 to provide that a waiver under an interest rate adjustment clause on a small issue bond shall not be treated as resulting in a new issue for purposes of determining deductibility of interest by a financial institution.

Sponsor: Rep. Rowland, J. Roy [D-GA-8] (Introduced 06/14/1988)

Cosponsors: (2)

Committees: House - Ways and Means

Latest Action: 06/14/1988 Referred to House Committee on Ways and Means.

LAW

45. H.R.1811 — 100th Congress (1987-1988) Radiation-Exposed Veterans Compensation Act of 1988

Sponsor: Rep. Rowland, J. Roy [D-GA-8] (Introduced 03/25/1987)

Cosponsors: (84)

Committees: House - Veterans' Affairs | Senate - Veterans' Affairs

Latest Action: 05/20/1988 Became Public Law No: 100-321.

BILL

46. H.R.3790 — 100th Congress (1987-1988) A bill to establish certain limitations on the approval of hydropower projects at Lake Tobesofkee in Bibb County, Georgia.

Sponsor: Rep. Rowland, J. Roy [D-GA-8] (Introduced 12/17/1987)

Cosponsors: (0)

Committees: House - Energy and Commerce

Latest Action: 01/22/1988 See S.2102.

RESOLUTION

47. H.Con.Res.108 — 100th Congress (1987-1988) A concurrent resolution expressing the sense of Congress that medicare reconciliation legislation take into account the plight of rural hospitals.

Sponsor: Rep. Rowland, J. Roy [D-GA-8] (Introduced 04/22/1987)

Cosponsors: (51)

Committees: House - Ways and Means

Latest Action: 04/28/1987 Referred to Subcommittee on Health.

BILL

48. H.R.1933 — 100th Congress (1987-1988) Long-Term Care Insurance for the Elderly Act of 1987

Sponsor: Rep. Rowland, J. Roy [D-GA-8] (Introduced 04/02/1987)

Cosponsors: (28)

Committees: House - Energy and Commerce, Ways and Means

Latest Action: 04/09/1987 Referred to Subcommittee on Health and the Environment.

BILL

49. H.R.4095 — 99th Congress (1985-1986) A bill to amend title 28, United States Code, to make changes in the judicial divisions in the Southern District of Georgia.

Sponsor: Rep. Rowland, J. Roy [D-GA-8] (Introduced 01/30/1986)

Cosponsors: (1)

Committees: House – Judiciary

Latest Action: 10/14/1986 See H.R.5674.

BILL

---

50. H.R.5255 — 99th Congress (1985-1986) Long-Term Care Insurance for the Elderly Act of 1986

    Sponsor: Rep. Rowland, J. Roy [D-GA-8] (Introduced 07/24/1986)

    Cosponsors: (9)

    Committees: House - Energy and Commerce, Ways and Means

    Latest Action: 07/31/1986 Referred to Subcommittee on Health and the Environment.

BILL

---

51. H.R.4876 — 99th Congress (1985-1986) A bill to amend section 9528 of the Consolidated Omnibus Budget Reconciliation Act of 1985 to hold States harmless, during fiscal year 1987, against a decrease in payment rates under the medicaid program resulting from enactment of that section.

    Sponsor: Rep. Rowland, J. Roy [D-GA-8] (Introduced 05/21/1986)

    Cosponsors: (64)

    Committees: House - Energy and Commerce

    Latest Action: 06/05/1986 Referred to Subcommittee on Health and the Environment.

RESOLUTION

---

52. H.J.Res.538 — 99th Congress (1985-1986) A joint resolution to designate the week of May 11, 1986, through May 17, 1986, as "Senior Center Week".

    Sponsor: Rep. Rowland, J. Roy [D-GA-8] (Introduced 02/26/1986)

    Cosponsors: (221)

    Committees: House - Post Office and Civil Service

    Latest Action: 05/09/1986 See S.J.Res.281.

BILL

53. H.R.3473 — 99th Congress (1985-1986) Federal-Aid Highway Reform Act of 1985

Sponsor: Rep. Rowland, J. Roy [D-GA-8] (Introduced 10/01/1985)

Cosponsors: (14)

Committees: House - Public Works and Transportation

Latest Action: 10/17/1985 Referred to Subcommittee on Surface Transportation.

BILL

54. H.R.3144 — 99th Congress (1985-1986) A bill to amend title 39, United States Code, to require that the United States Postal Service prescribe regulations relating to the delivery of mail to physically handicapped individuals.

Sponsor: Rep. Rowland, J. Roy [D-GA-8] (Introduced 07/31/1985)

Cosponsors: (1)

Committees: House - Post Office and Civil Service

Latest Action: 08/06/1985 Referred to Subcommittee on Postal Operations and Services.

RESOLUTION

55. H.J.Res.295 — 99th Congress (1985-1986) A joint resolution to designate July 16, 1985 as "National Atomic Veterans Day".

Sponsor: Rep. Rowland, J. Roy [D-GA-8] (Introduced 05/22/1985)

Cosponsors: (229)

Committees: House - Post Office and Civil Service

Latest Action: 07/16/1985 Indefinitely postponed by Senate by Voice Vote.

RESOLUTION

56. H.J.Res.146 — 99th Congress (1985-1986) A joint resolution to designate the week of May 12, 1985, through May 18, 1985, as "Senior Center Week".

Sponsor: Rep. Rowland, J. Roy [D-GA-8] (Introduced 02/07/1985)

Cosponsors: (228)

Committees: House - Post Office and Civil Service

Latest Action: 05/15/1985 See S.J.Res.60.

BILL

57. H.R.1283 — 99th Congress (1985-1986) A bill to amend the Highway Improvement Act of 1982 to provide additional funds for the completion of certain priority primary projects.

Sponsor: Rep. Rowland, J. Roy [D-GA-8] (Introduced 02/26/1985)

Cosponsors: (7)

Committees: House - Public Works and Transportation

Latest Action: 03/11/1985 Referred to Subcommittee on Surface Transportation.

LAW

58. H.R.4201 — 98th Congress (1983-1984) A bill to provide for the rescheduling of methaqualone into schedule I of the Controlled Substances Act, and for other purposes.

Sponsor: Rep. Rowland, J. Roy [D-GA-8] (Introduced 10/24/1983)

Cosponsors: (3)

Committees: House - Energy and Commerce | Senate – Judiciary

Latest Action: 06/29/1984 Became Public Law No: 98-329.

BILL

59. H.R.3012 — 98th Congress (1983-1984) A bill to designate the building known as the Veterans Administration Medical Center in Dublin, Georgia, as the "Carl Vinson Veterans Administration Medical Center".

Sponsor: Rep. Rowland, J. Roy [D-GA-8] (Introduced 05/12/1983)

Cosponsors: (9)

Committees: House - Veterans' Affairs

Latest Action: 11/03/1983 Committee Consideration and Mark-up Session Held.

BILL

60. H.R.1097 — 98th Congress (1983-1984) A bill to place methaqualone in schedule I of the Controlled Substances Act, and for other purposes.

Sponsor: Rep. Rowland, J. Roy [D-GA-8] (Introduced 01/31/1983)

Cosponsors: (46)

Committees: House - Energy and Commerce

Latest Action: 10/26/1983 See H.R.4201.

BILL

61. H.R.3909 — 98th Congress (1983-1984) Atomic Veterans Relief Act

Sponsor: Rep. Rowland, J. Roy [D-GA-8] (Introduced 09/15/1983)

Cosponsors: (1)

Committees: House - Veterans' Affairs

Latest Action: 09/15/1983 Referred to House Committee on Veterans' Affairs.

INDEX OF PUBLIC FIGURES

INDEX OF LEGISLATION